PETE ROSE

My Prison Without Bars

PETE ROSE

My Prison Without Bars

with Rick Hill

RODALE

Printed in the United States of America
Rodale Inc. makes every effort to use acid-free ∞, recycled paper ♻.

Except where otherwise credited, photographs appearing
in this book are from the personal collection of Pete Rose.

A special thanks to the *Cincinnati Post*, the *Cincinnati Enquirer*,
and the *Dayton Daily News* for source information.

Book design by Susan P. Eugster

Library of Congress Cataloging-in-Publication Data

Rose, Pete, 1941–
My prison without bars / Pete Rose with Rick Hill.
p.   cm.
ISBN 1–57954–927–6 hardcover
1. Rose, Pete, 1941–   2. Baseball players—United States—Biography.
I. Hill, Rick, 1953–   II. Title.
GV865.R65A297   2004
796.357'092—dc22   2003024769

Distributed to the book trade by St. Martin's Press

4   6   8   10   9   7   5   3   hardcover

RODALE
WE **INSPIRE** AND **ENABLE** PEOPLE TO IMPROVE
THEIR LIVES AND THE WORLD AROUND THEM

FOR MORE OF OUR PRODUCTS
WWW.RODALESTORE.COM
(800) 848-4735

To Gantry and Garrett Hill

and

Pete Jr. and Tyler Rose—

sons of the fathers

ACKNOWLEDGMENTS

Pete Rose and I wish to thank Rodale for their confidence and enthusiasm throughout the project and for what turned out to be a major sprint to the finish due to fast-breaking events. Specifically, Jeremy Katz, executive editor, whose counsel and strong hand in shaping the book was invaluable. Thanks also to Marc Jaffe, Amy Rhodes, Chris Krogermeier, Lois Hazel, John Reeser, Cindy Ratzlaff, Emily Williams, Susan Eugster, Andy Carpenter, Jan McLeod, Adrienne Kreger-May, and Jennifer Giandomenico.

I would also like to thank the following for their insights and direct or indirect cooperation: George "Sparky" Anderson, Mike Bertolini, Mike Brennan, Ron Cey, David E. Comings, Bob Costas, Bob Dupuy, Jim Eisenreich, Fred Fenster, Henry Fitzgibbon, Warren Greene, Mark Gubicza, Billy Guide, Danny Gumz, Billy "Catfish" Haas, Pete Hall, Charlotte Jacobs, Reuven J. Katz, Luther Kilness, Vic Lapiner, Earl "Scoops" Lawson, Jim Leyland, Wayne Lyster, Roger Makley, Arnie Metz, Joe Morgan, Paul O'Neill, Tony Perez, Frank Robinson, Cara Shea Rose, Carol Rose, Caryl Rose, Dave Rose, Fawn Rose, Pete Rose Jr., Tyler Rose, Jeff Ruby, Rickelle Ruby, Oliver Sacks, Russell C. Schalk, Mike Schmidt, Marge Schott, Jackie (Rose) Schwier, Bud Selig, Danny Sheridan, Charles Sotto, William "Big Bill" Staubitz, John Terosian, Andrew Vilacky, Arnold Wexler, and Don Zimmer.

A special thanks to Roger Kahn for his previous collaboration with *Pete Rose, My Story; The Sports Encyclopedia: Baseball 2003*, written by David S. Neft, Richard M. Cohen, and Michael L. Neft, which provided statistical information; Sisley's Italian Kitchen for catering and conference rooms; *Boss Cox's Cincinnati*, written by Zane Miller; my literary agents, Joel Gotler and Scott Waxman; and my attorney, Barry Felsen, for encouragement and sound advice.

A special thanks to my wife, Barbara Kilness Hill, and our three children, Gantry, Garrett, and Hayley, whose love and patience, during a hectic year, were major blessings.

—*RICK HILL*

CONTENTS

FOREWORD   ix

PREFACE   xiii

CHAPTER 1   **HINDSIGHT IS 20/20**   1

CHAPTER 2   **BETWEEN THE RAILROAD AND THE RIVERBANK**   9

CHAPTER 3   **MY OTHER PASSION**   24

CHAPTER 4   **BREAKIN' IN**   37

CHAPTER 5   **HIGHLIGHTS**   69

CHAPTER 6   **THE FIRST TIME**   101

CHAPTER 7   **IN TOO DEEP**   124

CHAPTER 8   **BUSTED**   144

CHAPTER 9   **THE LONG HOT SUMMER**   168

CHAPTER 10   **MY PRISON WITH BARS**   191

CHAPTER 11   **LESSONS**   207

CHAPTER 12   **PUSHING THE ENVELOPE**   228

CHAPTER 13   **THE LONG ROAD BACK**   244

CHAPTER 14   **MY PRISON WITHOUT BARS**   267

CHAPTER 15   **TURNING POINT**   287

CHAPTER 16   **THE MEETING**   306

EPILOGUE   **MY DREAM**   318

FOREWORD

It was a crisp autumn night, perfect for playing football on Cincinnati's lower west side. It was the kind of night I grew up dreaming about. As I trekked along the muddy banks of the Ohio River, I paid no attention to the mélange of red, yellow, and orange that shrouded the branches of the oaks and silver maples. I stopped only occasionally to chuck a fallen buckeye at some appealing target. After all, it was Sunday night. And that meant the proud folks and I from Anderson's Ferry would descend on Hampton Field, as they had for years, to watch a legendary halfback wreak havoc on the opposition. At five feet ten, 195 pounds, my dad, Harry Francis Rose, or "Big Pete" as he was called, was simply impossible to stop. He was known for delivering bone-jarring tackles and breaking highlight-reel runs of 60 and 70 yards, which dazzled the fans. Hold on. Wait a minute . . . wait just a goddamn minute! Does anyone out there in the book-reading public believe for a minute that I'm actually writing this stuff? I didn't think so. Hell, I flunked the 10th grade. I can't even spell "mélange" let alone use it in a sentence. So, before we get off on the wrong foot, let's just back up and start all over again.

I was born on April 14th, the day the Titanic went down . . . the same day Lincoln was shot. Hell, do you think I might've had a dark shadow hanging over my life? I never cared much for big words or the folks who used 'em, but I'd like you to remember the word "shadow" because I'm going to refer to that word later in this book. Rick Hill—he's my writer—says that "shadow" represents a strong metaphor in my life. Like me, Rick grew up in Ohio and spent his summers playing baseball with his favorite uncles. Unlike me, Rick got his college education and was nominated for a Rhodes scholarship. I told Rick that he must've been pretty smart but not as smart as the feller who actually won the damn thing. Anyway, you're going to hear some words that I don't use in my day-to-day talk in here. Words like *obsessive-compulsive* and *risk-craving behavior*. And even a few brain chemicals such as *dopamine*. Since I don't use or even understand most of those words, I'll have to rely on some help from the experts. You see, I've made some discoveries about myself in the last few years and I'm going to try and talk about them as best as I can. I was involved in the most controversial scandal in baseball history and it's time I told the truth about what really happened. I know what you're thinking—why now, Pete, after 14 years? The answer is simple. Because it's time. Because I'm a little older and maybe a little wiser. Because it's what the fans want. Because it's what my dad would've wanted. Because maybe, just maybe, someone else might benefit from my mistakes.

So, before I go on, let's get one thing straight: I don't blame anyone else for my problems and I sure as hell don't want your sympathy. I'm not going to break down and beg your forgiveness like a TV preacher. I ask no quarter and give none—that's how I was raised and that's how I played baseball. Truth is, I've hurt myself and my family far worse than I've hurt baseball or any of its fans. I lost a career that I loved, a million-dollar-a-year job, and the respect of my peers—all because of gambling. That's right—gambling, which means we've gotta get another thing straight—I don't have normal hobbies like most folks. I don't play golf, tennis, or chess. I don't tinker with cars, fix furniture, or plant flowers in the garden. I don't go fishing, hunting, or hiking. I don't play the piano, listen to music, or read good books. I don't drink, smoke, or chase wom—er, well, like I said—I don't drink or smoke. Outside of baseball and my family, nothing has ever given me the pleasure, relaxation, or excitement that I got from gambling. Gambling provided an escape from the day-to-day pressures of life. And for me, gambling was just plain fun. I started going to the racetrack with my dad when I was 6 years old and I've been going ever since. I love going to the track with friends and I love watching them have a good time. Over the last 30 years, I've hit over a dozen pick-six tickets—all totaled, more than a million bucks in winnings. Ask any gambler and he'll tell you that's pretty damned exciting . . . except when you start to figure in my losses, and not just in money. I'll watch just about any sport on TV—football and basketball are my favorites. And if I had a wager on the game, it made it that much more exciting to watch. But there was a time in my life, after my playing career ended, when my gambling got outta control. It came after breaking Ty Cobb's record and at a time when I needed more thrills in my life. The more I gambled, the more I needed to gamble. And the more I lost, the more I tried to double-up to win back what I'd already lost. But ask any real gambler and he'll tell you: "It ain't about the money—it's about the action!" I kept pushing the limit until I was so mixed up, I didn't know whether to wind my ass or scratch my watch.

I'm gonna talk about things I've never talked about before. Like what it was like spending 5 months in federal prison . . . about losing a fortune and hitting rock bottom . . . and about living in exile for the last 14 years. I'll talk about how and when and what I did . . . and even what I didn't do— that part may surprise a few of you. And for that, I'm going to need some help from those experts I told you about. According to David E. Comings, M.D., director of medical genetics at the City of Hope National Medical Center in Duarte, California, gamblers experience something called *risk-craving* and *sensation-seeking behavior*. I can't speak for anyone else, but those words sure describe how I felt when I placed my bets. It might also explain why Winona Ryder got herself into some trouble. Do you think a millionaire actress couldn't afford to pay for all of those expensive clothes? It might also explain why Robert Downey Jr. kept snorting cocaine, even though it meant going back to jail. Do you think he preferred living in jail to making movies? I don't think so. You see, I've been to jail, so I'm qualified to talk about that subject. Now don't get me wrong. I'm not making excuses for myself or anyone else, and I'm sure as hell not pointing the finger. Those two kids are talented actors—at the very top of their profession—just like I was. I'm just trying to explain that nobody—I mean nobody—actually makes a conscious effort to screw up his life.

According to the experts, there are more than 40 million active gamblers in the United States and more than 3 percent have a real problem. Gambling is considered pathological when an individual is chronically and progressively unable to resist the impulse to gamble and it disrupts or damages personal and family life. I denied having a problem for many years. And because of my success in baseball, my friends and family let me get away with it. But in the end, can you imagine anything more damaging than being banned from your profession for life?

I've had a lifelong battle with something called ADHD—Attention Deficit Hyperactivity Disorder—which made it impossible for me to concentrate on schoolwork or anything else I didn't love doing. And oh yeah, there's something else: ODB—Oppositional-Defiant Behavior, which I got from my mom, Rosie. Hell, that one's obvious—it means I love to fight. I love conflict. Always have. That attitude paid off big-time on the baseball fields of America but it sure as hell wreaked havoc in my personal life. After you get to know more about my family and me, I think you'll come to understand why. You see, I just don't think the same way as most civilized folks—call it "Pete Rose logic."

I'm not proud of what I did, but I'm ready to take responsibility for it. I want to make my peace with the game of baseball—a game I worshipped for 24 years. A game I miss being a part of. A game I'd like to get back into . . . if they'll have me.

PREFACE

I first met Pete Rose during the summer of 1986 in Pittsburgh's Three Rivers Stadium. He was the celebrated player/manager of the Cincinnati Reds, having broken Ty Cobb's record for career hits. At the time, I was costarring with Mike Connors in the ABC-TV series *Today's FBI* and was in town to play a softball game against the Pittsburgh Steelers before that evening's Reds–Pirates game. Along with actors like Michael Keaton, Carl Weathers, Tony Danza, and Mark Harmon, I played for a team called the Hollywood All-Stars, which traveled the country playing softball games against teams from the NFL and NHL for a host of charitable causes.

The All-Stars, who played more for competition than entertainment, were on a 25-game winning streak and led the Steelers by 7 in the late innings. I knocked a gapper that bounced off the warning track, which caught the attention of Pete Rose. "Give that kid a baseball," yelled Pete. At the end of the inning, I was surprised to find Jim Leyland and Pete Rose waiting for me at the dugout. Jim Leyland was in his first season as manager of the Pirates, and along with his brother Bill, coached my Little League baseball team in our hometown of Perrysburg, Ohio. Following introductions, Jim Leyland told Pete that I had spent my college years playing football at Georgia Tech, an institution known as much for academics as for athletics. Much to my surprise, Pete just smiled. "1973 . . . Georgia Tech played Southern Cal in Atlanta," said Pete. "The Trojans were National Champs but Tech had a great defense and covered the point spread. I won a bundle on you guys." I was pleased that Pete won money from my team's efforts but was much more impressed by his remarkable memory—a talent I would become more familiar with in the years that followed. After we laughed and shook hands, I watched as a shot of me and Charlie Hustle appeared on the stadium's Diamond Vision screen—an image still etched fondly in my mind.

Years later, I was reunited with Pete Rose through a mutual friend, who had given Pete a copy of my screenplay, *The Longshot*, based on the life of baseball star Jim Eisenreich. The script intrigued Pete because, first, Eisenreich was a great hitter. Second, it dealt as much with Jim's inner struggles as his accomplishments in baseball. Within days, Pete and I began discussing our ideas for a tell-all book. I learned early on, that Pete, through no fault of his own, is not really capable of emotional exposure. He uses a relentless sense of humor to deflect even the most traumatic experiences. Trying to peel away the layers of self-preservation and defiance for the purpose of a cathartic reading experience has proved challenging indeed. Nevertheless, as both friend and collaborator, Pete has spoken with me honestly and openly on an array of personal and sensitive subjects, which I have tried to capture in a manner consistent with his irrepressible personality. Pete Rose may be tragically flawed in some ways, but like many of America's greatest heroes—the flaws are what make him interesting.

During the ensuing years, I came to know and appreciate Pete Rose for what he is—a hard-hitting, head-first-sliding baseball legend, who parlayed lightning-quick hand-eye coordination and a compact swing into 4,256 major league hits—a record that may never be broken. Rose is also a charismatic, cantankerous, fun-loving man-child, who, like Sinatra, did it "his way."

I salute Pete for coming forward with the truth and I thank him for giving me the opportunity to tell his story—one that should appeal to any red-blooded American baseball fan. But it is more than that. His story should appeal to any husband, wife, or enabler of an obsessive-addictive mate. It should appeal to any parent, teacher, or sibling of an oppositional-defiant child. It should appeal to anyone who seeks an understanding of the human condition. And with understanding comes hope . . . and with hope, anything is possible . . . even the Hall of Fame.

—RICK HILL

HINDSIGHT IS 20/20

"When they take your freedom—
there is nothing scarier in the whole world."
—PETE ROSE

Of the 17 baseball players who have been banned for life, none have ever been reinstated. But since I have seven major league and 12 National League records, you'll understand why I would like to add just one more "first" to my tally before I settle in for the big dirt-nap. Not that I think I deserve better than those other guys—I just love to win. I had only met Commissioner Bud Selig once before, but on November 25, 2002, Mike Schmidt and I stood in his office in Milwaukee waiting for a meeting that I hope will bring me back to baseball. Actually, I wasn't sitting. I was pacing. I'm what you call a "hyperactive" person, which means I can't sit still for any length of time. I was pacing back and forth, thinking about how to talk about something that I had kept secret for 13 years—hell, longer than that. I don't know why the Commissioner agreed to reconsider my case. Perhaps he thought it was time to mix justice with mercy and some good old common sense. Maybe he was struck by the endless chants of "Let Pete in" at the 2002 World Series where I appeared on the Master-Card All Century Team. Maybe he thought that after 13 years, the so-called deterrent value of punishment was firmly in place. I did know what Mr. Selig wanted to hear but didn't know how he would react after he heard it. Finally, my friend and Hall of Famer Mike Schmidt got frustrated by watching me wear out the carpet and offered some words of encouragement: "Look at all these photos, Pete," he said. "Just about every Hall of Famer in baseball is hanging on these walls and Pete Rose has more hits than any of them. Mickey Mantle's dead. Jackie Robinson's dead. Joe DiMaggio, Ted Williams, Satchel Paige, and Babe Ruth—all gone. You're one of the last men standing from the old regime. So just remember: Baseball needs Charlie Hustle." Most folks know that I'm not a warm-and-fuzzy guy. I don't pick up stray dogs or send thank-you cards, and I don't cry at weddings—unless it's one of my own. But I'll be damned if I wasn't a little bit moved by what Schmidt had to say. So hell, I took his advice. I started looking at the pictures and it took my mind off the business at hand. I looked at a picture of Willie Mays—the greatest player I ever saw. Then I looked at Sandy Koufax—who could throw a baseball through a goddamn carwash without getting it wet. And I looked at Hank Aaron—the man who broke Babe Ruth's home-run record.

I kept pacing until finally I came face-to-face with another familiar face—Ty Cobb, and you can imagine what that reminded me of.

The year was 1985, a warm September night, and I was one swing away from breaking Ty Cobb's career record of 4,191 hits—a record that stood for damn near 60 years. People have often tried to compare me to Tyrus Raymond Cobb but I just don't see the resemblance. Cobb idolized his strong-willed father and was pretty chilly toward his mother. As a rookie, Cobb was hated and shunned by the veteran players on his team. Cobb loved baseball with a passion and absolutely hated to lose. Cobb was involved in an alleged gambling scandal that drew a suspension from the American League president. Now, honestly, folks, does that really sound like Pete Rose? Aw hell, let's just get back to the night of the record-breaking hit. As y'all know, I've always been a media-friendly guy. But during the weeks leading up to the big night, I got radiation burn from all the cameras that were constantly stuck in my face. They were camped out at my house on Indian Hill. They were camped out at the ballpark, and they pretty much followed me everywhere I went. For 3 straight weeks, I did a press conference, TV, magazine, or newspaper interview every day of the week and twice on Sunday. I did an in-depth interview with Rick Reilly of *Sports Illustrated* and with Lesley Stahl of CBS. But to be honest, none of that stuff bothered me. I was feeling strong, calm, and confident about the whole situation. I had become the most media-experienced athlete of my generation. In fact, when asked where I got my strength to perform under such intense pressure, I just opened my jersey and exposed my T-shirt, which read: "Wheaties, Great out of the Box!" Everyone busted up laughing, which kept the press right where I wanted them.

Top of the first, Browning, our starting pitcher, retires the San Diego Padres in order. Bottom of the first, Milner flies out. Then I step into the box against Eric Show in front of a sold-out crowd of over 47,000 Cincinnati fans, who were screaming and shouting like crazy. I looked back at umpire Lee Wire and he said: "Time to make history, Pete." The first pitch was high, which I took for ball one. I swung easy and fouled off the second pitch and then held off again for ball two. Show's 2-1 pitch was a slider, down and in, which I drove to left-center for a single. Then the fireworks erupted and all hell broke loose. I rounded first and slapped hands with Tommy Helms, my longtime friend and coach. Then the fans just went berserk. Steve Garvey of the Padres stepped in and said: "Thanks for the memories!" First, they took away the baseball and then they took away first base, which I assumed was being sent to the Hall of Fame for posterity.

Marge Schott ran onto the field and presented me with the keys to a new red Corvette with a license plate that read "PR 4192." Then I looked over and saw Tony Perez and Dave Concepcion—two of the best teammates in the world. Yes, sir, it was a pretty special night. I was doing just fine throughout the first several minutes of all the hoopla. But after they left me alone, I began to feel strange. I had no glove, no base, no ball, and no bat. It was the only time I was ever on a baseball field and didn't know what to do! Then while hugging Tommy Helms, I started to choke up. Helms gestured for my son, Pete Rose Jr., and while hugging Petey, I just lost it. I remembered all the men who helped me reach that milestone in my career, but during the 9th minute of the standing ovation, I looked up in the sky and saw the face of the only man I ever idolized—my dad, Harry Francis Rose.

In 1947, when I was 6 years old, my dad, or "Big Pete" as he was called, was the fiercest damned competitor the Feldhaus Football League had ever seen. On the night of the big game, I trekked along the banks of the Ohio River to get to the field, but like I said, I don't remember seeing a "mélange." I was the team waterboy and assistant equipment manager—jobs I loved because they kept me on the field, close to the action. I hated sitting in the stands with my mother and my two older sisters, Caryl and Jackie, because even back then I had no interest in the idle gossip of women. In fact, the only time I ever went into the bleachers was to "pass the hat" for donations to help pay for the stadium lights and referees. Dad only got paid about 15 or 20 dollars for the entire semipro season. So everybody else had to chip in to help pay for the extras. But after the Great Depression, there was never much in the hat because nobody really had any money. I would usually get to the field 2 hours before kickoff to set up the water buckets and help my uncle, Buddy Bloebaum, chalk the field. Buddy was a real flamboyant man who wore a fur coat and fedora hat. He also had a secret identity, which I will talk about in detail later. Before chalking the field, I'd run routes, catch passes from Uncle Buddy, and imagine myself breaking long runs and delivering bone-jarring tackles just like my dad. But in my mind, I wasn't playing between the railroad and the riverbank. I was playing at Soldier Field in Chicago before a sold-out screaming crowd. Even back then, I had big ideas about my future in sports, ideas fueled by my dad's encouragement.

During this particular season, my dad was playing for Trolley Tavern, one of the five different semipro teams in the area. Dad played semipro football for 23 years including one year with the Bengals long before they joined the NFL. On this night, Trolley was ahead of the Comets by three points, late in the fourth quarter. Since none of the roster's plumbers, bartenders, or bankers could kick, a field goal was not considered a threat. Come to think of it, I'm not sure if the "field goal" had been invented yet. Anyway, Dad kicked off to the other team, fought off a block, and got blindsided really hard by some big burly-ass player. Dad's teammate, Shorty Goings, heard the bone crack and could see the pain in Dad's face as he pulled himself from the ground. "Damn it, Pete," screamed Shorty. "Your goddamn leg is broke. Take yourself out of the game!" "It's just a scrape for chrissakes," said Dad. "I'm fine." Shorty knew better than to argue because Dad wasn't about to sacrifice a year of Cincinnati's bragging rights over something as trivial as a broken leg. I ran into the huddle with the water bucket and offered the ladle to my dad, who just waved me off. As team captain, he never drank water until the other players had a chance to drink their fill. Then I looked up, expecting to hear a balls-to-the-wall pep talk. But all eyes were glued on Big Pete, who was very calm. But that was my dad—a man of strong presence. He had a square jawline and piercing steel gray eyes. When he spoke, people listened. He looked at his teammates and said: "I don't intend to lose on the last play of the game. So let's put on a big rush and stick somebody!" As they broke huddle, each Trolley player tapped Shorty on his special leather helmet, which was designed to protect the metal plate in his head—the result of shrapnel wounds Shorty got during the war. I laughed my ass off at that good-luck ritual, then raced off the field, where I watched Dad from the sidelines. It was cold as hell and Dad's breath looked like smoke in the night air—an image I can remember just like it was yesterday. The Comet's quarterback stood behind center and barked out the signals: "Blue 22, blue 22!" The wide receivers were lined up for what is now called a "Hail Mary." But Dad must've sensed a sneak play because he screamed, "Red Dog" to his teammates, which meant the linebackers were supposed to blitz. Sure enough, instead of the drop-back pass, the quarterback gave a pump-fake and then handed off to his fullback on the draw play. But the middle was all clogged up because Dad played his hunch correctly. He got knocked down while fighting off a blocker, but Dad crawled over, wrapped his arms around the fullback's legs and joined in on the game-winning tackle. As the final seconds ticked off the clock, a dozen other fans and I stormed the field in celebration. My dad had just won the big game and the Schultes' Fish House keg of beer that went with it. Dad limped toward the sideline, removed his helmet with his bloody hands, then looked into my eyes and gave me a smile—one of the biggest thrills of my life.

Forty-two years later, I was looking down into the eyes of my own 6-year-old son Tyler. But instead of celebrating a victory, I was trying to explain why I was going away. No, this was not just another spring training in Florida or 3-week stint on the West Coast to play the Giants, Dodgers, and Padres. I had been convicted of filing false income tax returns and was being sent to the prison camp at the U.S. Penitentiary in Marion, Illinois. I decided to tell the truth and when I did, Tyler started to cry. He was not old enough to understand what was happening. But I didn't want to lie because I knew that sooner or later, he'd find out the truth. I swallowed the lump in my throat and thought about the pain my dad must have felt while making that tackle with a broken leg. But Dad's pain was physical and what I felt this day was emotional—a helluva lot harder to deal with! I grabbed Tyler by the shoulders and tried to explain that everything would be okay. But nothing I said made that little boy feel any better. The next few minutes felt like hours. I had no answer for the betrayed look in Tyler's eyes. My dad never let me down on any level and failing my own son was just too tough to handle. So hell, I started to cry, too—rare for me because, like I said, I'm not a warm-and-fuzzy guy. But I'm speaking from experience when I tell all of you dads out there—no pain is worse than when you let down your kids. Finally, my wife, Carol, ushered Tyler into the kitchen for some ice cream and a promise that he could come visit me on Sundays. Now ain't that a bitch? Trying to cheer up your son by telling him he can come visit Daddy in prison on Sundays.

As you can imagine, this was the lowest point in my life. I walked out onto the lawn and took one last look at my 10-acre Indian Hill estate and stared toward the barn that housed my prize quarter horses—knowing that it would all have to be sold to pay the seven figures I owed to lawyers, taxes, penalties, and interest. I felt more like an outcast than Cincinnati's favorite son or baseball's all-time Hit King. At just about that time, I saw my wife's closest friends, Rickelle Ruby and Charlotte Jacobs, pulling into the driveway. The two attractive blondes were invited along to help my wife share the drive back from Carbondale, Illinois. Years earlier, Johnny Bench and I provided the seed money for Rickelle's husband, Jeff Ruby, to open the Precinct and Waterfront restaurants—sites where we all spent many nights celebrating during the 1980s. But as soon as Carol saw her girlfriends, I knew I was in for trouble. The three of them huddled up and started hugging and crying and talking about how they had to be strong, which left me no option but to step right in and straighten things out. The last thing I wanted to see was a bunch of crying women. So I walked toward the girls and looked them squarely in the eye. "I have a serious question to ask and I'd appreciate an honest answer," I said. The girls wiped their tears and responded to the serious tone in my voice. "Do you know why they can't keep Jews in prison?" I asked. "Because they eat all the lox," I replied. The punch line took a moment to sink in but the girls started laughing at my corny joke, which provided some much-needed relief from what was already a grim atmosphere. I figured a little humor would help to keep things in perspective. After all, I faced Sandy Koufax, Nolan Ryan, and Bob Gibson—I could damn sure face 5 months in southern Illinois.

I had 6 hours before I was required to surrender to the authorities at Marion—a 5-hour drive from Cincinnati. The word "surrender" was never part of my vocabulary but ever since that day in Judge Spiegel's courtroom, the prison sentence had been hanging over my head like that "shadow" I mentioned earlier. But in some strange way, I was eager to get on with the challenge. As we drove down I-75, I caught a glimpse of Riverfront Stadium along "Pete Rose Way"—a sight that . . . well, you can just imagine how that sight made me feel. Hell, they should've named an alley after me based on the things I'd done. The Queen City, which had been my oyster for 30 years, never felt so lonely. As we crossed the Ohio River, I settled into my seat and took a little nap. I didn't wake up until we passed through Louisville, where, contrary to published reports, I did not stop to bet on the ponies at Churchill Downs.

Within a few hours, I caught a glimpse of a huge concrete structure with cinderblock walls and barbed wire fence—the U.S. Penitentiary in Marion. So, without fanfare or media attention, I said my good-byes and surrendered to the authorities, who would take control of my life for the next 5 months. I was immediately taken to a holding area to await "orientation." Some re-porters called this place a "country club." But let me tell you, when they take your freedom, there is nothing scarier in the whole world. The sound of iron bars closing at the main prison damn sure caught my attention—a sound that caused me to ask myself a question: "How did I get here?"

2

BETWEEN THE RAILROAD
AND THE RIVERBANK

"A man who doesn't take care of his own family ain't a real man."
—HARRY FRANCIS ROSE

Back in the 1940s and 1950s there were three big things in Cincinnati culture—baseball, other sports, and sports gambling. I'll get to the other two
a little later. But first, I want to tell you about how I became obsessed with
my first true love—baseball. I was born and raised in a clapboard house
30 yards from the New York Central Railroad tracks, which ran along the
banks of the Ohio River. We lived on the lower west side, in the
Sedamsville section of Cincinnati, in a little area called Anderson's Ferry.
It was named after some feller named Anderson who operated a ferryboat
back in the early 1800s, which is the entire history lesson you're going to
hear out of me. Anyway, the Ohio River flooded so bad in 1937 that my
Mom, LaVerne, or Rosie as she was called, just sat on the front porch
smoking her unfiltered Luckys, contemplating how to deal with such a
devastating natural disaster. Our house had 12 steps that led from the

front door down to the steep hillside along River Road. The river had swelled up all the way past the third step. After watching a chest of drawers from our neighbor's house floating down the street, Rosie got a great idea. She went inside, grabbed her fishing pole, baited up a hook, and caught one of the best fish dinners our family ever ate. Yes, sir, the Roses might have been poor, but by God, we were resourceful!

My dad worked for the Fifth Third Bank & Trust in downtown Cincinnati. In his 40 years as a teller and bookkeeper, he was never late and never missed a day of work. I don't think Dad ever earned more than 10,000 dollars a year, but I can honestly say that we never lacked for anything. What we missed in material things, we made up for in other ways. Dad was not a "hug-and-kiss" type of father. Hell, nobody behaved like that in the 1940s. It just wasn't natural—not like it is today, where parents feel obliged to videotape every second of their kids' lives and dote on their every word. I never heard my dad say "I love you." But I knew that he did, more than anything in the world, by the way he treated me. He just couldn't express those feelings because he was too macho. All of the folks from his generation lived through the Great Depression, which made them iron tough, not soft. They had a different way of doing things. They took stock in the value of hard work and a hot meal. Soft-hearted emotion just didn't put food on the table.

In his prime, Dad was one of the best and most respected athletes in Cincinnati history. At age 21, he boxed under the name of Pee Wee Sams, trained at the Danny Davis Athletic Club, and won the state special-weight championship at 106 pounds. Twenty years later, he was still winning championships as a 195-pound semipro football player. In 1985, after breaking Cobb's record, I said "I'm the next generation of my father, with an opportunity to show what he could have done." But if my dad had been the baseball player—he would've gotten 5,000 hits. Even after everything I accomplished with the Reds, I'm not sure I ever earned the respect that my dad received. Throughout my life, Dad's friends gave me a constant reminder of their expectations: "If you grow up to be half the man your father is, you'll be one helluva man."

Instead of pursuing a career in professional sports, Dad married LaVerne Bloebaum and settled down to raise a family, supporting us with his job at the bank. Mom was the daughter of a local trolley operator and along with her three older brothers, one damn good softball player. The 1930s was not a popular era for women's sports. But that didn't stop LaVerne one bit. She could really swat that ball and was not above talking trash long before Allen Iverson made that particular trend fashionable. You see, Mom was outspoken and opinionated—filled with piss and vinegar. Traits I have to admit, I inherited from her. Even as a teenager, Mom had a pretty tough reputation. She never took nuthin' off nobody and she never backed down from a fight. While in junior high school, she had a little run-in with one of her girlfriends, who was saying stuff that really bugged my mom. LaVerne followed her home and just whupped the living hell out of her. Apparently, the girl tried to put up a fight but she was no match for LaVerne.

But Dad still loved sports with a passion and after having two daughters, Caryl and Jackie, he was understandably thrilled to have a son who shared that passion—me, Peter Edward Rose. I came into this world on April 14, 1941, at Cincinnati's Deaconess Hospital. I weighed in at over 9 pounds and was almost 20 inches long. I reckon my sister Jackie was as thrilled as my dad to see me join the family because until then my parents cut her hair really short and dressed her up like a boy. Of course, Jackie didn't really mind. She was only 5 years old at the time and happy to get the extra attention.

I got my first baseball glove before I could walk, and I got a new glove every year thereafter. By the age of 4, I was swinging a bat and throwing a baseball. As long as I could remember, just about every activity in our

life revolved around sports. In fact, Dad used to set his watch to the time
I'd be in the front seat of his car every Saturday morning. He'd be sitting
at the dining room table, reading the sports page, and having his coffee
and doughnuts. Then he'd walk to the living room, poke his head through
the curtains, check his watch, and look at me. I'd be sitting in the front
seat of his car, 20 minutes early, waiting to go play ball with one of his
teams. I was the ballboy for his basketball teams at Christ Church, the waterboy for all of his semipro football teams, and the batboy for every one
of his baseball and softball teams. At the end of every game or practice,
Dad would take time to play catch, shoot baskets, or run drills with me.
In fact, folks in the community used to call us "Pete and Re-Pete" because
rarely was one of us seen without the other.

During the summer, Dad used to pitch batting practice to me over at
Boldface Park or Hampton Field. He'd not only pitch but he'd teach the
finer points of playing the game. Dad would show me how to position my
hands on the bat, teach me how to run the bases, or turn the double play.
We'd spend hours of repetition with every single aspect of the game. On
days that Dad went to work, I'd continue to practice until I learned what
he taught. My mom never had to worry about where I was during the
summer. I was always playing baseball. I'd walk 3 miles to find an open
field. If I couldn't find a pickup game at one of the fields, I'd toss a baseball
against the brick wall at Schultes' Fish House. The wall was painted with
a big walleyed pike, and I used the fish's eye as a throwing target. I'd toss
the ball at different angles, field the rebound, and make a play against imaginary base runners—my way of taking infield practice without the infield!
Even as a 9-year-old kid, it was not unusual for me to toss the baseball
against the "fish" for hours at a time or until my hands started bleeding.
Truth is, the bleeding didn't bother me because it meant that I'd never get
blisters during the Knothole League season. Over the years, I've read
where reporters took the stories out of context and twisted them around to

make it sound like my dad pushed me too hard toward sports. Nothing could have been further from the truth. My dad was always encouraging—obsessive but not abusive. He coached and taught, but he never screamed or yelled. Besides, I loved playing sports as much as he did and if I practiced until my hands started bleeding, it was because I wanted to!

Throughout my childhood, I never lacked for activities or entertainment. In those days, sneaking off to the filling station to get a 2-cent deposit for our pop bottles and then applying the money toward a nickel Coke was about as big a treat as any kid could want. Occasionally, we'd climb the grain silos or the steps of the Ashland Oil refineries. But mostly we just swam in the river, went fishing and boating, or made up our own games for fun and entertainment. We had baseball and hot summer days, and I wouldn't have traded that for the world. During the summers, Dad would take us hiking or horseback riding 2 or 3 days a month. We'd hike up steep Anderson's Ferry Road, through Delhi, and down Sister's Hill. Jackie and Caryl would sing songs or play "kick the can" along the way. My brother, Dave, was 7 years younger than me so he had trouble keeping up. But Dad was a fast walker and insisted that we never fall behind his pace. He always set a time schedule for the hike. Even in leisure, Dad had a purpose. On some nights, we'd take our sleeping bags and camp out in our backyard or on the riverbank near the ferryboat landing. Dad would build a bonfire and we'd roast hot dogs and catch lightning bugs. Mom, by now called Rosie by everyone, would make hot chocolate and tell some pretty outrageous stories, which kept the entire neighborhood entertained. Being married with children didn't slow down Rosie's fiery personality one bit. At the time, Rosie was tending bar up at Trolley Tavern and the VFW Hall to earn extra money for the family. Apparently, there was some lady named Hazel, who was spreading rumors that Mom was running around with her husband. Of course, Mom never ran around on my dad and didn't take too kindly to Hazel's accusations. Rosie got so pissed off that she grabbed Hazel by the hair, pulled her out of the tavern, and beat the livin' hell out of her. After that ass-whuppin', Hazel and everyone else in the neighborhood stopped spreading rumors about Rosie! Of course, hearing those stories directly from Rosie's mouth kept everybody entertained while sitting around the campfire.

Dad was always the strong, quiet type and Mom was outspoken and opinionated. So they got along just fine. In fact, the only time I ever heard my folks argue was just after my sister Caryl's 12th birthday. I was 6 years old at the time and taking a lot of teasing for being about a foot shorter than most kids my age. Dad wanted to make sure I learned to stand up for myself and fight back. Rosie saved up a few extra dollars from tending bar at Trolley Tavern and gave the money to Dad so he could buy a nice pair of shoes for Caryl. Dad brought home a gift box, but when Caryl opened it up, she started to cry and ran out of the room. I looked inside and pulled out a brand new pair of boxing gloves! I reckon I was about as thrilled as I could be. But Rosie threw a fit. "Harry Francis Rose!" she screamed. "What in the hell did you do? I gave you that money to buy Caryl a new pair of shoes!" Dad just snapped right back at her. "It's 100 degrees outside, Verne," he said. "Caryl can go barefoot but young Pete's got to learn how to defend himself!" The two of them went at it for quite some time. Since neither one of them could ever back down from a fight, I thought the ruckus might go on for a while. Finally, Dad realized he couldn't win an argument with Rosie. He just walked out of the house and joined me in the backyard, where he began teaching me the art of self-defense. Later that night, I knew peace had been restored to the Rose household when I saw Mom and Dad sitting on the couch listening to Waite Hoyt, the radio voice of the Cincinnati Reds. Dad loved to listen to Reds games on the radio—a ritual he rarely missed. Caryl got her new shoes the very next day, but I got to keep my boxing gloves!

Over the years, Dad continued to train me for a career in the ring, paying close attention to see if I had the heart and moves of a champion. He taught me how to jab, punch, and bob 'n' weave. But the very first time I let down my gloves, Dad cuffed the back of my neck with his open hand. It didn't hurt but it sure caught my attention. It taught me never to drop my guard, a lesson I never forgot. I didn't realize it at the time but Dad was preparing my attitude as much as my technique. He always told me that sports were 90 percent mental toughness . . . that if I made fewer mistakes and out-hustled my opponent, I'd win every time. Dad also knew that the technique used in throwing a punch was very similar to throwing a ball or swinging a bat. All three involved coordinating the use of the legs, hips, arms, and back. Even though Dad had no way of knowing which sport I'd take to, he knew that boxing would be a valuable experience.

Just before my 16th birthday, Dad arranged for my first amateur match at the Finley Street Neighborhood Club. I fought Virgil Coles, an experienced boxer from the inner city, who pretty much used me as his punching bag. At 115 pounds, I wasn't much of a physical specimen. But I took everything Coles dished out and on occasion landed a few wild punches myself. In between rounds, my mom and sisters got upset by the sight of my bloody face and asked my dad to stop the fight. But Dad reassured them that I was doing just fine. Fine, hell, I was getting my brains beat out! Dad knew it, too, but didn't want me to see that he was concerned. I stood on my feet for the full five rounds and never once hit the canvas. But I was no Pee Wee Sams. I lost the match by unanimous decision. Afterward, I took a lot of teasing from my friends but I was proud of my effort. "At least I didn't get knocked out," I said. But my bruised and swollen face was more than Mom could handle, so she and Dad decided that I was better suited for something less violent, like football or baseball—wise decision!

At that time, going to Crosley Field to watch the Reds was the biggest thrill in my life. We usually sat in the "cheap seats" down the right field line. But any seat to a Reds game was a great seat as far as I was concerned. Cincinnati was rich in baseball tradition, boasting the world's first professional team—the 1869 Red Stockings, which finished their first season with an amazing 57–0 record. Sometimes Dad got tickets through the bank. But on other days, I'd hitch a ride downtown, stand outside the stadium, and beg for an extra ticket. In fact, if I had a ticket to a game, the principal would let me out of school early. I'd catch the bus and get to the stadium in plenty of time to watch batting practice. I was in awe watching the star players—Stan Musial, Ted Kluszewski, Gil Hodges, and Duke Snider. I knew from the first day I set foot in that stadium that I would some day play for the Reds. Don't ask me how. But I just knew.

Although not as thrilling as football or baseball, The evening meal was always the biggest event in the Rose family. Dad usually got off the bus from work at 5:45 P.M. and Mom would have dinner waiting on the stove. As we all sat around the dinner table, we'd tell stories about our day. And we'd sit still until everyone was finished with their meal. We never got up from the table early or sassed back—not like kids today, who come and go as they please and talk disrespectfully to their parents. Although most of our dinner conversations centered on sports, Mom and Dad were interested in everything that was going on in their kids' lives. Dad loved the girls as much as the boys. Caryl and Jackie would talk about school and how well they did on their tests. My younger brother, Dave, loved cars and motorcycles, so he'd talk about races and such. Of course, Dad and I would always talk sports because that was our main interest. During the winter, we'd discuss football and the Cleveland Browns. During the summer, we'd discuss the Cincinnati Reds and their chances of winning the pennant. But by the time I turned 9 and began playing Knothole baseball, most discussions shifted to me. Dad loved watching me play baseball, but he was always a nervous wreck. He'd shift from seat to seat depending on how well I did at the plate. If I got a hit, he'd stay for good luck. If I struck out, he'd shift to another seat to break the jinx. He did the same thing years later when I played for the Reds. He'd drive everybody in his section crazy changing from seat to seat. And no matter how well I did, Dad would only comment on what I didn't do. If I went 2-for-4, he'd say I should have gone 4-for-4. If I went 4-for-4 and made an error, Dad would really get agitated because he looked at errors as preventable mistakes. Dad had no interest in discussing what I did well. He was only interested in helping me improve on my areas of weakness. His style of coaching never bothered me because I felt the same way he did. I hated making mistakes and Dad's attitude kept me focused on getting better and better as a player.

I got my desire and strong work ethic from my dad. But I got my knack for hitting and 20/20 vision from the Bloebaums—Mom's side of the family. Her older brothers, Buddy, George, and Al, were all-star players in their prime. Buddy, in particular, was a standout in the AA Marx League in northern Kentucky. At six feet three, Buddy was tall, strong, and loaded with talent. He went to the minor leagues right out of high school and played for a while in the Cincinnati chain. But the money was so meager that he left the team and went to work. As the oldest of four siblings, and coming out of the Great Depression, Buddy felt obliged to stay close to home and help support the family. At the age of 30, he became a switch-hitter and had his best success at the plate, leading the amateur leagues in Dayton year after year. Along with my dad, Buddy played hardball well into his 30s. By the time I started playing Knothole ball, Buddy retired from the active roster and, along with my Dad, spent a great deal of time coaching me. In fact, it was Buddy who came up with the idea of making me a switch-hitter. He and my dad went to my coach and struck a deal. "My son's going to be a switch-hitter," said Dad. "I want him to bat right-handed against left-handed pitchers and left-handed against right-handed pitchers—regardless of the circumstances—men on base, cham-

17

pionship on the line, whatever. Promise me you'll enforce that rule and he'll never be late, never miss a practice, and we'll never take a family vacation during the summer." The coach agreed. At that point, I became a switch-hitter at a younger age probably than anybody ever had. But just switch-hitting in the games was never enough for me. You can't become great just playing twice a week. So I practiced my hitting every day. Uncle Buddy gave me a leaded bat, which I would swing religiously morning, noon, and night. I took over 100 swings a day from each side of the plate for several years. I'd stand in front of the mirror and call out imaginary pitches. "Down and away," I'd say. Then I'd swing accordingly. High and inside . . . swing accordingly.

At 12 years of age, I became old enough to play rover—the fourth outfielder on Dad's softball team. Not only was it a great thrill but it was a great learning experience. As much as I learned from Dad's lectures, I learned twice as much from watching him play. He had great speed and was very aggressive on the base path. If an outfielder was lazy, Dad took advantage and got an extra base. He didn't care if we were down 7–0 in the ninth inning—he'd steal a base or break up a double play.

I learned more from Dad than I ever learned from any of my big league managers. "Baseball is not played game by game," said Dad. "It's not played inning by inning. Baseball is played pitch by pitch. You gotta watch the ball come out of the pitcher's hand. You gotta watch the ball hit your bat. You gotta watch the ball into your glove, because the player who watches the ball wins the game—and baseball is all about winning."

Dad also showed me when to make certain plays. For instance, most folks think a triple is earned by digging hard from second base to third. But Dad taught me that a triple is earned while coming out of the box. As soon as you hear the crack of the bat, and you know it's well hit, you've got to come out of the box thinking third base. It's not that the last 90 feet aren't as important as the first. But if you don't make the first, you'll never make the last. You've got to know when to gamble. One simple rule—never make the first or third out at third base! If you reach third with one out, you'll score easily on a fly ball. You never want to try for third with nobody out— too risky. Stop at second base. You've got at least three more batters who'll have a chance to drive you home. With two out, stay at second! You'll always need a solid base hit to score and the same hit that scores you from third will almost always score you from second. Not surprisingly, I led my minor league in triples for 2 straight years. And my first major league hit? A triple against Bob Friend of the Pittsburgh Pirates in 1963.

I was never much at school and frankly didn't much care. I talked too much in class and always disrupted the teachers. I never did it on purpose but I was too hyperactive. I'd try to sit still but my leg would start bouncing up and down so fast that I couldn't contain myself. I had to be outside playing ball. Notice I didn't say that I "wanted" to be outside. Hell, every kid in class wanted to be outside—I had to be! I had trouble comprehending information when I had no interest in the subject. As a result, I got distracted easily—and then I became frustrated. When the teacher asked the class a question, I'd usually know the answer. But by the time he called on me, I'd not only forget the answer, I'd forget the question as well! Then to cover my embarrassment, I'd usually crack a joke, which drew big laughs but also got me sent straight to the principal's office. In those days, principals were allowed to use a paddle on the kids—a lawsuit in today's world. But back then, it was totally acceptable. I remember attending the Saylor Park School and getting sent to the principal—Mr. Leyland T. Jones. Ol' Leyland would use a leather strap to whack me on my ass! It got to the point where I spent almost as much time in Leyland's office as he did. Like any kid, I did my share of teasing the girls and cutting up—nothing really bad. But some kids were pretty mean to me. They'd call me "dumb," which probably hurt my feelings, but I had too much pride to show it. I just buried myself in sports, which became my way of coping with anything in life that didn't go my way. And because I loved sports so much, Dad never made schooling a big priority. In fact, I never really had any responsibilities outside of playing ball. I never had to get a job or a paper route or anything like that. I just spent all of my time playing sports.

Throughout high school, I was much better at football than baseball. I had a great year as halfback and defensive back for the Western Hills freshman football team. I led the team in scoring, ran back kicks, and even handled all the kicking assignments. A quick little scatback with swivel-hips and deceptive moves, I'd break long runs of 50 and 60 yards. My mom was so pleased that I was following in Dad's footsteps that she promised me 50 cents for every touchdown I scored. But after earning $2 from one game, Dad informed her that I shouldn't get paid for doing what I was supposed to do. During our big rivalry game against Elder High School, I slid into their sidelines after making a tackle. I was so gung-ho that I came up swinging . . . challenging anyone who dared to fight. I can't remember if they were scared or just thought I was crazy. At 120 pounds, I was the smallest kid on the team—not what you'd call a physical threat. But nobody took me on. I reckon they thought anybody that small who wanted to fight must be pretty tough. Truth is, I didn't know I was too small. In my mind, I was five feet ten and 190 pounds.

By my sophomore year, I was excited at the prospect of playing for the varsity. But I still weighed only 125 pounds and the coach thought I was too small to play. He chose just a few kids from the frosh team and I wasn't one of them. At that time, there was no junior varsity, so I had to spend a whole year of my life without football—a major crisis! I was the star of the freshman team and the son of the best football player in the area, yet I wasn't even allowed to try out for the team! I was so heartbroken that I started to skip classes. If I couldn't compete for a spot on the football team, I wanted no part of that school. It was my first experience with being treated unfairly and I didn't like it one bit. The pain stayed with me for many years and provided me with strong motivation to prove the bastards wrong whenever they underestimated me. Even as a big league manager, I'd get into arguments with our baseball scouts, who only measured talent with stop watches and radar guns. "Radar guns don't measure heart and desire," I'd scream. "What good is being big and fast if the player has no guts?"

Not being allowed to try out for varsity football really took its toll on my life. I not only cut classes but started running the streets. I didn't break the law or run with gangs. I just found other things to occupy my time. I jumped the freight trains that ran along River Road, or I swam the choppy currents of the river across to Kentucky. I hung out with a group called the River Rats—or "greasers" as we were known back then. We were all pretty tough kids who started playing by our own rules. One day I marched right into the Gay Nineties bar, which was owned by one of my dad's friends, Danny Gumz. I just decided I was gonna beat their pinball machine, which had never been beaten. I went up to Danny Gumz and got 10 bucks worth of change. Danny told me that nobody could beat that machine. "I'm gonna beat it," I said. Sure enough, I stood there for hours and just beat that pinball machine to death. That's how I felt about challenges. If I made up my mind to do something, I knew I could do it. And nobody could tell me differently.

On the few days that I actually went to school, I didn't fare too well. I remember sitting in Mr. Dunkel's science class and taking a test. The kid next to me was looking over at my desk and copying all my answers. It was a multiple-choice test. So when I wrote down an A, he wrote down an A. If I wrote D, he'd write D. I helped him through the entire exam, yet he got a "B" and I got an "F" on the test. Afterward, I went to the kid who copied my answers and asked how it was possible for him to get a "B" and me to get an "F" when we both had the same answers? He just shrugged his shoulders. "I can't figure it out, Pete," he said. "The teacher saw us both. Maybe he has a grudge against you because you skip classes." At that point, I just said "Screw it!" I gave up and quit going to school altogether. That's why I flunked, not because I was dumb but because I never went. Hell, you gotta flunk if you don't go to class! Dad never found out that I was skipping school. But even if he had, he would have understood because he knew how I felt about getting aced out of the opportunity to play football. Hell, he was just as heartbroken as I was! I got up in the morning and rode the bus but I got off downtown, where I roamed the streets. I refused to go to school because I hated the teachers—just hated 'em! I hated the football coach because he wasn't fair to me.

"Even today with all our knowledge and experience, most teachers will fail to understand a kid like Pete Rose," says David E. Comings, M.D. "They only notice that he can't pay attention and that he is disruptive. So instead of understanding his personality and working with him, they ignore him or label him a troublemaker. Although there was not much awareness in the medical profession in the 1940s and 1950s, Pete's personality as described by his teachers is very telling: A bright kid but bored by classroom activities, sensitive to criticism or rejection, stubborn and strong-willed, will not comply with the rules, tests the limits with every adult, short tempered, inattentive, and aggressive—textbook ADHD, Attention Deficit Hyperactivity Disorder, which is genetically linked to gambling in adults.

"As far we know, ADHD is caused by a deficiency of dopamine and other neurotransmitters in the frontal lobe of the brain, which is responsible for behavior and the control of our emotions. ADHD kids will typically have problems paying attention to things of only peripheral interest. They will sometimes show poor judgment and react impulsively to various situations. But this has no effect on IQ. ADHD kids are typically very bright people who will shine when given a good teacher or mentor. When given a bad teacher, they will lose interest and drop out. But this doesn't mean they will fail in life. There are millions of kids who suffer from these symptoms—many very gifted. Bill Clinton supposedly had characteristics of ADHD. He had trouble concentrating during cabinet meetings or staying organized on things of only peripheral interest. But he was arguably a great president. NFL Hall of Famer Terry Bradshaw has ADD. He was a disaster in school yet won four Super Bowl Championships and became an Emmy-winning sportscaster.

ADHD kids are very strong-willed. They don't like anyone telling them what to do. They are going to be their own person and do it their own way regardless of the circumstances. In Pete's case, these characteristics helped him to become one of the greatest hitters in baseball history. So the ADHD can be a great advantage. Although they can't sit still or focus on subjects of little or no interest, their restless energy when focused can be dynamite. In fact, Pete Rose is not unlike Einstein, who flunked English but excelled in math. When these personality types find something they love, they will excel far, far beyond normal expectations.

"Without going into complex medical detail," Dr. Comings said, "the genetics are really quite simple. There are many genes that regulate any given personality trait. Each person gets half from their father and half from their mother. Most people will inherit a blend of these genes, which keeps their behavior in a spectrum commonly referred to as normal. But if by chance you get too many genes of any one trait, you're over threshold and have problems. In Pete's case, his parents' lives are very telling. In fact, the entire Rose family is a geneticist's dream. Given an 'oppositional-defiant' mother, who never backed down from a fight, and an 'obsessive-perfectionist' father, a legendary semipro athlete Pete Rose was virtually destined for greatness . . . as well as tragedy."

<u>3</u>

MY OTHER PASSION

*"This Kentucky Derby, whatever it is—a race, an emotion,
a turbulence, an explosion—is one of the most beautiful
and violent and satisfying things I have ever experienced."*
—*JOHN STEINBECK*

Cincinnati was very conservative during the era of my youth, molded in the image of Proctor & Gamble, makers of Mr. Clean and Comet. When it came to entertainment, the Irish-Catholic and German population were very buttoned down. But the Sedamsville–Riverside part of town where I came from was just the opposite. It was loaded with saloons and nightclubs and chock-full of craps games, poker, roulette wheels, and blackjack tables. Most of the local men, like my dad, routinely bet the horses and occasionally shot craps over at the Glen Rendezvous or at one of the joints up on Price Hill. The saloons were the hub of social activity, both legal and illegal. Prostitution was commonplace. The madams posted their signs right out in public for all to see. Most of the downtown pubs had in-house bookmakers and a few slot machines. Al Schavel, a friend of my dad, had a popular downtown restaurant called the Rib Pit Barn, which occupied an entire city block. The Rib Pit Barn provided the best live jazz bands, a great roast beef sandwich, and a wire service, which broadcast horse races from every track around the country. If you wanted action, the Rib Pit Barn was the place to go. But if a man wanted even bigger action, he could always go across the river. Newport and Covington, Kentucky, featured strip joints and casino-style gambling 24–7, just like Las Vegas. The bigger action was rumored to be run by the syndicate—folks up north in Chicago and Cleveland. But I had no way of knowing anything about that—I was just a kid back then. But from what I've heard, the casino bookmakers took action on all kinds of sports—college and pro. Players from the National League teams would come into town, go across the river, and place bets on games—not their own but on games throughout the league. The authorities heard about it and tried to clamp down but the syndicate people were just too strong and too organized. But in 1950, everything changed. Senator Estes Kefauver of Tennessee formed a commission, and held televised hearings on illegal gambling. They investigated the connections between organized crime and local politicians, which eventually caused crackdowns on illegal gambling throughout the country—not just in Cincinnati.

As a young kid, I played Knothole baseball against Mike Brennan, whose father, Bill, was a bookmaker during my dad's era. Mr. Brennan lived up on Price Hill and ran a respectable operation—nothing big, just routine sports and horses. Due to the cold weather conditions, the horse-racing season only lasted for 5 months in Cincinnati. Most folks worked long hours, so if a guy wanted to lay down a bet, he'd use a local book-maker, whose job was to get to the track during business hours. Bill Brennan came from a nice Irish Catholic family and made his rounds on Sunday mornings to collect his debts and pay off his losses. He'd visit the saloons up and down River Road then stop off at the church to collect from the nuns and priests who gambled as much as everyone else and sometimes more. Father Niehaus of Saint Vincent DePaul was the head of the local parish, a guy you could count on to get you out of a jam. But he skipped Mass regularly to go the track. When I asked why he spent so much time at the races, Father Niehaus just gave me a sly grin. "Jesus went out among the sinners and so must I." But if he got a tip on a horse, Father Niehaus was just as likely to place a bet as the next guy. "After all, Petey," he said with his Irish accent, "even a man of the cloth is tempted by a sure thing at 20–1 odds!"

Like Father Niehaus, Mr. Brennan was a good man with good intentions. If a gambler was getting in over his head, Mr. Brennan would alert the other bookmakers on the west side to let them know not to take his action. Nobody wanted to lecture a guy who was out of control, but nobody wanted to take advantage either. And if a guy got behind in his debts, they'd give him some time to make good. But that's not to say that folks were easy. They weren't. Sedamsville was filled with rough trade—guys who'd just as soon fight as look at you. One of my teenage friends, Howard Stein, got into some trouble and got killed in a local bar called Five Points. So, I learned early never to let down my guard. If you showed any weakness at all, you'd get taken. I grew up learning to be tougher than the next guy. And knowing my family, I think you can understand why.

On Friday nights, Dad pitched horseshoes for Gumz Café. He'd pitch against the 50-60 Bar, Renter's Café, Saylor Park Grill, Houck's Café, and ironically, the 4192 Club, which was named after their address on River Road—not my record-breaking hit. I went along with Dad every Friday night, carried the horseshoes, and whenever there was a break in the action, pitched a few ringers myself. Usually, the men wagered a dollar a game but mostly they just played for beer. Dad got a big kick out of winning at horseshoes even though he didn't drink. Occasionally, he'd bring home a six-pack of Hudepohl, Weideman's, or Burger beer because those were the sponsors of Cincinnati Reds baseball. But they'd sit in the refrigerator for weeks. You see, Dad considered drinking a "weakness." Years later, I found out why. When my sister, Caryl, was having some problems with her husband, I witnessed dad's convictions firsthand. At the time, Caryl had four kids, named Randy, Sandy, Andy, and Candy. "Damn, girl," I'd ask Caryl. "Whattaya gonna name the next one—Dandy?" Caryl and the kids always took the teasing in good spirits. They had a tough life due to no fault of their own. Dad didn't like the way Caryl's husband, Chub, took care of his family. Chub came walking up our front lawn one day and made the mistake of running his mouth. Dad smelled booze on his breath and just saw red. BAM! BAM! BAM! Dad hit him with two left jabs and a right cross and Ol' Chub went down like a sack of potatoes—out cold! I never saw any of Pee Wee Sams' boxing matches but I saw why he won the championship in his weight class. Dad had a haymaker that would have made Rocky Marciano proud. When I asked dad why he knocked out Caryl's husband, he replied, "A man who doesn't take care of his own family ain't a real man."

On Sundays, Dad played softball for Gumz Café with all the other "real men." Among them, two of the greatest guys I ever met—Dud Zimmer and Eddie Brinkman Sr. Along with their sons and me, we were two generations of father-son ballplayers from the same neighborhood. Mr. Brinkman played shortstop just like his son, Eddie Jr., who went on to play in the majors for 15 years. At the time, Mr. Zimmer's son, Don, played American Legion ball for Bentley Post and was tearing up the league with monster home runs. Don was later drafted by the Brooklyn Dodgers and has since become a household name in Major League Baseball, long before getting wrestled to the ground by Pedro Martinez during the 2003 ALCS between the Yankees and Red Sox. Now don't get me wrong, Pedro is one of the greatest pitchers of all time. His ball has unnatural movement—almost unhittable. But if Pedro had come up against Don Zimmer in his prime instead of at age 72, Pedro would've been the guy who got carried off the field on a stretcher.

Mr. Zimmer owned a very successful downtown produce business and parlayed a good deal of his profits on the ponies. Everyone called him "Dud," but I called him "Mr. Zimmer" because I always treated my elders with respect. Whenever I was downtown, I'd stop by his produce store and say hello. Mr. Zimmer would greet me with a great big smile and shake my hand. He'd give me a free apple or a slice of watermelon and we'd talk baseball for hours. Mr. Zimmer just loved talking about sports. He'd remember a certain double play or a hit that I got in my last ballgame. He always made me feel like I was the most talented ballplayer in town.

When Dad, Mr. Zimmer, and Mr. Brinkman weren't playing sports, they'd sneak over to River Downs Racetrack or Old Latonia Raceway to play the ponies. And they always took me along. Mr. Zimmer had a strong passion for horse racing but my dad was just a recreational gambler who stayed within his means. Dad only went to the track two or three times a month and bet between two and four dollars per race. Dad never bet every race on the program because he knew the odds would stack up against you.

Other than Crosley Field, I'd never seen anything quite like the racetrack. The energy and the atmosphere fascinated me. The men wore suits and ties during that era, which really added to the experience—conjured up images of Bing Crosby, Red Grange, and Jack Dempsey, who I'd seen on the newsreels. Bing Crosby opened the Del Mar Racetrack in the 1930s and always invited celebrities, athletes, and political dignitaries to the races. Anybody who was "anybody" in that era was at the track.

I would get right up against the fence and watch the ponies bust out of the gate. There weren't many kids at the track in those days, so I usually stood by myself or with my younger brother, Dave. But sometimes Dad would take me to the stable area, where the owners would come and talk with the jockeys, trainers, and even the college kids, who galloped horses in the morning to help pay for their schooling. It didn't matter that we were from the wrong side of town. Everyone was equal at the track and everyone had something interesting to say—the jockeys, trainers, groomsmen, and exercise riders, and even the kids who mucked out the stalls. There was a special type of camaraderie at the track, which is like no other place I've ever found save for the baseball field.

My first trip to the races was my most memorable. I sat in the bleachers with my Dad, Mr. Zimmer, and Mr. Brinkman and tried to follow along as they laughed and told jokes. They'd study the program before each race and talk about the trainers, jockeys, and previous races. Before each race, I'd walk up to the window with Mr. Zimmer and stand on line. Mr. Zimmer knew everyone in town and always struck up a conversation with friends like Rick Meyer and Henry Lapp from Schultes' Fish House. After Mr. Zimmer placed his bets, we went back to the bleachers with our tickets and screamed and hollered for our horse. After the fourth race, Mr. Zimmer had to leave the track to take care of some business at his produce store. But just before he left, Mr. Zimmer gave $200 to my dad to place on the number six horse at 9–1 odds in the fifth race. Dad sent me up to the window with the money and asked me to give the bet to Rick Meyer, who was already standing at the front of the ticket line. I gave the money to Mr. Meyer and asked him to place it on the number six horse, just like Mr. Zimmer requested. It was my first trip to the ticket window alone and I remember feeling nervous and excited . . . like I was "one of the guys." Rick Meyer paid the money to the teller and gave me four $50 tote tickets, printed on shiny red paper. When I got back to our seats, I handed the tote tickets to my dad and watched as he turned white as a ghost! "I told you to place the money on the number six horse to win," said Dad. "Win—not place!" My heart dropped down to my stomach. I was just a kid but I knew I screwed up big time. I bought four $50 "place" tickets instead of four $50 "win" tickets! Anyone who saw *The Sting* with Paul Newman and Robert Redford will identify with my dilemma. In the movie, Newman and Redford established a "past-posting" con to sucker Robert Shaw into betting bigger and bigger stakes. Once Shaw took the bait, Redford told him to place a million dollars on a particular horse—a guaranteed winner. After he called to verify his bet, Robert Shaw freaked out when he discovered the bet was for a "place" showing—not a "win." My mistake was just the opposite but no less reason to panic. Two hundred dollars was not a million but it was a lot of money to a guy who bet just twos and fours. In 1947, $200 was more than 2 week's take-home pay for my dad. And since he'd given his word to Mr. Zimmer, Dad was responsible for the money—not just the $200 but the $1,860 if the horse came in! There was only one ticket line back in those days, so the wait was really long. It was a lot of trouble to try and exchange tickets, so Dad didn't want to tie up the line and potentially cause someone else to get shut out at the bell. Most gamblers were pretty sophisticated and didn't want to be embarrassed by admitting they made a mistake. But Dad didn't panic . . . and he didn't blame me. He just looked around the track, saw a friend from the bank, and borrowed $200 in a heartbeat. Then, Dad took the money, ran to the window, and placed Mr. Zimmer's bet just in the nick of time. When Dad came back with the tickets, I blew out a sigh of relief. Then I thought, damn, what if the horse doesn't win? Mr. Zimmer will lose his money but Dad would still owe the $200 that he borrowed from his friend. Geesus, my little ol' heart started pounding like a jackhammer! You never heard so much commotion in all your life as when those ponies broke out of the gate. Between Dad, Mr. Brinkman, and me, we were riding right along with our jockey all the way down the backstretch! The six-horse and the nine-horse were striding neck and neck all the way and we were screaming and yelling at our jockey! "Use the whip! Wiggle the goddamn reins!" Finally, the six-horse and the nine-horse closed at the wire—photo finish! My heart dropped down to my knees while waiting for the results. You could've heard a pin drop in the stands. Hell, I was thrilled, scared, amused, and angry all at the same time. When they finally posted the results, we started whoopin' and hollerin' like we'd just won the Kentucky Derby! The number-six horse won by a nose and paid $1,860 to win and $980 to place. Dad and I ran up to the window and collected on both bets. Talk about exciting! We thought we were the richest folks in town . . . and the luckiest! Dad paid back the $200 loan to his friend and, just as Mr. Zimmer requested, parlayed his winnings on another horse in the sixth race, which lost. But Dad placed his personal winnings on a 7–1 horse that won in the seventh. So, at the end of the day, we went home with over $2,200—big money in 1947! When we got outside to the parking lot, Dad gave me the lecture of my life. "We were lucky today, Pete" said Dad. "But this is exactly why you have to listen and do as you're told. If the coach says 'bunt'—you don't hit away—you bunt. Make a mistake in sports or in life and you lose!" I nodded my head. Lesson learned. Then, Dad used the pay phone in the parking lot and called home to speak with my mom. "Put on a dress, Rosie," said Dad. "I'm taking the whole family to Trolley Tavern for a victory dinner!" After that, it was all hats and horns.

I continued to go to the track with my dad and Mr. Zimmer throughout my teenage years and even more frequently after I broke in with the Reds in 1963. The track became my sanctuary—a place where I could go to relax and escape the day-to-day pressures of life. Sure, gambling was a big part of the attraction. The race is a competition with money as a prize. But while I enjoyed the races, I enjoyed the camaraderie even more. The track was filled with wonderful characters who reminded me of the folks I grew up with—folks who lived hard and played hard.

Mr. Zimmer played as hard as anybody I've ever met. He considered himself a great handicapper but more often than not, the real handicap was Dud's advice. Dud was what you call a "hunch gambler." He bet with his hunches, which always provided me with some good laughs if not winning tickets. "I had an incredible dream last night, Pete," said Dud. "When I got to the produce store, I saw nothing but hats. Hats everywhere. When I drove home, I saw thousands of hats just floating down the Ohio River." I just grinned. "Hats, huh?" "Yeah, Pete, hats," said Dud. "Nothin' but hats—same dream three nights in a row! Everywhere I looked, I saw hats. When I got to the track, I opened my program and saw a horse named 'Top Hat' at 20–1 in the fifth race—Providence. I just knew it! Dreams are for a reason. They're not just random. The Race Gods were trying to tell me something! So, I plopped down five hundred on Top Hat at 20–1 odds! Sure enough, Top Hat broke out of the gate and just dusted the competition. As he was streaking down the backstretch, I was jumpin' up and down, just going crazy! Then, all of a sudden, Top Hat ran out of gas. Finished dead last! I just stood there feeling shocked . . . betrayed. Five hundred dollars down the goddamn toilet! I mean . . . what about my dreams?" Finally, I had to ask. The suspense was killing me. "Who won the race, Mr. Zimmer?" "Sombrero!"

Throughout the 1950s, it seemed like every time we went to the track, something strange happened. Dad had a long shot coming down the backstretch all alone, when suddenly a deer ran onto the track and knocked our jockey ass-over-elbows onto the rail. Our horse and jockey were okay but that damn deer was a little shook up. On another occasion, my dad, Mr. Zimmer, and I were sitting right in front of the starting gate at Hamilton Raceway when our horse broke out of the gate and took the lead. But some stupid sonafabitch from the crew tied the horse's tail to the gate. So, when he busted out, the force tore off his tail. I don't know whether the horse was scared or shocked but he ran like the wind until he hit a bad spot on the track. Then, with an eight-length lead, the horse fell and broke his leg. Everybody was just shocked. You could have heard a pin drop in the bleachers. Today, they have an ambulance for such things but in those days, they brought out a tractor, hooked up a noose, and pulled the horse onto a tarp, then dragged him all the way around the track and off to the stable area. The horse's tail was still hanging from the gate! Finally, I looked over at Mr. Zimmer, who was just as sad as he could be. "What will they do with the horse?" I asked. "Well," said Dud with a straight face, "I reckon they'll have to wholesale him . . . damn sure can't *re-tail* him."

Dad, Mr. Zimmer, and I would go over to Latonia every year for the Donkey and Harness Races, which were always a lot of fun. Today, donkeys like Taz and Black Ruby win up to 25 races a year. But the donkeys were totally unpredictable back in those days. Every year, the same driver would use the same stubborn donkey as his lead Sulky in the Post Parade. And every year that damn donkey would pitch a fit, start bucking and kicking, which always brought the house down. But I'd get frustrated because his antics always delayed the races. "Why in the hell does he do that?" I asked. Ol' Dud shot me a grin and in a high pitched voice replied, "Oh, Hee-Haw, Hee-Haw-ways does that."

Over the years, I continued my friendship with Mr. Zimmer. And long after I became a major league star, I went to the hospital to see him when he was on his deathbed. But Mr. Zimmer wasn't afraid of death. He looked up at me and grinned just like always. "Pete," he said. "I promise you this—I'll get back to the track and see the ponies just one more time before I die." The very next day, Dud pulled the "pillow-under-the-sheets" trick on the nurses, got dressed, called a cab, and went over to

Turfway Park one last time. The doctors and nurses freaked out when they discovered the scam. But afterwards, they just smiled. "At least he died with his boots on."

Mr. Zimmer was as good as they come. His was one of the only funerals I ever heard of that wasn't sad. Everyone had such great memories of Dud Zimmer that they couldn't help but smile. To this day, I honestly believe that's why Don Zimmer and I love the ponies so much. We grew up going to the races with our fathers.

Throughout my adult life, I still thought of myself as an "average Joe," just going to the track and feeling the same excitement I felt as a kid. Even though I became famous I could walk into the clubhouse at any track in the country and be equal to anyone else. Whether a guy is a $2 or $2,000 bettor—we'll both share the same information. We may not stand in line to place our bets at the window but we'll talk about horses, trainers, and jockeys. We'll talk about owners, breeders, and track-bias and speed figures. We'll talk about Derby and Breeder's Cup prospects and we'll both be talking the same language. The average Joe can't go to a Lakers game and mix with Jack Nicholson. He can't go to a Ravens game and mix with Art Modell. But the average Joe can go to the track and feel like a king. Some guys may be down on their luck and touting horses to catch a break. But the millionaire will stop and listen because the advice he receives may net him a fortune. The average Joe can't go out and buys a professional basketball team. But he can get a bunch of friends together who love sports and excitement, buy and train a racehorse, and have a ton of fun—and maybe, just maybe, make some money. Jim McKay once said, "I've never seen anybody walk to the winner's circle. They all run like it might disappear before they get there."

When it comes to gambling on horses, everyone has their own system—the Sheets, Thoro-Graph sheets, or just plain ol' superstition. None are fool-proof. That's why they call it gambling. If it were a sure thing—it wouldn't be any fun! Women and children might bet their favorite colors or lucky numbers, which can be as good a system as any. Some folks study the program for hours, going back 10 races to chart every statistic in the world. Others study Beyer Speed Figures and breed-lines. But my system is simple. I like speed. A fast horse is going to win a lot of races in much the same way a fast runner will steal a lot of bases. I also like winners. I'll bet on Bob Baffert and D. Wayne Lucas, Pat Day, and Jerry Bailey. I'll look at the breeder, turf conditions, and pole position if things are close. I'll bet a mudder on a wet track every time. But mostly, I bet the ponies the same way I used to bet football—Elway and Marino. Go with the winners or go with your gut.

This is how it works: In the year 2000, I attended Gulfstream Park, when the Breeder's Cup Classic was a wide open race. The Classic was the final race of the day with a $4 million purse. I was in Miami as a celebrity guest and I was too busy entertaining corporate guests to spend a lot of time handicapping the horses. There was a big field that day and my friend Russell Schalk who owns Raintree Racing in Maryland, had been handicapping the races throughout the week. Russ started out by winning with a longshot on the very first race. So, with money ahead, Russell decided to have a good time and enjoy the whole scene—no pressure to hit the jackpot. I looked at the program and noticed that D. Wayne Lucas entered a horse called Cat Thief—always the bridesmaid but never the bride. Cat Thief won his share of small races but never quite made the jump to big time respectability. Since there were very few times that Cat Thief started off as a favorite, he was listed at 19–1 odds. Cat Thief, with Pat Day on board, was owned by W.T. Young of Overbrook Farm in Lexington, Kentucky—one of the top breeding facilities in the world. I'm thinking "D. Wayne Lucas, Pat Day, and W.T. Young are looking pretty strong at 19–1." I saw another West Coast horse I liked named, Bud Royale, who was trained by Ted West and claimed for

35

$40,000—low for a claimer but not a good indication of his speed or his heart. Bud Royale was listed at 20–1 odds. So, based on my gut reaction, I made up my mind that Cat Thief and Bud Royale were my one-two picks. If they actually finished one-two, it would make for a great exacta. Also, if they become the first two on a trifecta—it would pay off big time. So, I bet $2,000 on my exacta and got ready to enjoy a great Breeder's Cup. Russell Schalk was even more ready. Russell bet $200 across the board on Cat Thief and another $40 exacta box on Cat Thief and Bud Royale. Then he bet Cat Thief, Bud Royale plus the field. He had maybe $800 in tickets but since he'd hit his first longshot, he was still dollars ahead—playing with the track's money. The field broke out of the gate and by the first turn, the favorites hadn't even picked up their feet. Cat Thief broke out into the early lead, which was consistent with his style of racing. Bob Baffert and John Orsino also had horses in the race but the two or three heavy favorites were nowhere to be seen. By the time they hit the far turn, I knew I was looking good. As Cat Thief and Bud Royale made the final turn, I cheered all the way down the backstretch. Cat Thief won by about 2 lengths and Bud Royale finished a strong second. Golden Missile finished third at 75–1 odds, which capped off a great trifecta. Cat Thief paid $40 to win, $20 to place and $16 to show. The $700 exacta paid 20 times. The trifecta paid $39,000 plus what Russell Schalk won across the board—all totaled over $150,000 from just $800 worth of tickets. That's what you call a good day at the races.

4

BREAKIN' IN

*"Don't ever give up on your dream because
you never know what the future might bring."*
—PETE ROSE

Over the years, I have often read that I got my gambling from my dad. "Pete's daddy was a gambler, so Pete became a gambler," they'd say. I've just never understood the connection. I got my desire and work ethic from Dad—not my gambling. But that's not to say that gambling doesn't run in the family. In his prime, my Uncle Buddy Bloebaum was one of the best baseball players in the state. While playing for the AA Marx League in Kentucky, he made no errors at shortstop and finished with a batting average of .500 in his best season. At the age of 30, he became a switch-hitter and led the Amateur league in Dayton, Ohio, with a .440 batting average. At six feet three, Buddy was tall, strong, and loaded with talent—best all-around hitter in the family. Buddy was a few years older than my dad, so the Great Depression affected his life as well. He was offered a minor league contract at an early age but the money and opportunity was so meager that he turned it down. As the oldest of three brothers and three sisters, including my mom, Buddy felt obliged to stay close to home and help support the family. But Uncle Buddy also had another talent, which earned him more money and recognition than playing baseball. Buddy could shoot pool as well or better than anybody in the state of Ohio . . . or Kentucky . . . or Indiana. And being ambidextrous, Buddy could shoot right- or left-handed. After earning a pretty good reputation as Cincinnati's best pool shark, Buddy found that nobody dared play him for money because they knew they'd lose! So Buddy took his show on the road. But after a few months, Buddy ran into the same problem: Nobody was foolish enough to play him for money. Being resourceful and flamboyant, Buddy Bloebaum was not to be denied. If his identity struck fear in the hearts and wallets of his opponents then by God, he'd change his identity! Buddy began traveling the Midwest as "The Masked Marvel." He wore a colorful mask, put on trick-shot demonstrations, and challenged all comers to high-stakes games. Those who feared Buddy Bloebaum found themselves attracted to the challenge of the Masked Marvel. I was too young to remember but I heard that the Masked Marvel actually beat the great Willie Mosconi in a game of nine-ball, which earned Buddy enough money to put a big down payment on his house in Dayton.

Over the years, Uncle Buddy enjoyed his adventures as a marquis pool hall attraction. But to imply that he was somehow a "pathological gambler" because he enjoyed high-stakes excitement would be misleading. Buddy worked for National Cash Register in Dayton, Ohio, for more than 30 years, wore nice clothes, always carried himself with style, and was the greatest uncle a kid could want.

If Uncle Buddy, who was a scout for the Reds, hadn't begged Phil Seghi to take a chance on me, I never would have received a pro contract. Phil Seghi was the farm-club director for the Reds, who liked my attitude but thought I was too small to play in the big leagues. He was right. I *was* too small. Uncle Buddy convinced Mr. Seghi that all the men in the Rose and Bloebaum families were late bloomers. He reminded Phil that "Big Pete" Rose didn't grow to be 195 pounds until he was 23 years old . . . and wouldn't he feel just awful if I turned into the kind of player my dad was, and he let me slip away just like he did with Don Zimmer? Zimmer was another undersized baseball player from my neck of the woods who signed with the Dodgers back in the early 1950s. Zimmer was a real sore spot with the Reds, who misjudged his heart by the size of his body. At that time, Zimmer was having some pretty good success in the majors and might have become a big star had they been able to slow down his swing. Ol' Zimm used to swing from his ass on every pitch. But when he made contact, the ball went right out of the park. That sumbitch could really swat. Zimm got beaned in the head a couple of times, which really hurt his career. But he is still one helluva coach and one of the greatest guys you'd ever want to meet—a real asset to major league baseball.

On the day after I graduated from Western Hills High School in 1960, Dad, Uncle Buddy, and I drove over to Crosley Field, where we met with Mr. Gabe Paul, the Reds' general manager, and Phil Seghi. I signed a minor league contract that paid me $400 per month, a $7,000 signing bonus, and an extra 5 grand if I was to stick with the big league squad for up to a month. I didn't tell the Reds but I would've signed for free just for the opportunity to play baseball. All I wanted was a chance. I would've carried the bats, washed the uniforms—anything.

I arrived in Geneva with only 2 months left in the season, so it took me awhile to catch up with the other players. I had some problems adjusting to faster pitching, fielding grounders . . . and, for the first time in my life, being lonely! I was away from my family, Mom's cooking, and all the day-to-day comforts of home. I traveled on buses for hours at a time, slept in broken-down motels, and ate whatever grub was available at the greasy spoon diners—typical life in the minor leagues. Finally, Mom got worried about me and rode the bus to Geneva, where she stayed for 2 weeks. She brought a care package loaded with home-cooked food and plenty of snacks. She also sat in the bleachers and cheered during my ball games, which helped me get adjusted to my new surroundings. I played with two talented teammates, who also became good friends—Tony Perez and Art Shamsky. Tony had just escaped from Cuba and was the nicest guy in the world. But he spoke with that thick Cuban accent and I couldn't understand a word that sumbitch said! But in all fairness, I couldn't speak a word of Spanish either. But we had no trouble communicating on the field. Baseball is a universal language. Catch the ball, throw the ball, hit the ball—"No problema!" Shamsky was from St. Louis, more experienced, so he showed us the ropes. Together, we'd go out for a milk shake or see a movie but mostly we just played baseball. Geneva was a small town with nothing much else to do except play baseball. And all three of us took baseball very seriously. This was our first taste of real competition—not like high school, where you only played twice a week. This was the real deal. We played every day—7 days a week. We played through pain and injuries and we played for keeps. If you couldn't cut the mustard, you just got cut. They gave you a road map and a hamburger—"Hit the road, Jack." Tony and Art and I each had our own dreams of making it to the big leagues. But given our size and lack of experience, nobody could have ever predicted that any of us would make it—let alone become stars. Truth is, very few players make it past the minor leagues—and at 155 pounds, I was more than a little nervous about my chances.

My uncle Buddy was still a bird-dog scout, so the Reds paid for him to come visit. He and his wife, Maggie, stayed for a few days and helped me with my personal business—starting a bank account—that sort of thing. We went down to the local pool hall and shot some billiards—er, Buddy shot and I watched as he ran the table. Buddy also gave me a few hitting pointers. "Look for a good pitch to hit," said Buddy. "Don't swing at bad pitches." But I did swing at a lot of bad pitches. Like most 19-year-olds, I had more energy than patience. At one point, Dad drove to Erie, Pennsylvania, and watched me play in a road game. He was disappointed that I wasn't making better progress but he knew that my enthusiasm would eventually pay off. Dad wrote me a letter once a week and signed each one "Keep Hustlin'." After his trip to Erie, Dad spoke with Mr. Blomski, another one of the Reds scouts, and asked him to keep an eye on me. So Mr. Blomski wrote me a letter of encouragement. In his letter, Slugger Blomski tells me not to get down in the dumps . . . reminds me that I'm a fair hitter. "Fair?"—some encouragement!

Tony Perez played third base. I played second and Art Shamsky switched time between first base and the outfield. Of course, I made a big impact right away. In just 85 games, I hit .277 and committed 36 errors—a league high! Yes, sir, I might've been too small but I made up for it by being clumsy! We finished the season in last place, so not much went well for anybody on the Geneva Redlegs. But regardless of my shortcomings, I was known for my aggressive play and positive attitude. I was voted the most popular player by the fans and received my first-ever performance bonus—Samsonite luggage. At that time, my worldly possessions consisted of two pairs of blue jeans, four pairs of socks, and five T-shirts. What the hell did I need with a suitcase? A TV would have been nice!

After the season, I moved back to Cincinnati and within a few days, Uncle Buddy got my first scouting report from the Reds and brought it over to the house. The report said I couldn't hit left-handed, couldn't run or throw, and I couldn't make the double play. I was disappointed but not disheartened. I knew that I was still in the process of growing and maturing. I reported to the Florida Instructional League and began a rigorous practice regimen that I maintained throughout my career. In order to play right, you gotta practice right. And nobody ever practiced harder than me. I spent hours every day taking grounders, fly balls, and batting practice. But still, I was not what you'd call a promising big league prospect. "Pete's got tons of desire," said the scouts. "But not much talent."

After winter ball, I got a job working for Railway Express on the shipyards in downtown Cincinnati. I worked the graveyard shift—midnight to 8 A.M. loading and unloading boxcars—great bodybuilding exercise. Mom brought home-cooked meals every night, which helped me to put on weight. During the day, I continued to work on my hitting and fielding. I took batting practice and fielded grounders for hours at a time. I even worked on making the proper pivot move while turning the double play— something the scouting report said I couldn't do. And again, Dad kept reminding me to hustle. "Hustling can make up for a lot of things you might lack in the way of natural ability," he said.

By the start of the 1961 season, I had grown 2 inches and gained 23 pounds. The Reds invited me to play with the Tampa Tarpons of the Class-D Florida State League. I got off to a slow start but gradually picked up momentum. I was coached by former Reds pitcher, Johnny Vander Meer, who in 1938 pitched back-to-back no-hitters in the big leagues. No one else has ever done it—before or since. Johnny played in the majors for 13 years and had a pretty good eye for talent. At first, I played for the B-squad, which was made up mostly of players who were on the verge of getting cut. After my poor showing in Geneva, I wasn't too high on anybody's talent list. But Johnny saw something special in me and decided to take a chance. I ran out every play, slid headfirst, and had enough energy and enthusiasm to play all day without ever getting tired. Johnny put me in the lineup at second base and just turned me loose. My defensive skills were still a bit raw but the extra size I gained from loading boxcars made all the difference in my confidence. I hit .331, set a new league record with 30 triples, and won league MVP honors. But my biggest thrill came when I hit two inside-the-park home runs on the same day, one each in a doubleheader. I told Mr. Vander Meer that it might not be as special as his back-to-back no-hitters in the majors . . . but for me, it came pretty damn close! "Every time I looked up," said Vander Meer, "Pete was driving one into the alleys and running like a scalded dog and diving headfirst into third." For my efforts, I received another performance bonus in the form of a Zippo lighter. Of course, I thought it was the greatest gift in the world. In just 2 short years, I had new luggage and a cigarette lighter even though I didn't smoke and never took a vacation! So I gave the lighter to my Mom and the luggage to my Dad as a way of thanking them for all their support.

I was proud of my statistics in Tampa but not satisfied. After tasting a little bit of success, I wanted more. I had my goal set on the big leagues and was anxious to get on with the challenge. I continued my work ethic throughout the winter and was soon regarded as one of the brightest prospects in the Reds organization. I grew 2 more inches in height and put on another 10 pounds. By the time I reported to Macon, Georgia, in the South Atlantic League, I was five feet eleven and 185 pounds. I became part of the "Dynamic Duo" with teammate Tommy Helms who was another major league prospect. In an article by Earl Lawson in the *Cincinnati Post*, Tommy Helms described his feelings. "Pete Rose is a physical freak," said Helms. "I've never seen a guy with his energy. He never gets tired. He jumps out of bed in the morning, goes into his hitting stance, and takes batting practice in the hotel room with an imaginary bat. I'm just lying there, rubbing my eyes, wishing I could go back to sleep for a couple more hours!" Tommy was right. I had a love and enthusiasm for baseball that I can't even begin to describe. Full of life and energy—like a pot of boiling water on the stove. And for me, enough was never enough. If I got two hits—I wanted three. If I got three—I wanted four. During one particular game against the Greenville Spinners, we batted around four different times and won the game, 32–5. But I never let up just because the game was out of reach. I started out 0-for-2 but went 6-for-8 on the day with a home run, triple, and six RBI. Afterward, my manager, Dave Bristol, grinned and called me the "greediest" player he ever saw. Coach Bristol wasn't knocking me—he was paying me a compliment. He loved the fact that I was never satisfied with just a little success. By season's end, I had just as good a year in Macon as I had in Tampa. I hit .330, led the league with 136 runs, 17 triples, completed 9 home runs, and won league MVP honors.

Along with my success on the field, I grew more and more confident as a young man. Art Shamsky, my teammate from Geneva, Tommy Helms, and I became known as "The Bad Boys." We tore up the baseball league during the day and did our fair share of damage at night. Instead of Macon, Georgia, we just called it "Makin' Out," which is what we set out to do. We were 21 years old and discovering the best of what the Peach State had to offer—girls! Shamsky and I got a room together and began dating the prettiest girls in town. Well, at least I did. The phone operator where we were staying was real sweet but not the prettiest of girls. As I recall, she was a little "deficient in the dental department," if you know what I mean. But I convinced Art that he needed to date that girl in order for us to get free long-distance telephone calls. We both liked to call home every day but with just $3.50 a day for food, there was nothing left in our budget for Ma' Bell. And I wasn't about to let something as trivial as "poverty" interfere with talking to my folks and giving them an update on my progress! Art put up a fuss but within time, he understood that free phone calls were more important than nice teeth. "For the good of the team, Art!" Shamsky was a pretty smart feller and one helluva good ballplayer. But I still can't understand why Ol' Shamsky didn't ask *me* to date the girl with bad teeth! I reckon I had a pretty persuasive personality even back then. I had energy and enthusiasm. Other folks called it "charisma." But after spending my first 18 years being too short and too slow, I was really enjoying my newfound confidence.

After saving my signing bonus and most of my salary from the previous 2 years, I bought my first new car—a custom-order Corvette from a Chevy dealer. Being 21 years of age and the proud owner of a new 'Vette, I decided to open up the four-barrel carburetor to see what she'd do. While roaring down I-75, I got pulled over for speeding in Calhoun, Georgia, by one of them good ol' boys with the State Patrol. Or maybe it was the sheriff's department—I can't remember. Either way, I tried my best to persuade the officer to let me off with a warning. I explained that Tommy and I were playing baseball in the Sally League and had to get back to Macon for a night game at Luther Williams Field. But that big cop wasn't the least bit impressed. "Y'all are in a whole heap o' trouble, boy," he said in that deep Georgia drawl. "We don't cotton to no out of state drivers coming 'round here breakin' our speed laws!" And with that, he made Tommy and me empty our pockets. Together we had $77 in cash, which turned out to be the exact amount of our fine! After taking our money, the cop just grinned. "Y'all come back now, y'hear?" Fortunately, we had just filled up our tank with gas. Otherwise, we would have been shit outta luck. We cruised into Macon, sputtering on gas fumes but we were laughing all the way.

Pushing the speed limit with my new Corvette was fun. It was the first of many expensive sports cars that I would own over the years. I always drove 'em fast and hard but never got into accidents. I had great hand-eye coordination and quick reflexes. I could see the road the same way I saw the baseball field—peripheral vision. You might say that I had a strong appetite for speed and adventure, which sometimes went beyond a typical nine-inning game. That's why I loved playing doubleheaders—another chance to hit, run, field, and throw. Sometimes the team traveled to Florida and the Carolinas by station wagons, not buses. We'd cram seven or eight players into each wagon and hit the road. And those 10-hour road trips drove me nuts! I'd talk, chatter, and crack jokes to the point where I got everybody annoyed. After a couple hours, I'd usually ask the driver to pull over to the side of the road so I could get out and play catch, burn off some steam. But the other guys always wanted to stay on the road and get to our destination. They had no trouble sleeping in the car. But I was too hyperactive to sleep or even sit still for any length of time. During one particular trip to Florida, we'd been on the road for hours and hours and I was just going crazy. I asked my teammate, Marv Fodor, to pull over so I could get out and stretch my legs. But Fodor said "no." He was in a hurry. Actually, he said something a little more expressive than "no" but it's been so long that I really can't remember exactly what it was. So I took it upon myself to vent my frustration. I slid out of the back window, climbed onto the roof, held onto the luggage rack, and waved my hand in front of the windshield. Fodor was still driving at 70 mph but I damn sure got his attention. "Rose," he screamed, "Are you crazy?" Everyone in the car busted up laughing. But I made my point. Finally, Fodor pulled over to the side of the road and let me blow off some steam. I didn't think too much of it at the time because that was just the wild side of me. At that age, I had tons of energy and needed challenges to keep myself entertained. I got bored when I didn't have a ball game to play and nothing was more boring than sitting in the backseat of a station wagon for 8 hours at a time. Looking back on it now, I can just imagine what might have happened if I had fallen off.

In December of 1962, I was back in the Florida Instructional League, where I hit .326, sixth best in the league. During the winter meetings, Reds manager, Fred Hutchinson, was really impressed with my statistics and work ethic. "If I had any guts," said Hutch, "I'd stick that Rose kid at second base and just forget about him." Even though I was invited to the Reds spring training in 1963, I was told that I had no chance of making the team. "I'd like to try just the same," I told Hutch. The Reds Don Blasingame, or "Blazer" as he was called, was the star of the team and the starting second baseman. Nobody ever expected a brash young rookie to come in and take his place. Nobody except me and my dad, who packed his clothes in his new Samsonite suitcases and drove to Tampa to watch his son play in his first-ever major league spring training. After 21 years of coaching, teaching, and willing his work ethic into me, Dad finally realized his lifelong dream—the Big Leagues. Not semipro, Trolley Tavern, or the Feldhouse Football League. I was playing for the Cincinnati Reds—"The world's first professional baseball team." Do you think Dad was proud? Hell, the buttons were popping off his shirt!

Most folks remember the story of how I was dubbed "Charlie Hustle" by Whitey Ford. But few remember the events leading up to that particular event.

Hutch took a liking to me right away but my gung-ho attitude didn't sit too well with the veterans on the team. They were annoyed by my "constant chatter" and maybe a little jealous that Hutch started bragging about me openly. At that time, Hutch was good friends with Gene Mauch, who managed the Phillies. Before our next exhibition game, Hutch and Mauch were standing behind the iron batting cage, watching me hit. "You see that kid," said Hutch. "He's as hard as this goddamn cage." Mauch just grinned. "Yeah, but can he run?" He asked. "He goes to first base in 4.1 seconds," said Hutch. "But that's only after a walk!" I don't know if Ol' Hutch was in on the scheme but Gene Mauch decided to have a little fun at my expense. I got a real surprise when I came up to the plate in the first inning of our doubleheader. The Phillies catcher looked up at me and said "Hey, Pete, Mauch told me to tell you every pitch so you could be sure to hit it. The first pitch is a curve ball—good luck!" Well, I was about as shocked as I could be. No catcher had ever told me what pitch was coming before it actually came! Sure enough the pitcher threw me a curve and I swung and missed! "Next pitch is a fastball, low and away," said the catcher. Sure enough, the next pitch was a fastball, low and away—and again, I swung and missed. Throughout the game, the catcher told me each pitch before the pitcher threw the damn thing. He confused the hell outta me. You see, each hitter has his own strategy or rhythm—and when a catcher interrupts that rhythm, he's breaking your concentration. Years later, I would have no problem with such things. In an article from the *Cincinnati Post*, Earl Lawson talked with umpire Bruce Froemming. "No hitter in the league can match Rose's concentration when he's at the plate," said Froemming. "There are catchers in the league who like to talk to batters. Gary Carter of the Expos is one. Dave Rader of the Cubs is another. So is Steve Yeager of the Dodgers. Yeager especially, who does it on purpose, hoping he'll break a batter's concentration. They don't talk to Pete Rose, though. I've seen them try. And I've seen Rose back out of the batter's box and tell 'em to 'shut up, I'm hitting!'" Of course, as a rookie, I wasn't experienced enough to tell the catcher to shut up. But finally, I decided to take matters into my own hands. I was never a "guess-hitter," which means I never tried to guess what a pitcher might throw. Guess-hitters strike out a lot and I hated to strike out. I just focused on the count, base-runner situation, and then looked for the pitcher's best pitch. During the second game of the doubleheader, I listened as the catcher told me the pitch. Then I plugged that information into my own mind as if I was looking for that particular pitch because it fit the situation. Sure enough, the catcher continued to give me the pitches. "Fastball, low and away," he said. So I told myself to "look for a fastball low and away." CRACK! I knocked that sumbitch into the gap for a stand-up double! The catcher looked into the dugout but Ol' Gene Mauch just grinned. He knew I had caught on to his tricks. The catcher continued to tell me the pitches until the seventh inning—after I'd gone 3-for-3 with two doubles and a triple. I stepped to the plate waiting to hear the next pitch but the catcher was speechless. I waited for a moment and then stabbed him with a look. "What's the next pitch?" I asked. "Hey, Pete," said the catcher, "Mauch told me to tell you to go fuck yourself!" Of course, I felt pretty good about myself after that. I proved that I could hit big-league pitching and could hold my own with the big boys. And within days, I drew a walk against Whitey Ford of the New York Yankees. Whitey and Mickey Mantle were seasoned veterans at the time and didn't think too much of a brash young kid who ran to first base on a walk. So Whitey looked over at Mickey and said "Hey, Mick, look at Charlie Hustle!" Everyone laughed but I didn't care. I was there to make the team—not win a popularity contest. Later, I got a game-winning hit, which caught the attention of the New York media. The headlines in next morning's paper read: "Charlie Hustle beats Yankees!" The name stuck. The name also caught the attention of Earl "Scoops" Lawson, who was the Reds beat writer with the *Cincinnati Star*, which later became the *Post*. Scoops had been writing sports for 10 years and had seen a lot of players come and go. He liked my aggressive style of play and thought my attitude was just what the team needed. Scoops wrote several articles about me and often went to Hutch and suggested he keep me in the lineup. Of course, that didn't go over too well with the veterans on the team. They thought my intensity was phony—just a put-on to impress the sportswriters and coaches. But I was never phony when it came to playing baseball. I played all-out because I didn't know any other way. I had a burning desire to win and wasn't shy about expressing it.

Throughout spring training, I made more and more progress until Scoops Lawson decided to take a poll among the veteran players. At the time, our team stayed at the Causeway Inn, which was about 5 miles from our practice field. The Causeway Inn had a nice lounge where all the players hung out during the evening. Scoops went into the lounge and gave a slip of paper to each player and asked them to vote "yes" or "no" if they thought I was going to make the team. Everyone answered "no" except Blazer. "There's no way Pete's not making this team," said Blazer.

"He's just too good." By the end of spring training, Hutch felt the same way. He called me into his office and gave me the news. "Rose!" he said. "You're my new second baseman."

Hutch put himself on the line by giving a chance to an untested rookie. But Hutch knew that a certain amount of dissention could motivate the other players. If the manager was willing to bench his star player—nobody's job was safe! Hutch played his strategy correctly. Everybody got off to a good start—except me. I went into an immediate slump, hitting just 3-for-25. Finally Hutch sat me on the bench. He knew I was pressing . . . trying too hard to make an impact. I was the local boy whose father and uncle were in the bleachers watching every inning of every game. So Hutch gave me some time off to escape the pressure. Within a few days, I was back in the lineup and started hitting like I did in Macon and Tampa—ripping singles and doubles into the gap. I approached each at-bat as if the game was on the line, which drew heavy criticism from my veteran teammates. They thought I was trying to "show them up." They called me "Hot Dog" and "Hollywood." But I never changed my style just to fit in. As much as my aggressive attitude offended my teammates, it sure as hell impressed the fans. They cheered every time I slid headfirst or squeezed an extra base out of a routine hit. When Earl Lawson asked me why I ran out my walks, I just grinned. "There's no sense hanging around homeplate when you could be on first."

Besides Hutch, the only friends I had on the team were the black players—Frank Robinson and Vada Pinson, who understood what it felt like to be shunned. Frank and Vada were both star players who took me under their wing, and showed me the ropes. They were the only ones who treated me like a human being. They taught me how to dress, where to eat . . . how to act like a big leaguer. I'd talk baseball with them for hours. But Frank was surprised by how naïve I was. "Baseball is all Pete ever talked about," said Frank. "It's all he ever wanted to do . . . or dreamed about. Baseball, baseball, baseball, baseball." Compared to me, Frank and Vada were both sophisticated guys. So just before my first trip to the West Coast, I figured it was time to put away the blue jeans and T-shirts and start dressing like a major leaguer. I splurged and bought myself some nice jackets and slacks, dress shirts, and ties. You should've seen the looks when I drove back to the old neighborhood in my lime green Corvette, dressed in a suit and tie. Nobody could believe it was me!

I was living my lifelong dream and loving every minute. Every day was an adventure. I'd spent much of my youth going to Crosley Field to watch the stars and now I was playing against them—Stan Musial, Duke Snider, and Ernie Banks. I faced some of the greatest pitchers who ever lived—Sandy Koufax, Juan Marichal, and Bob Gibson. And there was even one great pitcher I didn't face—Satchel Paige. During my first trip to the west coast, I went to Dodger Stadium during an off day, where I met Satchel Paige, who was pitching for the Braves at the time. Satchel was getting up in years but hadn't lost his sense of humor. I was still a skinny little crew-cut kid—not an impressive physical specimen. Satchel took one look at me in my new suit and tie and just frowned. "Hey, kid, are you out here to watch a ball game?" he asked. "No sir," I replied. "I'm playing second base for the Reds." Satch broke into a toothless grin and took a big bite out of his egg salad sandwich. He didn't believe I was really a major league ballplayer! Satch shook my hand, said, "Nice to meet cha'," then just walked away. At first, I was a little disappointed by the snub. But then, I looked down and saw that my hand was covered with egg salad! The wily old veteran had given me something to remember him by. But that didn't bother me one bit. I was just so thrilled to be in the big leagues. I wiped off my hand and thought about how much I would have loved to face Satchel Paige in his prime. He had velocity and control but I would have found a way to get a hit off him. I would've found a way . . .

During our first road trip to Pittsburgh, I went out to eat with Frank and Vada. I was still pretty green but I was learning how to enjoy the perks of being a professional ballplayer. While coming out of the fancy restaurant, I saw a gorgeous woman who was built like nobody I'd ever seen. I went right up to her and introduced myself and told her that I played baseball for the Reds. She was several years older than me but I reckon she thought I was cute. "Nice to meet you," she said. "I'm Elizabeth Goodneighbor." I asked if she'd like to come to the ballpark to watch me play. Ms. Goodneighbor just smiled. "I'll come watch you, if you'll come watch me," she said. Then Elizabeth gave me a funny-looking ticket and later that night, I took a taxi cab to the address and watched my first-ever live burlesque show! Ms. Goodneighbor was performing under the stage name of "Irma the Body"—and, man, did she ever have one! Irma put on a great show and I had the time of my life. The next day, I was shagging fly balls during batting practice when Irma—er, Ms. Goodneighbor, showed up on the field, wearing Spandex pants, spiked heels, and a halter top that didn't halt much of anything! All the players started whistlin', cat-callin', and hollerin'. But Irma didn't mind. She just smiled, jiggled past Roberto Clemente and Willie Stargell—strutted right up to the dugout and called out to Fred Hutchinson, who wore #1 on his uniform. "Hey, number one," screamed Irma! "Which one of those cute boys out there is Rose?" Needless to say, Hutch did a double take when he saw Ms. Goodneighbor live and in person. She was something to behold! Hutch just turned to the outfield and screamed at the top of his lungs: "ROSE!" I ran right up to the dugout and stood at attention. When Hutch spoke, you listened. "Who in the hell is that?" asked Hutch. "That's Irma the Body," I said. "She's here to watch us play!" Hutch just rolled his eyes and shook his head. "Rookies!" It was a good thing I'd busted out of my slump because Ol' Hutch looked like he was gonna send me back to Macon right then and there. Folks were pretty conservative in those days and they didn't take too kindly to seeing a stripper on the baseball field. This was many years before Morgana, "the

Kissing Bandit," started the trend. But hey, a deal is a deal. Irma gave me a ticket to watch her, so I gave her a ticket to watch me! How was I supposed to know she'd walk right down on the field? I was in Hutch's dog house for several days. But the next time we flew into Pittsburgh, Hutch's mood changed for the better. Irma showed up at the ballpark with a string of balloons, which read "Happy Birthday Hutch!" After the game, Hutch and Irma left the ballpark arm in arm. Hutch just grinned and shot me a wink. "Thanks for the introduction, Rook!"

Sumbitch shot me right outta the saddle! As it turned out, that was my biggest setback of the year. By July, Blasingame was traded to the Senators and I became the everyday second baseman. I finished the season with a .273 batting average, scored 101 runs, and hit 25 doubles. Then, on November 26, 1963—just 4 days after President John F. Kennedy was assassinated in Dallas, I earned 17 of the 20 votes cast for the National League Rookie of the Year award.

Throughout my rookie season, I spent a good deal of my spare time at the track. It was one of the few places I could go to relax and forget about the pressures of day-to-day life. I usually went with my dad, Mr. Zimmer, Earl "Scoops" Lawson, or with one of my long-time friends from the west side, Danny Gumz and Al Esselman. Danny, along with his brothers Billy and Mo, owned a nightclub, and Al was a car dealer and a damn good horse handicapper. After a game or on an off-day, I'd usually head over to River Downs or old Latonia, join my friends, and enjoy the excitement of the racetrack. I usually carried binoculars to get a closer look at the horses as they made their way past the far turn. But on one hot summer day in July, something else caught my attention. I noticed a really attractive young girl with long brown hair standing by the fence. She was dressed in a blue mini-skirt and wearing plenty of jewelry—a real looker. I went down to the track and introduced myself as Pete Rose. Of course, she already knew who I was. And I knew her, too—kind of. Her name was

Karolyn Engelhardt and she just happened to be from the west side of Cincinnati. After the races, I drove Karolyn home in my lime green Corvette, went inside, and met her family. As it turned out, we knew all the same people and had a lot in common. Karolyn was fun to be with and in many ways, just like my mom—outspoken and opinionated. We started dating right away and within a few months got pretty serious. At first, Dad was against the relationship because he thought we were too young. He wanted me to spend a few more years concentrating on baseball. But after we set a wedding date, Dad went along with the program. Hell, he had no choice. Karolyn's parents had already rented the church!

I got off to a poor start early in the 1964 season. I'm not sure why. Karolyn was pregnant at the time, and I was probably just a little over-whelmed with all the pressure. At 23 years of age, I was just a kid, and not a very patient one at that. When my batting average dropped to just over .200, Hutch had no choice but to put me on the bench—a move that brought strong reactions from the fans. They unfurled huge banners in the outfield protesting the move, "A Rose Cannot Bloom on the Bench." Scoops Lawson and Si Burick even wrote articles in the local papers, de-manding that Hutch put me back in the lineup. It was one of my first ex-periences with what would become a long-term friendly relationship with the press. Early in my rookie year, Scoops Lawson taught me to be acces-sible. "Don't be like those other guys, who snub the reporters," said Scoops. "Be friends with the reporters and they'll be friends with you." I followed his advice. Throughout my career, I made friends with the sportswriters—guys like Scoops, Si Burick, and Ritter Collett. I treated them with respect—didn't talk down to them or try to humiliate them like some of the star players. After a game, I'd usually be the first one to talk with the press. But I was no frontrunner. I genuinely loved talking about baseball. In those days, the reporters were the only guys who'd talk to me! I learned from watching Muhammad Ali, who charmed the press and looked like he enjoyed every minute. In return, the press almost always treated him fairly. Despite the protests, Hutch was right about sitting me on the bench. I was in a slump and I needed to break out. I've always been a positive thinker, and I still don't understand why I was so worried. Finally, I called my uncle Buddy, who pointed out that I was "slapping" at the ball—trying to punch rather than hit. "You gotta get aggressive, Pete," said Buddy. "Just go out there and attack the damn ball." Paralysis by analysis—thinking too much! Having a mentor like Buddy, someone in my corner, made all the difference in my confidence. I went on a hitting streak and raised my batting average to .269. I took the rest of the team with me. With just 2 weeks left in the season, the Phillies were out in front by 6½ games. It looked like they had a lock on the pennant. The Cardinals were in fifth place, which caused owner Gussie Busch to fire his general manager. Gussie threatened to fire everybody else if things didn't improve. His team took the hint. Back in June, the Cardinals acquired Lou Brock, who batted .348 for the rest of the year. Third baseman Ken Boyer won the MVP award, hit .295, and led the league in RBI. With Bob Gibson, Ray Sadecki, Curt Simmons, and reliever Barney Schultz, the Cards were unhittable. As fate would have it—the Phillies dropped 10 games in a row and finished one game out of the pennant race. The Reds went into the last game of the season tied with the St. Louis Cardinals for the lead in our division at 92–69. The winner went to the World Series. The loser went home. I was so pumped up by the idea of going to the World Series that I could barely contain myself. But we lost the final game of the season against the Phillies, 10–0, which taught me a very valuable lesson. Every pitch, every at-bat, every inning of every game should be played like it's your last. After the game, I heard some talk in the locker room that really pissed me off. One of our starting pitchers was bragging that he left his car running in the parking lot so he could get out of town as quickly as possible. Several of the veterans laughed at his stupid joke.

But I wanted to punch his lights out! Can you imagine, playing for a chance at the World Series and making a joke about losing as if it didn't matter? I sat at home and watched on TV as St. Louis beat the Yankees in the World Series, four games to three. Bob Gibson struck out 31 batters and Cardinals catcher Tim McCarver hit .478! I was so disappointed that I didn't sleep for 3 days. "That could've been me playing in the World Series," I thought. "That could've been me . . ."

By the end of 1964, at the age of 45, manager Fred Hutchinson developed lung cancer and died shortly thereafter. The Reds missed his leadership sorely and so did I. To this day, I can't help but smile whenever I think of Hutch and Irma walking arm in arm with those balloons . . . "Happy Birthday Hutch!"

The 1960s were filled with racial tension, riots in the big cities, and hatred. Whites were not supposed to associate with the Blacks in those days but that didn't stop me one bit. I was flattered that Frank and Vada made me feel like a friend of theirs. We even formed an off-season basketball team, which was made up of Reds players and a few local celebrities. We played during the evenings to stay in shape and sometimes traveled the area for charitable causes. Frank, Vada, and I drove to West Virginia for a charity basketball game, which almost turned nasty. Among the three of us, we got paid about $500 in cash for our appearance—big money in those days! On the way home, we decided to stop at Frisch's restaurant for dinner. Frank had a wicked sense of humor and decided to play a joke on the local townsfolk. He pulled out the cash and started counting it on the dinner table. This was long before ESPN and Fox Sports Net made every star player a recognizable face across the country. Hell, nobody even knew who we were. But here I was, a White guy, with two Black guys, counting out $500 in cash in a small West Virginia town in 1965. Everyone stared at us like we were from another planet. Finally, one of them ol' redneck boys went for the phone to call the cops. I stood up and told him not to worry. "It's not what you think," I said. "I'm Pete Rose and that's Frank Robinson and Vada Pinson of the Cincinnati Reds."

"Yeah right, and I'm the Easter Bunny . . . nice to meet ya." He walked straight to the phone but I took out my wallet and showed him my driver's license. He stabbed me with a look and then turned to his buddies. "It's okay, guys," he said. "They're not bank robbers, they're ballplayers!" Then, Frank and Vada just busted up laughing. Frank stood up and took a bow but nobody applauded. In 1961, Vada Pinson hit .343 and led the league with 208 hits. Frank Robinson hit .323 with 124 RBI. On the field, they were cheered, practically worshipped. Off the field, they were criminal suspects just because they had a wad of cash—go figure!

I started off the 1965 season on a tear. By the end of the year, I led the league with 209 hits, .382 putouts, and 670 at-bats and hit .312—the first of my 9 consecutive and 14 out of 15 .300-plus hitting seasons. I also made the All-Star team for the first of what would become 17 selections in 24 years.

In 1965, the Reds finished in fourth place and Dick Sisler was replaced by a young manager named Don Heffner. Before spring training of 1966, he took it upon himself to make some changes of his own. Now, don't get me wrong. I've got nothing against change. Change is inevitable. Sometimes "change" is better. Sometimes it's not. But he traded our best player, Frank Robinson, to Baltimore for a pitcher named Milt Pappas. Why? I have no idea! Heffner walked right up to me during spring training and told me that he was switching me to third base. He didn't ask—he told me. He was a rookie manager and I was an All-Star player, who had just led the league in putouts. I had never played the coffin-corner in my life and I wasn't too thrilled about the change. The Reds had just brought up Tommy Helms from Macon the previous year and offered second base to him. Tommy was a good friend and one helluva player. But why should I change positions after I had worked so hard to perfect the one I had? Truth is, I didn't work very hard at third base throughout that spring. I couldn't accept the change under those circumstances. I was just too stubborn. I know it doesn't sound like me—my work ethic and all, but it's true. The inexperienced manager ordered me to change positions. What was it the experts said about my mom's personality? Oh yeah— "oppositional-defiant."

The team got off to a terrible start. I was making errors left and right and we lost like 10 outta 16 games. By the end of April, Heffner realized the error in his ways and switched me back to second base. Tommy Helms took over at third, which turned out to be the best decision in Heffner's short-lived career. After just 83 games, Heffner got fired—replaced by Dave Bristol, who coached Tommy and me back in Macon, Georgia. Team chemistry was restored. Tommy won National League Rookie of the Year, and I led the team with a .313 batting average, and finished second in the league with 205 hits. In all my years as a manager, I never forgot the way I was treated during that spring. A manager has to lead, encourage, and motivate his players. You can boss around a rookie but you can't tell a seasoned player to change positions. You've got to ask him, and keep him motivated. A decade later, in 1975, I won the World Series MVP award—at third base. By that time, I was a more seasoned player and I busted my ass trying to learn the new position. The year before, I was an All-Star in left field. I led the league with 110 runs, played in 163 games, and made just one error during the whole year. I was a great left fielder but I changed positions willingly. What was the difference between 1966 and 1975? By that time, we had a seasoned manager named Sparky Anderson. Sparky knew how to talk to his players. He asked me to move to third base. He didn't "tell" me.

In 1966, Sandy Koufax and Don Drysdale pulled a dramatic "joint-holdout" during spring training. They were the two premier pitchers in the league and believed in "strength in numbers." Both were near the end of their careers and were holding out for long-term security. Koufax thought he deserved $200,000 and Drysdale wanted $150,000—huge salaries in 1966 dollars. But the Dodgers balked. The only leverage the duo had was to sit out the entire season, which didn't make sense. Baseball players have a limited career—especially pitchers. Any year they missed was a year they'd never play. Management knew it. Eventually, the two sides came to terms and Koufax became the highest-paid player in the game at $130,000. Drysdale settled for $105,000. Both pitchers earned their money. Afterward, Koufax went out in a blaze. In his last five seasons, he finished with a record of 111 wins against just 34 losses, winning five straight ERA titles. Along with every other hitter in the National League, I was happy to see that sumbitch retire. But I was inspired by his success. Not just with his pitching, but with his negotiating skills, too. I took his lead and went to our player personnel director, Phil Seghi, and asked for a raise. This was still the era before free agency, when lawyers and agents were forbidden from taking part in contract negotiations. Each player had to negotiate his own deal, which meant he was at the mercy of the owner. I wasn't a savvy businessman but after leading the league in several statistics and making the All-Star team, I thought I had some leverage. I wasn't going to stage a holdout but I figured I was worth about $100,000 less than Sandy Koufax. So I asked for a $25,000 salary. Mr. Seghi cringed. He knew that I was just as stubborn with getting my money as I was with getting my base hits. I enjoyed the nice things that life had to offer and I wanted to buy a new house for my wife and daughter. During the previous year, I made just $13,500 and had to sell used cars during the off-season to make ends meet. Hell, I was tired of selling cars—I wanted to buy a new one! Mr. Seghi tried to nickel and dime me down to $17,000 but I wouldn't budge. I reminded him that I was really popular with the fans—someone who sold tickets—"put asses in seats." I also had great relationships with many reporters like Earl Lawson, Si Burick, and Ritter Collett. Surely, I could give one of those guys a call and ask them to run a nice little article about how "stingy" the

Reds were being with their money . . . about how the Reds were not willing to pay market value for their star player. Mr. Seghi blinked. Contract negotiations were never fun. But it was a necessary evil. I earned a reputation for being "difficult," which I took as a compliment. I wasn't trying to be difficult. I was just fighting to get what I deserved. Sure, I gave fits to the front office. But if I hadn't fought, I would've had to settle for less . . . and I never settled for less. Mr. Seghi relented and gave me the $25,000 salary. Afterward, I went out and did what I always did—earned my money. I hit .313, finished second in the league with 205 hits and 38 doubles, third in the league with 654 at-bats, and finished in the top 10 for league MVP.

With the added success came recognition. And with recognition came opportunity. Just after St. Louis beat Boston in the 1967 World Series, I received a phone call from someone in the State Department, who asked if I wanted to go to Vietnam. I reminded the caller that I already served with the Ohio National Guard at Fort Knox, Kentucky. "Besides, isn't there a war going on over there?" I asked. "Don't worry, Pete," said the caller. "We're not asking you to fight. We'd like you to entertain the troops during a goodwill tour." I had visions of telling jokes with Bob Hope or standing on stage with Raquel Welch and Barbara McNair. But since I couldn't sing or dance, I wasn't really qualified to entertain anybody. Then the caller clarified the situation. "This is strictly a morale-boosting mission, Pete," he said. "We took a poll among the troops and the soldiers picked Joe DiMaggio and Pete Rose as the two baseball players they'd most like to meet." "Did you say 'Joe DiMaggio'?" I asked. "Yes, Pete" he replied, "Joe DiMaggio." "When do I leave?" I asked. Joe had been retired from baseball for 16 years but I remembered watching "Joltin' Joe" as if it was yesterday. Besides Ted Williams, nobody—I mean nobody—could hit like the Yankee Clipper. The media made it sound like I was performing a very patriotic mission by going to Vietnam. But hell, I would have flown to Mars to meet Joe DiMaggio!

Within days, I was on a flight to the West Coast. In 1949, DiMaggio became the first baseball player in history to earn $100,000 a year and here I was having dinner with him at his restaurant in San Francisco! Joe congratulated me on my 1963 Rookie of the Year award and said that my hustle and aggressive style of play reminded him of the old-time players. "Baseball needs more players like Pete Rose," said Joe—one of the biggest compliments of my life. That night, we took a World Airlines charter from San Francisco to the former Saigon—17 hours in the air. While in Saigon, we met with military officials and got briefed on our itinerary. Since we would be in harm's way throughout the tour, we had to travel in small groups to avoid detection. Our mission was kept a complete secret. Nobody ever told us where we were going until we actually got there. Vice President Hubert Humphrey was in Saigon to celebrate the inauguration of the new South Vietnamese president. But security was so tight that all 15,000 of the local cops had been issued new carbines and machine guns. They were trying to prevent another attack by Communist terrorists, who bombed the ceremony a year earlier. From Saigon, Joe and I headed south, where a great deal of fighting had taken place. Joe had great respect for the military and was looking forward to getting out among the troops. "Don't worry about a thing, Pete," said Joe. "I'm a veteran myself and I'll show you the ropes." We flew a fixed-wing aircraft from Saigon and landed on the aircraft carrier USS *Intrepid*, which was en route to a location in the South China Sea so their pilots could fly bombing missions over Hanoi. At our briefing, we were given GS-14 Colonel credentials, which meant that if we got captured, we'd be treated as POWs and not shot as spies. DiMaggio went down on the flight deck and started talking with the young pilots right away. You should've seen the looks on their faces. Can you imagine being on an aircraft carrier and getting a preflight pep talk from Joe DiMaggio? Joe took a piece of chalk and wrote "Fuck Ho" on one of the bombs—referring to Ho Chi Minh, the enemy leader.

When the pilot returned from his mission, he reported that his "Joltin' Joe" scored a direct hit on its target—an ammunition dump! DiMaggio laughed his ass off.

We spent 2 days on the *Intrepid*. I learned to steer the ship and took part in the fueling operations. I also felt obliged to talk baseball with the ship's officers and sailors whenever they had a question. But with just 5 years in the majors, I didn't have that many interesting stories. It was DiMaggio they wanted to hear from. Joe played with the Yankees for 13 seasons, won nine World Series, and knew Lou Gehrig, Ty Cobb, and Babe Ruth personally. Everyone wanted to hear the inside scoop on all the juicy details of Joltin' Joe's life. But Joe wasn't talking. Except for his chats with the pilots, Joe kept to himself. He could be grumpy, short-tempered, and downright cold-hearted. But, hell, I was grumpy, short-tempered, and cold-hearted, so Joe seemed perfectly normal to me! I had plenty of opportunities to talk one-on-one with Joe. But I was taught never to meddle in another man's affairs. When Joe felt like talking, I listened. Otherwise, I gave him his privacy. Besides, I understood why Joe was feeling bitter. He never got over the death of Marilyn Monroe.

After 2 days, Joe and I boarded a chopper and flew in-country to visit with the ground troops at various hospitals and field stations. Our first stop was the toughest. We visited a triage hospital for the severely wounded. Most of the patients had lost arms and legs during battle. Some were still in shock or on their deathbed. I spoke with one soldier who got hit with mortar shrapnel, which was still lodged in his neck. The nurses had to rotate him every 20 minutes to allow the wound to drain. The doctors couldn't operate because the shrapnel was too close to his spinal cord and they were afraid the surgery might paralyze him. I felt terrible for the soldier but he didn't seem the least bit fazed. "Thanks for coming all this way to pay us a visit, Pete," he said. "I know it looks bad but don't worry about me. In a few days, I'll be back on the front lines and I'm gonna kill the sumbitch who did this to me!" I visited with several other patients, but one in particular caught my attention—an amputee who was holding a young Vietnamese baby in his arms. The hospital authorities kept trying to take the baby away so they could return it to a local village. But the soldier would not let go. He witnessed its parents' death in a bomb explosion and was committed to raising the baby as his own. Each time a nurse came by to get the baby, the soldier refused to let go. "The only thing you'll get from me," he said, "is my signature on the adoption papers!"

After visiting with our wounded troops, we were taken to the "Charlie Ward," where they kept the injured and captured Vietnamese. They had doctors and nurses working around the clock in air-conditioned hospitals. DiMaggio was furious when he saw how well the enemy was being treated. "Where in the hell's the air-conditioning for our soldiers?" screamed Joe. But our military escorts just shrugged their shoulders. "We're in the 'Nam, Joe," they said. "Nothing makes sense in the 'Nam."

Our next stop was Canto, where the Cong tried to overrun the village during a raid the night before. When Joe and I arrived on the battle scene, we saw six dead Vietnamese bodies wrapped in bamboo. I approached the bodies to take a closer look but I was immediately stopped by an escort. "Don't touch anything, Pete," he said. "These bodies are all booby-trapped with explosives. Charlie likes to come back at night to claim his dead . . . and when he does—KABOOM!"

From Canto, we flew by helicopter gunship at 130 mph at treetop level to avoid enemy fire. We landed in a battle area called Hill 84, about a mile or so from the front lines. As we approached camp, I counted a number of black bags, which contained the bodies of 21 dead Marines who were being loaded onto a chopper to be returned home. It was the most gruesome sight of my entire life—one I'll never forget. 1967 was also the year that Muhammad Ali was stripped of his world heavyweight boxing title for refusing induction into the armed services. "I ain't got nothin' against them Cong," said Ali. Three and a half years later, Ali's title was restored by the U.S. Supreme Court, which upheld his refusal based on religious grounds. I've never been a very religious person myself but after witnessing the horrors of war firsthand, I was starting to understand Ali's point of view. He was years ahead of his time.

By the time we arrived at Hill 84, DiMaggio was getting worn down by all the activity. At 52 years of age, he was not as energetic as the rest of us. We were always in harm's way and the constant sound of mortar fire was taking its toll on Joe's nerves. While in camp, Joe and I were talking to a colonel when one of our guns fired down a road from just 30 yards away. It was the loudest blast I'd ever heard in my life. I damn near had a heart attack as DiMaggio hit the dirt! I thought we were under attack but the blast turned out to be a warning shot—fired at regular intervals to provide protection for our patrols.

That night, Joe and I sat in camp just staring up at the sky, which was lit up by the glow of tracer fire and explosions. I could tell that Joe's nerves were frazzled, so I talked baseball for as long as possible. I reminded him of the four great things that happened in 1941. "It was the year I was born, the year Eddie Arcaro rode Whirlaway to the Triple Crown, the year Ted Williams hit .406, and the year of DiMaggio's 56-game hitting streak!" Joe just grinned. He knew that I had no interest in probing into his personal life, so he felt comfortable talking with me. He scoffed at the idea that he just had to "show up" at the ball field—as if his natural talent was the key to his success. "Nobody ever worked harder than me," said Joe. "In spring training, I'd take hundreds of grounders and fly balls every day. Sure, I had talent. But the key to my success, like all the great ones, is hard work."

Ironically, just 2 years later, I would meet Ted Williams for the first time and hear essentially the same philosophy. "The reason I became a great hitter," said Ted, "is trial and damn error . . . trial and damn error . . .

trial and damn error!" Ted believed that I could be the league's next .400 hitter because I was a switch-hitter with great vision. (It was no coincidence that the two best hitters in their era had the same work ethic as me.)

Finally, I asked DiMaggio which feat was more difficult—hitting .407 or his 56-game hitting streak? Joe liked Ted Williams as a hitter but then he just raised his 10 fingers. "It all comes down to rings, Pete" he said. "I've got nine World Championships and Ted Williams has none. Besides, I won the MVP award in 1941—not Ted." After listening to DiMaggio, I realized one thing. Like me, Joe DiMaggio believed he was put on this earth to play baseball.

By 2 A.M., Joe was getting tired. But between the sound of mortar fire and the jungle temperature of over 100 degrees, he just couldn't sleep. Finally, Joe got up and asked for permission to take a shower. Every activity in the jungle was done in tandem. But since the guards had to stand post with their weapons drawn, nobody was available to give Joe an escort. So I volunteered. I walked down to the creek and poured buckets of cold water into a bamboo trough. Then, I stood on a chair and pulled the shoot-handle, which released the water over Joe's head. It would have been the perfect opportunity to crack a joke or make some half-assed comment. But Joe wasn't feeling too good and there was nothing funny about the war in Vietnam. So I gave him the privacy he deserved. But as I stood there listening to that mortar fire at 3 A.M., I was struck by one strange thought: "I'm probably the only man on the planet to give a shower to Joe DiMaggio!"

I saw a lot of disturbing things during my 19 days in Vietnam, the most unpopular war in American history, not even sanctioned by Congress. But you'd have never known from the morale of our soldiers. They were all heroes putting their lives on the line. When I returned to the United States, I had a new attitude toward baseball. I was determined to put it all on the line. I won back-to-back batting titles in 1968 and 1969, hitting .335 and

.348 respectively—clinching each title on the last game of the season. I didn't receive a lot of national recognition because the Reds were a small-market team. But my headfirst style of play and blue-collar work ethic became synonymous with the city of Cincinnati. The Reds finished only fourth and third in our division during those 2 years. But we were in the early stages of putting together the roster for the Big Red Machine.

Throughout the 1960s, I established myself as one of the most consistent players in the major leagues. I was a four-time All-Star, Golden Glove winner, and five times voted in the top 10 for league MVP. I drew my share of walks and hit doubles and triples with power. Despite having to learn three different positions in 2 years, I raised my game a notch at each position. Most players would have been thrilled with the success I achieved. Many would've called it a career. But I wasn't satisfied. I wanted more—an obsessive work ethic I shared with my dad. After a sloppy effort at Crosley Field, I was reminded of my shortcomings. We'd just lost a game to the Cardinals and my dad was waiting next to my car in the parking lot. I knew something was strange because Dad never waited outside the locker or in the parking lot. He always went straight home after my games. Without even saying hello, Dad asked me if I was sick. "No, sir, I'm fine," I replied. "You sure you're not sick?" he asked. "Yeah, I'm sure," I replied. "I feel just fine." Satisfied that I had no excuse, Dad looked me square in the eye. "Well, if you're not sick," he said, "Do you mind telling me why you dogged your way to first base with your head hung down like a scolded dog?" Then, I remembered the play that he was talking about. Early in the game, the pitcher threw high and inside—a little chin-music, which got me riled up. The next pitch was a changeup, which caught me off-guard. I swung too hard and hit a blooper, which was easily caught by the shortstop. "It was a can o' corn, Dad," I replied. "I had no chance." "You're damn right you had no chance," said Dad. "If the shortstop had lost the ball in the sun, he still would've had time to pick it up and throw you out." Dad was right. I fell for one of the oldest tricks in the book—I got anxious and swang right outta my jock. But even worse, I did not hustle down the base path. Then, Dad looked me square in the eye. "You embarrassed me out there today," he said. "Don't ever do that again." Having spoke his piece, Dad just walked away. Lesson learned.

Certain things between men are understood but never spoken. That's the way things were between me and my dad. I understood his way of thinking because I thought the same way. Dad was just as rugged as they come, but he had a thirst in his life that never got quenched. Although he never complained, Dad did not advance up the ranks at the bank like he did with sports. He was dedicated, hard-working, and ambitious—just like me. And everyone who ever worked with him had nothing but great things to say about him. If one of his tellers came up short at the end of the day, he'd stay late and help them balance their till until every dime was accounted for. That was Dad—meticulous with everything. Perfectionist. But still, he struggled with his work. In the early years, Dad enrolled in the IBM school, where he learned new technologies in the banking business. Then, he attended the American Institute of Banking for 1 year and eventually received his biggest promotion—assistant manager of the bookkeeping department, which came in 1963, the same year that I broke in with the Reds. I remembered all of his bad headache nights and how he strained over those bank numbers all day long. I'm sure he could have done better if he'd had the opportunity to attend college. But he went about his business with great diligence. Although we never discussed his career, I could sense that he was frustrated by not making advances or earning a bigger salary. But he never complained. Instead, he put all his energy into my career. And in many ways, I learned to pursue my dreams with a vengeance because Dad was not able to pursue his.

Most folks remember the frog-hop catch I made out of Bob Boone's glove during the 1980 World Series—the catch that put the nail in the coffin of the Kansas City Royals. But I was doing the same thing in 1968, just not in front of a national television audience. While playing against the Atlanta Braves, I followed my teammate Alex Johnson to the left field wall, where I prepared to back up his play. Alex jumped in the air to grab a long drive, hit off the bat of Hank Aaron. But the ball popped out of Alex's glove and into mine. Alex just looked at me and rolled his eyes. He couldn't believe I hustled all the way over from right field. Then, with two out and a man on second in the bottom of the ninth inning, Rico Cardi of the Braves hit a line drive that hit Alex in the chest and dropped to the ground. Run scored—game over. As we ran off the field, Alex turned to me and threw his hands in the air. "Where the hell were you, Pete?"

5

HIGHLIGHTS

"I'd walk through Hell in a gasoline suit to play baseball!"
—PETE ROSE

Whoever said "It's not whether you win or lose but how you play the game" is full of it! Winning makes all the difference in the world. Winning is fun. Losing is not. Losing sucks. Just look at any player who ever lost a championship game and you can see how he feels by the expression on his face. On the other hand, look at the players who won the championship and you can see how they feel by the way they pour champagne over each other's head. Former University of Kentucky basketball coach, Adolph Rupp, said it best: "If it doesn't matter who wins, then why do we bother to have scoreboards?"

After the 1969 season, the Reds hired a 36-year-old manager named George "Sparky" Anderson, a strong leader who knew his personnel. He mixed role players with established stars, and he always put us in a position to win. Sparky came up in the Dodgers organization and never amounted to much as a player. But as a manager, Sparky won championships with four different minor league teams. And once he got a taste of the big leagues, Sparky had no intention of going back to the minors. Sparky began his tenure with the Reds by naming me team captain. "We're not giving Peter anything he hasn't earned," said Sparky. "With two batting titles under his belt, Peter deserves the honor." Sparky was putting his stamp on the team by delegating authority—creating a chain of command and uniting the players.

Just 2 months before spring training in 1970, I was called in to the front office for a meeting with the Reds director of player development, Sheldon "Chief" Bender. A knowledgeable guy, Bender had spent his entire career with the Reds. He and the team president, Bob Howsam, informed me that they wanted to sign the team captain first. Two hours later, I walked out of the meeting with a new contract worth $105,000. It was the smoothest negotiation of my life—one that completed a prediction I made after the 1966 season when I said that I expected to become the game's first "$100,000 singles hitter." Not only was I the first Cincinnati Reds player ever to earn six figures, but I was one of the highest-paid people in the state of Ohio. It felt good to be appreciated—not just for my performance on the field but for what I'd done promoting the Reds in general. Throughout the off-season, I gave baseball clinics, spoke at banquets, and made myself available to any organization that requested me. I often stopped by the University of Cincinnati and the Knothole League in my old neighborhood to give tips to the younger kids. Sometimes, I'd even give free hitting clinics at the ballgame batting cage, where I spent hours of practice. I considered myself the Cincinnati Reds good-will ambassador.

With the added money and recognition came perks, privileges, and opportunities. I began what would become a long-term relationship with a lawyer named Reuven Katz. Reuven was a Cincinnati native, about 20 years older than me, highly educated, and as honest as the day is long.

(Reuven always charged me by the hour when, in fact, he could have earned more money by charging a percentage.) Reuven went to Harvard Law School and specialized in trusts and estate planning. He became my lawyer, advisor, daily tennis partner, and father figure. Although he had many clients, Reuven represented just three ballplayers throughout his career—Johnny Bench, Tony Perez, and me. "My three adopted sons," he called us. I wanted to celebrate my new contract by buying a big house and a new sports car, but Reuven was more practical. "Let's put your money into a portfolio, Pete, and let your investments pay for your big house and new sports car." Hell, who was I to argue with a Harvard man? So, Johnny Bench and I bought a Lincoln-Mercury dealership in Dayton and a bowling alley in Fairfield—both profitable ventures. As soon as the money started pouring in from my "portfolio," I went out and bought my big house and new sports car—on the advice of my lawyer, of course.

In Sparky's first year as manager, we stole the division, winning 102 games. We left the second place Dodgers in a cloud of dust—15 games behind. I hit .316, ninth best in the league, and won the Golden Glove in the outfield with a .997 fielding percentage. I also led the league with 205 hits and led the team with 37 doubles—third best in the league. Tony Perez hit 40 home runs. Johnny Bench hit 45, led the league with 148 RBI, and won the National League MVP award.

And wouldn't you know it? Just when everything was going great, the bottom fell out. On December 9, 1970, I received a phone call from my sister Jackie that changed my life. I was sitting in the barbershop, getting a haircut, when the barber handed me the phone. "Dad died," said Jackie. "You mean Mom?" I replied. "You mean Mom died?" "No," said Jackie. "Dad died. He was feeling kinda sick at work so he left early and took the bus home. He made it all the way up the front steps and then dropped dead." I hung up the phone and just went numb. I couldn't believe or accept the fact that Dad was gone. Just the night before, he was playing basketball with me . . . running and jumping. How could he be dead?

By the time I got back home, I just ran to my room and cried. I was devastated. I always thought my dad was invincible. And oddly enough, if he hadn't been so tough, he might still be alive. He was working at the bank, going over his numbers like he always did. Then all of a sudden, he started to feel sick. One of his bookkeepers, Fran Carter, offered to call a cab, but Dad didn't think he needed one. He tried to get all the way home by bus, which took almost an hour. He should've just gone to the doctor. But he was too stubborn. He didn't want to inconvenience anybody. Dad got off the bus, walked up the hill toward our house, and made it through the front door. My mom was surprised to see him home so early. Dad looked at her and said, "I don't feel good." Then the blood clot went to his heart and killed him.

It didn't really hit me until I got to the funeral parlor. I handled all the other arrangements just fine. But when I saw him lying in the casket and realized he was dead, it hit me like a ton of bricks. Dad was 58 years old and I was just 29—too young for both of us. After looking at Dad, I still couldn't believe or accept that he was gone. The room was filled with dozens of our friends and neighbors, folks from the bank and from Dad's many sports teams.

After the funeral, I must have cried for 3 days. But I was left with the comfort of knowing that Dad got to enjoy a big part of my career. I took him to spring training in Florida every year. He saw me win back-to-back batting titles, collect my 1,500th hit, and score the winning run in the 1970 All-Star Game. He also watched me play in the World Series against the Baltimore Orioles. So in many ways, I felt like I had given something back to the man who had given me everything. Still, after Dad died, I kinda lost my way—not as a ballplayer, but as a person. I spent a great deal of my life trying to please my father, and not having him in my life left a big void.

◆ ◆ ◆

Throughout the 1960s, I always said that I was playing for my father. Now I was playing for myself and for my family. My daughter Fawn was born in 1964 and my son Pete junior in 1969. I accepted my role as a father and in some ways took on that responsibility with my teammates. I remembered what it felt like to be shunned by the veterans on the team when I was a rookie. I didn't care whether a guy was young or old, I made a point of looking out for his best interest. Tony Perez came aboard in 1965, Tommy Helms in 1966, Johnny Bench in 1967, and Bobby Tolan in 1968. Davey Concepcion joined the team in 1970. I took all of them under my wing, showed them the ropes, taught them how to act and live like major leaguers. Since I was from Cincinnati, I knew the city and could help them find nice homes and good schools for their kids. My wife, Karolyn, and I threw Halloween costume parties every year, hosted dinner parties—the whole thing. And if any of the players needed new cars, Johnny Bench and I would fix 'em right up!

At that time we had a relief pitcher named Clay Carroll, who we nick-named "The Hawk"—a big ol' country boy from Alabama. Hawk was coming off a good year and would eventually set a major league record for most saves in a season—37. Clay wanted to buy a new Cadillac with the raise he just got from the Reds. But Johnny Bench would hear nothing of the kind. No way he'd allow one of his pitchers to drive a Cadillac! Johnny took the Hawk aside and gave him the big sales pitch. "Look Hawk," said Johnny, "Why don't you buy this new Lincoln Continental? It's a much better car!" "Can't do it, Johnny," replied Hawk. "Ever since I was a young kid in Clanton, Alabama, I've had my heart set on owning a new Cadillac."

Bench immediately called for a changeup. "The Lincoln Continental is the only luxury car on the market that comes equipped with an automatic vacuum cleaner. Just think of the hours you'll save. You'll never have to vacuum your car again!" Hawk's eyes lit up like slot machines. He was so impressed that he plopped down his cash and bought that new Lincoln right on the spot. Bench just smiled and shot me a wink. But 2 days later, Hawk stormed back into the dealership loaded for bear. Bench slipped out the back door the minute he saw him coming and left me holding the bag. Hawk grabbed me by the arm and just gave me holy hell. "First of all, Pete," said Hawk, "This car is so slow that a dog was pissin' on my tire all the way over here! Secondly, I've been looking for 2 days and I still can't find that goddamn vacuum cleaner!" Well, I just stood there biting a hole in my tongue trying not to laugh! Finally, I just busted a gut and had to admit the truth. "Listen, Hawk," I said, "Bench didn't mean to lie; he was just having some fun at your expense. But since Johnny's your catcher and the guy most responsible for your success, I wouldn't get him pissed off if I were you. After we washed off Hawk's new tires, he saw the wisdom in my thinking and drove away happy—another satisfied customer.

The Hawk could afford his new car. He was one of every starter on our team who got a raise that year—every starter except me! Can you believe it? After winning the pennant in 1970, the Reds offered to re-sign me for my previous salary of $105,000. I was coming off a season where my batting average dropped from .348 to .316. But I led the league with 205 hits, scored the winning run in the Ray Fosse All-Star game, and hit 37 doubles. I asked for a $20,000 raise—a modest sum, given my statistics and stature in the game. The Reds said "No." This was 1971—before free agency. If any player in the big leagues wanted more money, he had no choice but to rely on the generosity of his owner. And anybody who followed baseball during that era will agree that the words "generosity" and "owner" didn't often collide in the same breath. I told the Reds that I wouldn't play for $105,000. I deserved to be paid like the top players in the game. Now don't get me wrong, I knew that $105,000 was a lot of money in 1971. But I wasn't asking for anything outrageous. I only wanted my fair share. Chief Bender and Bob Howsam from the front office knew that I could quote my statistics with a great deal of accuracy. So, as soon as I walked into their office for another negotiation, they hit me with a statistic of their own. "You didn't even lead our team in hitting, Pete!" I just rolled my eyes. Tony Perez went into the last game of the season just three percentage points behind me for the team's lead in batting average. He went 3-for-4 in the last game and finished with a .317 average. I finished at .316—tied for second with Bobby Tolan. "Yes, I did lead the team in hitting—for 161 games!" But the Reds were playing hardball. Bender and Howsam claimed that I had an "off-year," and even suggested that at 30, I might be "getting up in years." As much as their remarks pissed me off, they held all the cards. The only leverage I had was to threaten to sit out the season—just like Koufax and Drysdale. So I did. But the Reds called my bluff. They suspected that I wanted to play baseball a helluva lot more than I wanted to sit out the season. But I also wanted to be paid and because I wanted to be paid, the Reds labeled me "headstrong and stubborn, difficult to sign." So, I called my good friend, Scoops Lawson, of the *Cincinnati Post*. In those days, the only way to get my message to the fans was through the press. Fortunately, the writers and players were allies. This was an era before huge salaries created resentment between players and reporters, an attitude I'd like to see changed with today's players. Besides Earl Lawson, I had great relationships with other beat writers like Hal McCoy of the *Dayton Daily News* and with freelance writers like Lou Smith, who wrote great articles for the *Cincinnati Enquirer*. If a writer needed a story, I was always available for an exclusive. On the other hand, if I needed a little boost around contract time, Earl Lawson was willing to write about my "hustle and determination" but only if he believed in my cause. Earl was as reputable as they come—never wrote puff pieces for anybody. He didn't get on your bandwagon unless he thought you were right. Scoops wrote articles praising my league-leading statistics, about how well I was doing financially with my car dealership and bowling alley, about how maybe I could afford to sit out the season to take care of all my "successful business ventures." Scoops even insinuated that the Reds were being "stingy" with their money—something no owner wants to read in the newspaper. Scoops was pulling out all the stops to get my story to the fans, who in turn, could put pressure on the owner by writing letters and calling in on talk shows. Although the feud made for great headlines and public debate, the owners had all the leverage—either accept their terms or sit out the season. The Reds refused to budge on my raise. I stuck to my guns, too. What was I suppose to do? Beg the Reds to take me back? No way! I had my pride. It was the principle of the thing. If they weren't going to give me a substantial raise, I'd sit out the season. End of story. "Good luck, fellas, have a great year without my league-leading hits and 37 doubles!"

At that time, Whitey Willenbourg, the general manager at my car dealership, was looking forward to a big spring season. "Sales are going to be brisk," said Whitey. So I went to work. "If you wanna great deal, go see Pete!" That charade lasted for about 2 days. I wanted to play baseball, not sell Lincoln Continentals! In early March, when spring training got into full gear, I got antsy. I didn't like missing spring training and the Reds knew it. Suddenly, the principle of the thing didn't seem so important. I ran home and got on the telephone. I called Scoops, who was staying with the team in Florida, and asked him to get in touch with Chief Bender. I reduced my demand for a $20,000 raise by 75 percent. Scoops thought I was being reasonable and relayed the message to the Chief. Can you imagine—a sports reporter negotiating a contract on a player's behalf? Today, the whole scene seems totally outrageous. Still, the Reds refused to budge—no raise at all. If I wanted to play baseball, I'd have to accept the same salary as the previous year. At that point, Scoops got pissed off because Bender had told him that if I had asked for a $5,000 raise in the beginning, he would have given it to me. "So, what's the big deal?" asked Scoops. "Give him the $5,000 raise." But the Reds were trying to make me squirm—set a hard-line example for the other players. Finally, I called Chief Bender myself and reminded him of my league-leading statistics and overall contributions to the team. "You gotta give me something," I said. "You can't expect me to play for no raise at all when you've given every other starter a raise." Bender and Howsam offered to settle the dispute for a simple cost of living increase, $2,500. I got on a plane and flew to Tampa, where I joined the team for the remainder of spring training. Was I happy? Hell, no. But once I put on my uniform and went to work, I never sulked or carried a grudge. I put the squabble behind me and never gave it a second thought.

The rest of the team didn't react too well to my contract squabble. But the Reds didn't care. They were sending a message to the other star players. If the Reds weren't going to pay me, they weren't going to pay anybody. And nobody likes playing baseball under those circumstances. Win the pennant—get a 2 percent raise! Wow, some incentive! The Reds hard-line economic strategy backfired. Either that, or Sparky Anderson got hit with the sophomore jinx. We finished in fifth place in 1971. No player on the team hit over .300 except me. I led the team with a .304 average, finished with 192 hits, played in 160 games, got 632 at-bats, and made the All-Star Game for the sixth time. Not bad for a feller who was "getting up in years." I reckon it's safe to say that I earned my $2,500 raise.

During the summer of 1971, I watched on TV as Satchel Paige was inducted into the Baseball Hall of Fame. Satchel played most of his career in the Negro Leagues, where he supposedly pitched more than 50 no-hitters and 300 shutouts. He didn't get a chance to play in the majors until 1948, when he was 40-something years old. But in his prime, Satchel was nasty and unhittable—not the toothless old man I met in California back in 1963. But by 1971, I was no longer a starstruck young rookie with porcupine hair and a goofy new suit. I was an established major league star, honing a talent that would become one of my trademarks—I studied a pitcher until I owned him. I studied his tendencies, his release point; I watched how and when he threw his best pitch and how and when he threw his junk. Like hitters, pitchers have tendencies. If a hitter can't lay off the high hard one, you can bet your bottom dollar the pitcher will throw the high hard one every time—work the advantage. Likewise, if a pitcher gets behind in the count, he will always throw his favorite pitch to get out of a jam.

The more I knew about a pitcher, the better chance I had at getting a hit. What is his strikeout pitch? How does he pitch with runners on base? What does he throw when he's ahead in the count? What does he throw when he's behind in the count? A great pitcher has to be able to throw the same pitch at 3-and-1 that he throws at 1-and-2. If he can't, he's got a weakness in his personality. And I wanted to know all about a pitcher's personality. An ass-kicker would come after you with his best stuff. A pussy would buckle under the pressure. I preferred facing the ass-kickers—more of a challenge!

In an ESPN television broadcast, former ass-kicker and Red Sox great Bill "Spaceman" Lee had this to say: "Pete Rose was the greatest two-strike hitter I ever saw. If I got two strikes on him, I knew he was going to hit it up the middle on me . . . and there was nothing I could do about it." Bill Lee was referring to what Sparky Anderson called my "tunnel vision," my ability to block out distractions. Throughout my career, I only struck out once in every 12 at-bats, or only 35 times per season. That means I was in position to put the ball in play 615 times per year. With so few opportunities, I wanted to take advantage of each one. I made just six adjustments to any given pitcher. I moved up in the box or back in the box. I moved closer to the plate or farther away from the plate. If I fouled off, I was either ahead of the pitch or behind the pitch. Then I'd make an adjustment in my swing. I could hit the same pitch to three different fields just by repositioning my hands. But the mechanics of my swing were always the same—consistent. Baseball is not complicated. You just have to work hard and concentrate. Prepare for success. In 1966, I went 13-for-15 off Bob Friend of Pittsburgh and 11-for-14 off Warren Spahn. I got 77 hits off Phil Niekro and 34 hits off his brother, Joe. That's 111 hits off one family—1/40 of my career total. Can you imagine how many hits I could've gotten if Mrs. Niekro had five sons?

Throughout that time, I made no secret about my love for horses or for gambling. I was never the type to stay in my hotel room during a road trip and watch soap operas. I didn't lie out by the pool or visit the local sights. I'd already seen the Statue of Liberty and the Golden Gate Bridge and once you've seen 'em, you've seen 'em. If I was in Chicago for a day game at Wrigley Field, I'd sneak over to Sportsman's Park or Hawthorne Race Course for the evening races. On a travel day between Los Angeles and San Diego, I'd stop off at Del Mar Thoroughbred Club or Hollywood Park. While in Cincinnati, I became friends with Arnie Metz, who worked in the Reds stadium operations. Arnie was about 15 years younger than me and just loved the ponies. We'd leave the ballpark, have dinner at the track, and review the program an hour before the first race. Arnie considered himself a great handicapper; but more often than not, the real handicap was Arnie's advice. When I really wanted to win, I'd pick the opposite ticket from what Arnie recommended. If Arnie told me to bet the 4–1 exacta, I'd bet the 1–4. Arnie was a great guy, but he hadn't picked a winner since Jesus was a corporal in the Salvation Army.

I bet more money at the races as my salary increased, but I didn't consider myself a problem gambler. I was a recreational gambler, someone who gambled for pleasure and diversion, not profit. If I laid a wad on a 7–1 horse, I loved watching him break high and wide off the last turn. I'd be rooting for the jockey to stand and wiggle the reins. But even if he pulled back against the rail—one of the dumbest things on the planet—I never got bent outta shape. I enjoyed the race itself—win or lose. Sure, I'd scream and cuss at the jockey, call him every goddamn name in the book. But after the race, I'd just tear up my losing tickets, throw 'em in the air, watch 'em fall to the ground like confetti, and laugh my ass off. And when I left the track, I left the races behind. I didn't take them home with me—didn't obsess over my winners or my losers. No guilt. No remorse. "Don't ever look back," said Satchel Paige. "Something might be gaining on you."

Within time, news and rumors of my racetrack gambling spread throughout the city and with certain members of local law enforcement. At that time, Bowie Kuhn, the commissioner of baseball, determined that he needed to bolster the league's security efforts against evidence of increased drug abuse among ballplayers. Mr. Kuhn was determined to keep the game clean, so he appointed retired FBI agent Henry Fitzgibbon as baseball's first director of security. (Apparently, the antidrug plan never took effect. According to 1989 statistics, there were over 8,000 newspaper articles written on drug abuse in professional baseball compared to just over 1,000 articles written about my gambling investigation.) Mr. Fitzgibbon was a big baseball fan whose wife was from the Cincinnati area. He began his duties by traveling around the major league cities talking with players, owners, and managers about drug abuse. He went to local law enforcement to get tips on problem players. And when he arrived in Cincinnati, Mr. Fitzgibbon heard from local sources that I enjoyed gambling and that I went to the track a lot. Hell, I did go to the track a lot. I never tried to hide it. Afterward, I was called in for a meeting with Mr. Fitzgibbon, Sparky Anderson, and Bob Howsam of the Reds. Mr. Fitzgibbon was very straightforward. He believed in helping players, not trapping them. Early in his investigations, Mr. Fitzgibbon caught Denny McLain of the Detroit Tigers, who provided financial backing to a bookmaking operation back in 1967. McLain won the Cy Young award 2 years in a row but got suspended for a half season in 1970 for associating with known gamblers. Mr. Fitzgibbon sat down with me and outlined the dangers of gambling and the similarities between me and Denny McLain. Mr. Fitzgibbon told me that he was concerned that I might get involved with "undesirables," or that I might be tempted to go beyond racetrack gambling. I understood and cooperated with Mr. Fitzgibbon completely and assured him that I was not betting on baseball or betting illegally. At that time, I saw no similarities whatsoever between me and Denny McLain. McLain was involved in an illegal bookmaking *business*. I wasn't in business—I played the ponies. And nothing interfered with my baseball career—nothing. Mr. Fitzgibbon seemed satisfied with my answers but he told me that he would keep his investigation open and report back from time to time to counsel me on "problem gambling." I continued to visit with Mr. Fitzgibbon over the years. I'd pick him up at the airport, we'd go to lunch, that sort of thing. I called him Fitz and he called me Pete. He was a great guy who loved baseball. At one point, Fitz told me that he received tips that I was betting through bookies and that I might owe them large amounts of money. He asked about my associations with Danny Gumz and Al Esselman. So I took Fitz over to the Gay 90s club and to Esselman's car dealership. I introduced Fitz to Danny and Al, and asked them point blank, "Do I owe you guys any money?" Both guys said "No." Danny and Al weren't choirboys but they weren't leg-breakers either. They were just long-time family friends, tough-ass guys from the west side of town. They discussed our racetrack gambling with Fitz. But there was nothing else worth discussing. Nobody was interested in talking about Monday Night Football or the Super Bowl—hell, everybody bet on that. And whatever money I bet on the ponies was perfectly legal. Afterward, Fitz stopped coming around as often.

We still had lunch or dinner once a year. We'd talk baseball but by the end, Fitz concluded that he had no evidence that I was a problem gambler or that I was betting illegally. He even stopped receiving tips on my gambling from his local sources. Fitz told me that he discussed his investigation with the commissioner and that Mr. Kuhn was satisfied that there was no evidence to sustain any violation of baseball rules.

◆ ◆ ◆

In November of 1971, team president Bob Howsam put together one of the best deals in Reds history. He traded Lee May, Jimmy Stewart, and Tommy Helms to Houston for Jack Billingham, Cesar Geronimo, and Joe Morgan, who provided the missing pieces to our team puzzle. If you look up the word "speed" in the dictionary, you'll find a picture of Joe Morgan. In his first 2 years, Joe stole 125 bases, played second base with phenomenal range, and was the smartest player I ever saw.

Between 1971 and 1978, the Cincinnati Reds became one of the most successful franchises in baseball history. With Sparky at the helm and a roster of stars, the Big Red Machine won back-to-back World Series Championships, four National League pennants, and six division titles. We averaged 95 wins a season and had more fun than any team in the league. During that span, the National League MVP award was won by a Cincinnati Red six times—George Foster and me, and Johnny Bench and Joe Morgan, who each won twice.

After the arrival of centerfielder Cesar Geronimo, Sparky asked me to switch to left field. My first instinct was to balk. I didn't like being told what to do—never have. But Sparky had a way of motivating people that confounded conventional logic. Sparky could sell ice to the Eskimos and make 'em feel like they got a bargain out of the deal. Like me, Sparky sold cars in the off-season during his years in the minor leagues. He knew that in order to make a sale, you had to get your buyer excited about the product, even if it meant telling a white lie—"automatic vacuum cleaner!" But I was Pete Rose, and I didn't like to be "sold" and Sparky knew it. *Tell* me what to do and you've got a fight on your hands. *Ask* me and I'll give you the shirt off my back. "I'm asking you, Pete," said Sparky. "I'm not telling you. I think the move would be good for the team, and it might add years to your career." I didn't want to go against Sparky's better judgment but I didn't think moving to left field would add anything to my career. I mean, the only thing it could possibly add is a longer jog back to the dugout. So I felt a bit insulted by Sparky's request. I didn't think my arm was that weak, and I had two Gold Gloves to prove it. Granted, I didn't have the arm strength of a Clemente or a Mays, but I threw out a lot of runners from right field. But Sparky didn't push too hard. He was too smart to make the same mistake Don Heffner made back in 1966. You see, Sparky had a certain way with his players—a presence. He dealt with each player individually and never tried too hard to prove his point—a method I adopted years later when I became a manager. "Treat each player in a way that he best responds," said Sparky. "Otherwise, you're working against yourself." Sparky was tough and aggressive but unlike me, he had a sensitive side. Sparky would go to the local hospitals once a week to visit young kids on the terminal ward. But Sparky always went unannounced. When it came to charity, Sparky had one hard and fast rule—No publicity! He did not want to embarrass any of the patients or their families by parading them on television or by making it appear like he was grandstanding. Sparky went to the hospitals for the kids, not the cameras. On my first visit, I found out why. I was standing in the hallway when a young boy called out my name. He rose up in his bed and grinned when I walked through the door. He was just 10 years old and dying of cancer. He was also a big Reds fan, and I happened to be his favorite player. I sat and talked with him and his parents for about an hour. His head was shaved and he looked really thin—just like Hutch during his last days. He had just barely enough strength to smile and talk a little baseball. He was impressed by the way I scored the winning run in the 1970 All-Star Game and wanted to hear all the juicy details. I've never been one to relish details of any kind, so I just said, "Hey, I wanted to win the game," which brought a smile to his face. Afterward I signed a baseball and promised to send him a new glove. "You can use the glove next spring when you start playing baseball again," I said. Then, his parents gave me a big hug. Afterward, I joined Sparky and went room to room, visiting with other patients, signing baseballs, shaking hands. Finally it was time to head back to the ballpark. Just before I left the hospital, I received news from one of the doctors that the 10-year-old boy I visited with had just died. Like I said, I'm not a warm-and-fuzzy guy, but I'd be lying if I said that I wasn't affected—I was. I went outside and dealt with my grief privately, where nobody could see me. From that moment on, I understood Sparky's philosophy. What if the media had filmed the young boy and shown it on the 11 o'clock news? Those private moments were meant for the family, not the general public! Sparky continued to visit the local hospitals every week. He always invited players from the team but never alerted the media. How could you not respect a man like that? How could you not play your heart out for a manager like that? Did I make the switch to left field? Damn right I did. Sparky had me convinced when he said, "For the good of the team."

Throughout that time, nobody had more fun than the Big Red Machine. We were the best baseball had to offer. We appeared in TV commercials and on the cover of every sports magazine in the country. With so much success, you'd expect strong egos. But our egos never got in the way of winning. Baseball always came first—fun second. Johnny Bench was the team bachelor, with a swarm of girls who followed him around. Joe Morgan was the smooth talker who set an example for all the black players on the team. Tony Perez was the leader among the Latinos and the only player without an ego. Tony never complained about not getting his fair share of magazine covers. Why? Because Tony just didn't give a shit! We laughed and joked on a daily basis, but nobody ever took the teasing personally. We had a player named Davey Concepcion, who was a great shortstop and a devout Catholic. But Davey struggled at the plate. Before each at-bat, he made the sign of the cross, which I never quite understood. I wasn't Catholic but since I got married in the Catholic Church, I went right up to Davey and posed a hypothetical question. "Hey Davey," I said, "What happens if you make the sign of the cross and then the pitcher makes the sign of the cross, and then the catcher, and the infielders, and the outfielders? Why would God take your side instead of the other players? I mean, with wars, worldwide hunger, and Siamese twins being born with two heads—does God really care who wins a baseball game?" Davey just stabbed me with a look and whispered something under his breath in Spanish. Then, after the veins stopped bulging in his forehead, Davey asked if I wanted to join him and a group of players who held chapel service in the clubhouse. "Why don't you come join us on Sunday morning, Pete?" asked Davey. "Might do you some good." Now, don't get me wrong. I have nothing against religion, but chapel service was meant for the church—not the clubhouse. Bench, Morgan, Perez, and I would show up early on Sunday morning, but not to pray. We came to get treatment for our injuries and to take extra batting practice. On one particular Sunday morning, while I was getting treatment on my elbow, I heard one of the guys carrying on during their service. Finally, I just looked over at Perez and said, "I hope he's thanking God for that piece of ass he got last night because he damn sure ain't had no hits!"

My philosophy was simple. When it came to playing baseball, I had confidence. I knew the game. I knew how to hit, and if given a chance, I knew I'd find a way to win. I knew that I wasn't blessed with great speed like Willie Mays or with power and grace like Roberto Clemente. But I was blessed with a great work ethic and something that is very essential to hitting a baseball—hand-eye coordination. I had strong arms and legs, a compact swing, and 20/20 vision. In hindsight, I don't know if attending chapel service would have made a difference in my life. But at the time, I was hitting .330 and Concepcion was hitting .215. Maybe Davey should have spent less time praying and more time in the batting cage. But like I said, nobody took the teasing personally.

After the New York Jets defeated Johnny Unitas and the Baltimore Colts in the Super Bowl, Joe Namath set new trends for professional athletes. High-top shoes and flattop haircuts were out; white shoes, mink coats, and the Fu Manchu mustache were in. Charlie O. Finley, the owner of the A's, was the ultimate showman. He followed Broadway Joe's lead and built a "Mustache Brigade" dynasty in Oakland with stars like Catfish Hunter, Sal Bando, Joe Rudi, Rollie Fingers, and, of course, Reggie Jackson. Even the manager, Dick Williams, had a mustache. I wasn't a full-blown hippy, but I grew a beard and a mustache during the winter just to fit in with the new trends. There was just one problem: I lived in Cincinnati, not New York or Oakland. The Reds had a long-established policy forbidding their players from growing facial hair. Why? I have no idea. Small market team with conservative values, I guess. I didn't agree with the Reds policy because a beard and mustache made no difference in how you played baseball. You don't want your players acting like maniacs, but you want them to be aggressive, and if growing a beard makes you more aggressive, then why not? Strength or not, I went along with the rules. The Reds paid my salary and I didn't want to buck tradition. I shaved my beard and mustache willingly, on national television for a Gillette razor blade TV commercial. As I recall, I got paid about $17,500 for the gig—about the same money the Reds refused to pay me during my previous contract holdout. Funny how things just seem to work out for the best, huh?

In August 1972, at the age of 31, I hit a single off Jon Matlack of the New York Mets—my 1,881st, which put me in first place on the Cincinnati Reds all-time list. At that time, I was starting to believe that I could realistically reach 3,000 hits—an automatic ticket to the Hall of Fame. I wasn't thinking about Ty Cobb. That record was just too far away— unrealistic. But my dad played football until he was 43. He was durable, never got hurt, and I had the exact same body as he did. I didn't drink or smoke, so I knew that I had a good shot at playing effectively into my late thirties, maybe even my early forties. I figured I had a better-than-good shot at reaching 3,000. The next day, I was surprised by an article written by Bob Hertzel, the Reds beat writer for the *Cincinnati Enquirer*. Hertzy had been a friend for years. He had prepared a chart on hitting statistics from the top sluggers in history and how they performed during their first 10 years in the league. Hertzy came up to me before practice and told me that Stan Musial and Paul Waner were the only two players in history to collect at least 2,000 hits in their first 10 years in the league. My 1,881 hits put me seventh on the list—ahead of Ty Cobb, Willie Mays, Ted Williams, and Honus Wagner. I was a tad surprised by the news, but it substantiated what I knew all along—I was *consistent*. I did the same things day in and day out. Even when I had an off year, it was still a pretty good performance. I always kept to my routine of practicing right and practicing hard. I took ground balls and fly balls constantly. I hit everything hard in batting practice and never let up. If we had a rain delay, I didn't go inside the clubhouse to play cards. I went into the batting cage to hit. That's why I always had such big arms. Nobody took more batting practice than I did. That's also why I never got tired during the season. I always worked hard to stay in shape. I never took myself out of games because we were too far ahead or too far behind. Some guys, like Joe Morgan, would only steal a base if it meant something. I'm not criticizing Joe Morgan—I'm just saying we were different in our approach to the game. I was out there to play every inning regardless of the score. I saw every pitch as an opportunity to get another hit and give the fans their money's worth. I never sat out the second game of a doubleheader because I didn't just play to win—I played to play!

After the 1972 season, I was back in the front office for another round of contract talks. We won two pennants in 3 years and had just reached the seventh game of the World Series and lost against Charlie O'Finley's moustache brigade. Home attendance was up close to 2 million per year, and the Reds were making money. Times were good. At that time, Johnny Bench was making about $155,000 a year and I wanted my fair share of the pie. It wasn't like I demanded to be the highest paid player on the team. But I was the Reds all-time leader in hits and I put up the most consistent numbers in the major leagues over the previous 10 years. I remembered my holdout in 1971 when Bob Howsam said that if I had asked for a $5,000 raise in the beginning, he would've given it to me. So, I followed his advice. I asked for a $5,000 raise. Mr. Howsam said, "No." He called me into his office and started off the meeting by asking me how old I was. When the president of the team starts talking about your age—you know you're in for a fight. Hell, the Reds knew my age. It wasn't like I was George Burns. I was only 32 years old and, based on the numbers I was putting up, I deserved at least a $5,000 raise—probably more. I liked Mr. Howsam personally and always agreed with his strict policies on discipline. But Mr. Howsam didn't seem to be my biggest fan. He took offense over the fact that I didn't back down, didn't just accept whatever money the Reds offered. He didn't seem to like that I negotiated my contracts the same way I played the game—to win. I fought for every penny and because I fought, I was labeled "stubborn, headstrong, and difficult." When all was said and done, the Reds refused to give me a raise. But I didn't complain. I went on with my life. I no longer had a beard and mustache to shave. But I had a new "Prince Valiant" haircut, which caught the attention of some folks on Madison Avenue, who offered me a TV commercial as the spokesman for Vitalis Dry Control hair spray. I was the spokesman who didn't speak. At that time, women were not yet allowed in the locker room, but the ad agency wanted to break new ground for the feminist movement. They hired a sexy young actress to strut through the locker room while a bunch of surprised ballplayers grabbed for their towels. I just stood nonchalant in front of the mirror, combing my hair—oblivious to the prospect of a woman in the locker room. The actress held up the product and spoke her lines into camera, take after take. Finally, after a few hours, I got a little bored. "Don't you want me to say anything?" I asked. "No, Pete," said the director, "Just stand there, comb your hair, and look sexy. Let the actress do all the talking. She's the trained professional." I was really good with spontaneous one-liners and improvisation, but I had trouble sticking to a prepared script. So I followed the director's advice and continued to comb my hair. "This is the year for sharing," said the trained professional. "So Pete Rose and I use the same thing on our hair." After she held a can of Vitalis Dry Control in front of the camera, the actress ran her fingers through my hair. "Nice hair, Pete," she said with a smile. "Now work on the gut." After my surprised double-take, the director yelled, "Cut, print! Sex appeal! That's why you get the big bucks, Pete."

1973 was a great year. I didn't have to say anything—I did my talking with my bat. Nolan Ryan did his with his arm. He broke Sandy Koufax's single-season record by striking out 383 batters. The American League adopted the designated hitter rule and Yankee legend, Yogi Berra became the only manager besides Joe McCarthy to win the pennant in both leagues. I led the league with 230 hits, 680 at-bats, and won my third batting title in 6 years with a .338 average. I hit 36 doubles, 8 triples, and got on base 301 times—first in the league. I scored 115 runs and won the National League MVP, which was highly unlikely for a guy who was considered a singles hitter. But I proved that a player who was consistently at the top of all the major categories was just as deserving as the guys who hit the tape-measure home runs. "Pete has helped me as a competitor to push myself every day," said Joe Morgan. "Pete's not the best player I ever saw. But he plays every game like it's the seventh game of the World Series—and I've never seen anybody else do that. I know it sounds corny, but playing with Pete Rose is inspirational."

◆   ◆   ◆

As a leadoff hitter my goal was to get on base. When I got on base, my goal was to run the bases aggressively and score runs. Before each pitch, I'd look at each outfielder to see if they were playing where they were supposed to be. If they were out of position, I'd look to take advantage. There is one play that best defines my career—not Cobb, Harrelson, Fosse, or Boone—although Boone comes damn close. It was a play that nobody remembers but me. I was on first base and feeling as good as I've ever felt. I picked up on the "steal" sign and as soon as the pitcher committed to his pitch, I darted for second base. The batter hit a medium ground ball that went through the hole and into right field. So, I kept running toward third. Out of the corner of my eye I saw the fielder approach the ball slowly and throw a lazy one-hop to the shortstop, who had moved to cover second base as the cutoff man. That was all I needed to see! I just kept right on running, rounded third, and slid headfirst safely into home. I went from first base to home on an easy grounder because I got the jump on the pitcher and a lazy outfielder who wasn't concentrating on the game. By the end of my career, I hit 746 doubles—second on the career list, 22 more than Ty Cobb, many of them coming at the expense of a lazy outfielder. That's how I define my career—taking advantage of every situation, pushing the boundaries, looking for an edge.

Unfortunately, the Reds lost their edge in 1974. We finished in second place, four games behind the Dodgers. Hank Aaron broke Babe Ruth's home run record and the Oakland A's won their third straight World Series crown. For the first time in 10 years, my batting average dropped to below .300—not because I slumped but because I was walked a career-high 106 times. The pitchers just weren't throwing to me and I'll be damned if I was going to chase bad pitches. Still, I got 185 hits, led the league with 110 runs scored, 45 doubles, and 163 games played. Throughout the season, I made just one error in the outfield, which was one error too many. My wife always said that she could never tell if I went 0-for-4 or 4-for-4 but she could always tell when I made an error. I hated making errors—no, I *really* hated making errors! I didn't throw water coolers or trash the locker room and I never took my anger out on my wife and kids. I took it out on myself, especially if I made a mental error like getting picked off or throwing to the wrong base. Let's say I made an error with two outs in the inning. Instead of the third out, the other team might get another hit or even a home run. They might score two, three, or even four runs—all of them unearned because of an error! So, if I made an error, I'd stomp around the house, obsessing over my mistake and how I should've prevented it. And then all of a sudden, I'd just blow up and scream at the top of my lungs. And then I was okay. I knew that I had another game coming up the next day. I forgot about the mistake and got excited about another opportunity to play, another opportunity to win. Fortunately, we played baseball every day. If I had been a football player, who only played once a week, I might have had some real problems waiting around for 7 days after a loss. I just might have thrown a few water coolers!

I've always been a perfectionist when it comes to playing sports. Right down to every last detail. I polished my shoes to a high gloss before each game, lined up the pinstripes on my Phillies uniform and even wiped my bats with alcohol, so after hitting I could see exactly where I made contact with the ball. Before each road trip, I'd pack my clothes in meticulous order, place every sock, shoe, and shirt in their proper place. But if I spilled a cup of sugar on the table, I wouldn't bother to clean it up—not because I was sloppy but because I had no interest in a clean table. The thought of cleaning up the mess never entered my mind! But if anything was out of place on the baseball field, I noticed right away and took immediate steps to correct the problem. I could calculate batting averages and fielding percentages in my head and never make a mistake. I could remember players, games, and won-loss records from 30 years in the past. I could remember every railroad crossing between Fort Myers and Tampa during spring training. But I couldn't remember to save a single receipt to give to my accountant for tax purposes. Deep down, in a place where I didn't want to go, I knew that I was different from the other players. But other players didn't have the single-minded focus that I had. They didn't get 650 at-bats, 200 hits, and average .300 year in and year out. So I took great pride in being different, and, to me, being "different" meant being better—something I enjoyed.

On May 1, 1975, Sparky Anderson gave me yet another chance at being "different." I was shagging fly balls during an off-day in Atlanta. I remember the date well because Gary Nolan was scheduled to pitch on Friday and I was calculating which of the Braves five right-handed hitters could get around on Nolan's fastball. The answer *None!* Sparky watched practice for about 5 minutes and then took a notion to make a change. After 4 weeks into the season, Sparky asked me to switch from left field to third base to allow for a starting outfield of Ken Griffey, Cesar Geronimo, and George Foster. "I'm not telling you, Pete," said Sparky. "I'm asking you . . . for the good of the team." As soon as Sparky asked, I nodded and headed straight into the dugout. No "automatic vacuum cleaner" this time. Griffey, Geronimo, and Foster were all power hitters. The move would give us more scoring potential in the lineup. As soon as I went inside, Tony Perez joked to the others that I was going inside to call my lawyer, Reuven Katz, to ask for more money. With all of my famous contract squabbles, they figured that I would demand a bonus for switching positions. Hell, I'd never played more than 60 games at the coffin corner—the most dangerous position on the field. With just 2 days to learn a new position, I didn't go inside to call my lawyer. I went inside to get a padded jockstrap. I'd switch positions for the good of the team but I wasn't going to lose the family jewels in the process!

It turned out to be a great move, as we put together an early streak of 41-9. With Bench, Morgan, Perez, and me on a hitting streak, the Reds won the West by 20 games. Don Gullett and Jack Bilingham spearheaded one of our best pitching staffs ever, and the Rose family jewels stayed intact. We swept Pittsburgh in three straight games, winning our third pennant in 6 years. The Boston Red Sox surprised everybody by sweeping the Oakland A's in the American League playoffs. We had lost the last two World Series we'd played in but were still the heavy favorites. Nobody expected the Red Sox to give us much of a fight, much less one of the most exciting World Series ever. Boston versus Cincinnati—old money, Harvard, and the Tea Party against Procter & Gamble's blue-collar river town. The matchup had all the makings of great drama.

Everybody remembers the excitement of that series . . . the great pitching of Louis Tiant and Bill "Spaceman" Lee. The 4 days of rain delay provided the World Series with Super Bowl-type media coverage. Five of the seven games were won by just one run. The sixth game was just incredible . . . Carbo's pinch-hit homerun in the bottom of the eighth to tie the score . . . and then Carlton Fisk's 12th inning homerun to win the game. The seventh game was even better because the Reds won in the ninth off Joe Morgan's RBI. Over 70 million viewers watched that seventh game. But what I remember like it was yesterday was the feeling I had throughout the series. I was in the best hitting groove of my life. Every pitch looked like a beach ball. Even when I made an out—it was a frozen rope that I hit right into some lucky fielder's glove. I came up to bat against Roger Moret late in the third game. Moret threw a fastball high and tight that must have ruffled my jersey. The umpire signaled for me to take my base. But I just stood there. I didn't want to take my base. I argued that a 2-1 pitch *didn't* hit me, even though it meant a hit batsman! Have you ever heard of anything so outrageous? But that is exactly how I felt. I was in the kind of zone that every hitter—no, every athlete—dreams of . . . when everything goes just right . . . when you can do no wrong. Eventually, reason ruled over impulse and I took my base.

When the seven-game series was finally over, most players said they were worn out—exhausted from all the drama. But I felt just the opposite—energized. I finally got my first taste of a World Series Championship and I wanted more. I was actually sorry to see the season come to an end. I was hoping spring training would start the very next week. I hit .370 for the series with 10 hits and won *Sport* Magazine's MVP award. But I would have given anything for another fastball from Roger Moret.

The 1976 season got off to a bumpy start with an owner-imposed lockout. But Commissioner Bowie Kuhn stepped in and saved baseball's 100th season. The Players Association and owners eventually agreed to grant "free agency" to players with six major league seasons—a ruling that was a direct result of the arbitration procedure won by pitchers Dave McNally and Andy Messersmith. As for the Cincinnati Reds—we just got better. We won our division by 10 games, led the National League in home runs, doubles, and runs, triples, and stolen bases! We swept Mike Schmidt and the Phillies and then swept the Yankees in four straight games and became the first National League team in 54 years to win back-to-back honors.

At the end of 1979, the Reds reached the very top of the baseball world. They were a dynasty. But rather than build on what we had, the front office took steps to dismantle it. They began by trading the driving force behind the Big Red Machine—Tony Perez. "If the game goes long enough, Tony Perez will win it," said Sparky Anderson. If I was on base, I wanted Tony Perez at the plate because I knew he'd find a way to get me over.

When Tony announced the trade at his press conference, he thanked the Reds for everything and conducted himself with class. Johnny Bench stood up, gave Tony a hug, and then started to cry. Bench was also expressing the feelings of the entire team. We all felt devastated by the loss. My kids, Fawn and Pete Jr., both cried when they heard the news. They played with Tony's kids, Victor and Eduardo, on a regular basis. I'd known Tony since 1960 when we played for Geneva and losing him was like losing a member of the family. The Reds could probably replace Tony's hits in the lineup. But they could not replace his clubhouse presence. When we lost Tony—we lost a big chunk of team chemistry and the Reds never fully recovered.

After losing Don Gullett to the Yankees through free agency, it appeared that I was next in line. Dick Wagner was the new assistant to team president Bob Howsam. Wagner was not a local guy and felt no loyalty to the team, the city, or its tradition. I suspect he was brought in to cut costs and tow the company line. But my philosophy is simple: "If it ain't broke, don't fix it!"

Our dynasty could have continued to thrive but the Reds didn't want to pay the price to keep us intact. Cincinnati was a small-market team and the Reds felt like they were unable to compete in the open market. Unable or unwilling—I'm not sure which. We had won our division five times, played in four World Series and won two of them. During that era, we had the best team in baseball—no doubt about it. We also drew more fans than any other club in the league. In 1976, our home attendance was 2.6 million—300,000 more than the Dodgers, who played in a city with five times our population! The Reds were a very profitable ball club. But they just weren't willing to spend their money on the players.

I earned $187,500 in 1976 and after compiling some of the best statistics in the game, I wanted to be paid what I was worth. The newspapers reported that I wanted to be the highest paid player on the team. But that was not true. I respected the talent of Bench and Morgan and I wasn't going to get into a pissing contest over who was better. All three of us were All-Stars. Each deserved to be paid. End of story. But Reggie Jackson had just signed with the Yankees for $580,000 a year. Now, don't get me wrong. I wasn't trying to compare myself to Reggie Jackson or demand the bigger money that came automatically with the New York market. But this was 1976—*before* Reggie hit three home runs on three strikes off three different pitchers! I was a World Series MVP, three-time batting champion, and had 14 years in the league. I might not have been worth *more* than Reggie Jackson. But I was not worth $392,000 *less*!

At that time, the Reds held my option for 1977. They could renew my contract for the same $188,000 salary that I earned in 1976. But then, I'd automatically become a free agent after the season. The Reds wanted to keep me in Cincinnati but at a reasonable salary. My lawyer Reuven Katz and I decided to ask for $400,000—very "reasonable" given my stature in the game. Reds GM Dick Wagner did not agree. What followed was weeks of one of the most hotly contested contract battles in baseball history. But when all was said and done, I had the Reds between a rock and a hard place. After trading Tony Perez, they could not afford to lose Pete Rose as well. Finally, the Reds caved in to the pressure. Just one day before the season opener, I signed a 2-year contract for $730,000. It was a long, hard-fought battle but the entire experience proved very satisfying. I stood my ground—didn't back down from threats or a challenge. I got what I was after and what I deserved.

They say that we build the future on experiences from the past.

Absolutely. I never backed down from a challenge and I enjoyed winning my battles, not because I was arrogant but because I was determined. Of course, there are some challenges you should ignore and some threats you should back down from, but I'm not too good at telling them apart.

The Reds finished in second place in 1977 but I earned every penny of my hard-fought contract. I played in every game of the season for the fourth straight year—hit .311, led the league with 655 at-bats, finished second in the league with 204 hits, and got on base 275 times. George Foster hit .320 with 52 home runs but that was the highlight of our season. Without Tony Perez, the Big Red Machine was sputtering.

Just before the start of the 1978 season, with 1 year left on my 2-year deal, Reuven Katz approached Dick Wagner with a proposal for a career contract. I was coming up on 37 years of age and wanted to finish my career as a Cincinnati Red. I was tired of the annual contract battles and wanted some financial security for my family. But Mr. Wagner balked at the idea of a long-term contract. He never actually said anything to me personally but I suspected he was concerned that my "off-the-field" activities were becoming a distraction to the organization. My marriage was on the rocks, and I was facing a legitimate paternity suit that wasn't playing well at home or with the folks in the Reds front office. Besides betting more frequently at the track, I was also betting on football and basketball through a friend from the west side of town. Mr. Wagner didn't like all the rumors and suggested to Reuven that he would try to get me to dial it back a notch before things got out of hand. During that time, Reuven and I played tennis early in the morning, five days a week. All of a sudden, Reuven suggested we start playing in the afternoons, which would have kept me from going to the track. Reuven tried his best to get me to cut back on my gambling but he was all too familiar with my rebel personality. The more Reuven talked— the less I listened—"oppositional-defiant" in action.

Still, I didn't take the contract snub personally. If the Reds didn't want to sign me to a long-term contract, there was nothing I could do about it. I didn't complain. I just did what I always do when faced with a challenge, I fought back. Early in the 1978 season, I rapped out my 3,000th hit against Steve Rogers of the Expos. The base hit put me in with some pretty exclusive company . . . with Hall of Famers like Ty Cobb, Hank Aaron, Roberto Clemente, and Willie Mays. After 16 years in the league, I was still going strong. In fact, I didn't feel any different at 37 than I did at 27. In many ways, I was stronger, more focused, even more relaxed. And as everyone knows, relaxation is the key to great hitting.

On June 14th, I got two base hits at Riverfront Stadium, which started a hitting streak that would last all summer. I wasn't *thinking* streak. I was just going up to the plate like I always did—focused and concentrating on getting a hit. Then, before I knew it, I was at 10, 15 . . . 20 straight games. As my streak continued, I got more and more attention . . . press conferences every day . . . swarms of reporters. But I never felt the pressure. I enjoyed the attention as much as I enjoyed the challenge. And I especially liked doing something that I wasn't supposed to do. Joe DiMaggio got his 56-game streak at age 26. Wee Willie Keeler got his 44-game streak at age 25. Ty Cobb hit in 41 straight games at the age of 24. I wasn't supposed to get all those hits at the age of 37, so every hit was like icing on the cake.

The hitting streak became the biggest sports story of the year. I spoke with an average of 50 reporters every day—guys who I'd known for 16 years, guys who were pulling for me to break the record. In an article from the *Cincinnati Post*, Earl Lawson talked with several major league umpires to get a handle on their opinion of my skills. "Super aggressiveness, determination, good eyes, and a desire to be the best . . . that's the capsule explanation offered by umpires Bruce Froemming and Dick Stello when asked what makes the Reds Pete Rose the hitter he is." "What amazes both of us," said Stello, "is that we've never seen Rose break a bat. And I've been in the league for 10 years now. To us that means that rare are the occasions when Rose doesn't get the fat part of the bat on the ball. Aggressive? There are hitters in the league who go the plate and wait for certain pitches before they'll swing. Not Rose. He'll go with the pitch. A lot of the pitches will be outside the strike zone. You'd be surprised how many base hits come on pitches that aren't strikes. When Rose is at the plate, he's not up there to take pitches. He's there to swing. I'm surprised that more hitters in the National League haven't learned from Rose just how much aggressiveness at the plate pays off. Rose is selective but to a point. If he sees a pitch he can pull or take to the opposite field, he'll take a rip at it even if it's not in the strike zone. If I weren't an umpire, I'd pay my way into a game to watch him. You never see Rose just go through the motions when he's out there on the field. With him, everything is life or death."

From June 14 through August 1, my aggressiveness paid off big time. I hit .385, with one four-hit game and six three-hit games, and only bunted four times throughout the streak. But all good things must come to an end. Mine came on August 1 in Atlanta Fulton County Stadium. I hit two line drives early in the game that were caught for outs. By the time I came up in the ninth inning, we were getting killed, 16–4. When I stepped to the plate, the full-capacity crowd cheered for over a minute. They were caught up in the moment and wanted to see me continue the streak. But relief pitcher Gene Garber had other ideas. He threw no different than if I had come up to bat with a toothpick in my hands. If I hadn't swung the bat, I would have walked on four straight pitches. With a 2-2 count, Garber threw another changeup, which I tipped into the catcher's glove. End of streak. I finished with a 44-game hitting streak, which broke the National League record set by Wee Willie Keeler back in 1897. But I was 12 short of Joe DiMaggio's 56— the major league record that I really wanted.

In September, I was invited to the White House to meet President

Carter, who had declared "Pete Rose Day" in Washington. I traveled with Reuven Katz and my children Fawn and Pete Jr. They were thrilled to be a part of such a big celebration and I was proud to have them with me. As I walked along the driveway leading up to President Carter's office, I stopped and stared in awe at the White House. I had flunked the 10th grade and 21 years later, I was being honored by the president of the United States—go figure! I spoke with President Carter in the Oval Office for about 10 minutes. We shook hands and exchanged gifts. He was very gracious. He told me that the whole country was proud of my accomplishments and that he was sorry my hitting streak had to end in Georgia—his home state! Afterward, I was escorted to the Capitol with Cincinnati's two congressmen, Willis D. Gradison Jr. and Thomas A. Luken. I sat in the house gallery as Mr. Luken read a Congressional Resolution in my honor. He praised my "irrepressible spirit, hustle, and rare sportsmanship . . . climbing to the highest level of achievement possible in baseball." After the presentation, a large number of congressmen stood in line for my autograph. I shook hands and took photos and thoroughly enjoyed the excitement. "I've been here 25 years and I've seen everybody—presidents, kings—but this is the greatest reception I've ever seen here," said Lt. Ralph R. Scalzo, a Capitol Hill police officer. "I think it's because Pete Rose is just a common guy who everyone can relate to." I was certainly honored that the president and all the congressmen took time out to see me. But I really wasn't expecting all the fuss. In an article in the *Cincinnati Post*, Barry M. Horstman wrote that I was given the kind of reception that was normally reserved for heads of state or foreign dignitaries. "While Rose spoke, a congressional page, seeing the swarm of television cameras, photographers, and onlookers, asked: 'Who's in there, the president or something?' 'Better than that,' replied a guard. 'It's Pete Rose.' "

6

THE FIRST TIME

"I wanted to astonish the spectators
by taking senseless chances and—a strange sensation—
I clearly remember that even without any prompting of vanity,
I really was suddenly overcome by a terrible craving for risk.
Perhaps the soul passing through such a wide range of sensations
is not satisfied . . . but only exacerbated by them . . ."
—DOSTOEVSKY,
The Gambler

It was so cold in Boston the other night that Ted Williams threw out the first pitch. That is why I want to be frozen when I die. Because if that sumbitch gets thawed out and comes back to play baseball, I'm coming back to get one more hit than Ted. I understand Ted Williams' attitude on that whole deep-freezer thing. He was thinking there just might be a way to come back and beat the odds. You see, a true competitor hates to quit doing what he loves to do. Quitting is unnatural. I never quit anything in my life. Hell, I never even "officially" retired from the active roster. I just couldn't accept that my playing days were over. I stepped into the box for the last time on August 17, 1986. I struck out against Goose Gossage, which left a sour taste in my gut. Just a few days before, I went 5-for-5—one of 10 times in my career that I went 5-for-5, a National League record. After that, I was tempted on several occasions to put myself into the lineup because I had a hunch that I might get a hit. But I never did. Although I honestly thought my black Mizuno had a few more hits left in it. At the time, my teammate Tony Perez was chasing the all-time home run record for a Latino player and I decided to give my roster spot to him. I already had my records. It was time for Tony to get his.

From that point on, I was in a major transition period of my life. Transition—my ass! I was pissed off. I was 45 years old and for the first time in my life, I was not playing baseball—the game I worshipped for over 30 years. I use that word "worship" because my daughter Fawn used to refer to baseball as my "religion." I was never around the house too much when she was growing up—at least not like normal fathers. Joe Morgan used to say that he felt sorry for me because when baseball was all over, I would have nothing else in my life to occupy my time. I never understood Joe's way of thinking. I always thought he was somehow less committed than me, that he didn't love the game as much as I did. Who in their right mind could ever put anything in life ahead of baseball?

I never thought my career would end. I always thought I'd be like that guy from *Damn Yankees* who plays baseball forever. Getting old was just another one of God's little practical jokes that I had no use for. It's not that managing the Reds wasn't exciting for me—it was. But it was a different type of excitement. There was just something about staring down a 95 mph fastball that I missed. I missed the feel of that lumber in my hands, the thrill of playing nine innings every day. I missed the headfirst slides and the competition. Hell, I missed the winning. I preferred to trust the outcome of the game to my bat and glove rather than giving the signal for a hit-and-run. It's not that I wasn't contributing to our wins. Hell, I loved building raw talent into great players, and I had a great group of young players on the Reds, guys who were getting better every day. In fact, 34 different players got their first major league hit while I was managing. Paul O'Neill was one of them. Paul went on to become one of the all-time greats with the New York Yankees. He played for 17 years and became a five-time World Series champion. But Paul was a tad slow during his rookie year with the Reds. We used to call him "Jethro" because he re-minded us of that TV actor on *The Beverly Hillbillies*. Paul would say things like, "Gee, Skipper, if I hadn't woke up, I'd still be asleep!" I'd just stare at him and say, "Uh, no shit, Jethro!" Paul took the teasing in good spirits. We'd never tease anybody we didn't really like and respect. Paul was just like me, a true competitor who hated to lose, but Paul had an-other talent that just amazed me. He was the only player in major league history who never made an out. Paul O'Neill was *always* safe! If an umpire called a strike, Paul would just drop his shoulders and shake his head as if the umpire was blind. And not just once in awhile—every goddamn call! During one particular game, O'Neill got thrown out at first on a routine grounder. Sure enough, O'Neill started arguing with the first base um-pire, Jerry Crawford. Tony Perez was coaching first base. He just looked over at me and shook his head. Tony knew that Paul was out by a mile and didn't have the energy to get into another fight. Well, it was early in the game and I needed O'Neill's bat in the lineup, so I ran onto the field to keep Paul from getting thrown out of the game. I stuck my nose right up into Crawford's face and gave him hell for missing that call. Satisfied that I had everything under control, O'Neill jogged back into the dugout, still thinking he was safe. The more I screamed at Crawford, the more the fans cheered. It was a real humdinger of a shouting match—one that would've made Billy Martin proud! But if you had been up close, you would not have heard an argument. I was sure screaming but this is what I said,

"That's the best goddamn call I've ever seen you make! O'Neill was out by a mile. Ray Charles could've made that call! The only reason I'm out here bitching at you is to keep that crybaby O'Neill from sulking the rest of the goddamn game!" Crawford jumped right back into my face and just gave me hell. "Thanks, Pete, I appreciate you taking the time and effort to voice your opinion," he screamed. "But we've been arguing long enough and if you don't get the hell off the field, I'm gonna have to throw your ass outta the game!" "Great!" I yelled. "Throw my ass outta here but make sure you show up at the Precinct restaurant after the game. We just got a fresh shipment of steak, and I'm buying your goddamn dinner!" Sure enough, Crawford threw me outta the game, which infuriated the crowd. As I walked back into the dugout, I got a standing ovation. O'Neill whispered to his teammate: "Now *that's* how a manager is supposed to stand up for his players!" I watched the rest of the game on the clubhouse television. O'Neill hit a home run, the fans got their money's worth, and Crawford had one of the best steak dinners he ever ate. Yes, sir, managing the Reds sure had its share of thrills—just not the same thrills I got from playing, which is *not*, contrary to public opinion, why I felt compelled to seek my thrills in other places.

◆ ◆ ◆

I first met Tommy Gioiosa, or Gio as I called him, during spring training in 1978. Tommy was a clean-cut kid from Massachusetts, who was down in Florida playing in a junior college baseball tournament. We all stayed at the same hotel, King Arthur's Inn in Tampa. Gio befriended my son Pete Jr., who was only 9 years old at the time. For a college kid, Gio was pretty level-headed. He didn't chase girls or go out drinking after the ball games like the rest of his teammates. He was really committed to baseball, which made a big impression on my son. He and Pete Jr. would meet in the parking lot of the hotel and play stickball every night. Gio was also really short—only five feet five, which kind of reminded me of myself at a young age. I reckon I had a soft spot for the hard-luck cases, aggressive kids who came from the wrong side of the tracks—kids who needed a break. After I got to know him better, I invited Gio to come stay at our house in Cincinnati after the end of the baseball season. Gio fit right in and became a good companion. He didn't have to pay rent or buy food. I loaned him one of my cars and even got him a tryout with the University of Cincinnati baseball team. He had a pretty good setup. He ran errands, babysat for Pete Jr., and went with me to the racetrack. My marriage was on the rocks, and I was looking for any excuse to get out of the house. I'd like to say that my wife, Karolyn, and I had grown apart, but we were never that close to begin with. Not that she didn't try. I just didn't respond. Being close was not something I had any experience with. I was only 22 years old and Karolyn was just 21 when we got married. So my dad was probably right—we were too young. Karolyn was also a lot like my Mom—outspoken and opinionated. We'd butt heads more often than not. Karolyn was a faithful wife and a good mother. She really didn't do anything to cause a breakup. I was just 36 years old and ready for a change. When it came to women, I was the restless type—always on the move. In an interview for *Inside America*, Karolyn told it like it was. "When I married Pete, I was his third love. First there was baseball, second there was his car, and third there was me. That was okay because all I wanted to be was a good wife and mother. Then our daughter Fawn was born and I was relegated to fourth place. Then our son Petey was born and I was in fifth place. Fifth place was too low in the standings."

When things didn't pan out with his baseball career, Gio started running some of my football and basketball bets during the off-season. I wasn't betting large at that time—just a grand a game—unless it was Monday Night Football, where I might bet two. If I was up a couple grand from Sunday's NFL games, I might sponge my bet and try to double up. But if I was down, I'd sometimes play it safe. I was making $376,000 in 1978, which was a lot of money but not so much to push me over the edge. Besides the ponies, football was always my favorite betting sport because I loved the excitement of the game. All the guys would come over to my place on Sunday. We'd order chicken and ribs from Montgomery Inn and make a whole day out of it. Like my dad, I loved watching sports on TV. If I put money on a game or a race, I wanted to watch it on television or listen to it on the radio.

During nights, Gio worked at Sleep Out Louie's, a local discotheque where I met a young waitress named Carol Woliung. Bernie Stowe of the Reds told me to get over to Sleep Out Louie's and check out "the best bottom in town." When I saw Carol, I realized Stowe underestimated. She had the best bottom in the whole state! Carol was 18 years old and a real "looker." She was also very nervous about dating a married man, so we decided to take it real slowly—something I had no experience with. I would stop off at the bar after a game and chat with her about this and that, just small talk. I'd order an orange juice and tease her about being a small town girl. Carol had just moved to Cincinnati from Indiana and she had never been to any of the Reds games. If it hadn't been for her roommate's poster of me, she wouldn't have recognized who I was. But I've got to be honest, that little girl really caught me off-guard. I was feeling things that I never felt before—that weird feeling in the pit of your stomach that guys just never understand. After a couple of weeks, I asked her roommate for Carol's shoe size and bought her some new boots as sort of a break-the-ice type gift. "Pete didn't just bring me some boots," says Carol. "He brought me five pairs of very expensive boots! I think that was his way of trying to impress me. Pete never did anything in a small way. His middle name was Excess—not Edward. I was shocked by the gesture, but I saw right through him. I saw what no one else had ever seen in Pete Rose—the charming little boy. Pete had a relentless sense of humor, which he used to keep anyone from getting too close to him. But deep down, Pete was shy and insecure—I could see that right away. It's part of what attracted me to him. In some ways, I think he used his aggression to hide his shyness."

So, being the shy romantic guy that I'm not, I invited Carol out on our first date to one of my favorite places—the track. "I had never been to the racetrack," says Carol. "It was one of the most exciting things I ever experienced. As we drove up to Beulah Park, Pete kept talking about how much fun we would have. I didn't understand what he meant until I saw those beautiful horses exploding out of the gate. Pete made it exciting for me. His energy and enthusiasm was contagious. He picked the horses and bought my tickets. He always picked the sure thing just to watch the expression on my face when I won. And it wasn't just me—it was everybody. Pete loves to see his friends having fun at the track."

I did for Carol what I rarely did for myself—picked the winners! Actually, the favorites win about 33 percent of the time at the track. So if you want to play it safe, pick the favorites. Most folks will bet quinellas, which pay off "either-or." But the odds are usually so low that you can't win any money. In some cases, you bet $3 to win just $3.50—not very exciting. So I prefer to bet exactas, where you pair any two horses in the exact order of finish. The odds are much better, which makes for a more exciting bet. For instance, say the number-7 horse is the favorite but the number-9 is a strong longshot. If I like the jockey, the trainer, and the horse, I'll buy a $50 ticket 20 times. The "7–9" exacta might pay 17–1 odds, which means a $1,000 ticket will pay $17,000 if it hits. Watching that "7–9" combination coming down the backstretch is very exciting . . . incredible energy . . . like riding right along with the jockey. If your horses finish "1–2," it's hats and horns. But if they finish "2–1" or if some other sonofabitch sticks his nose in at the tape—you're screwed! The bad news is you've lost $1,000. The good news is there is another race in 20 minutes—all part of the excitement of the track.

I continued to date Carol throughout the 1978 season and since word travels fast in a small town like Cincinnati, and it didn't take long before my wife found out about my girlfriend. I usually played early birds several days a week at the Luken Tennis Club on the east side of town. One morning at about 6 A.M., I left the house to go to the club, which must've raised Karolyn's suspicions. She got dressed, went over to Carol's apartment, snuck in through the gate, and forced her way in when Carol opened the front door. Karolyn was surprised to see that Carol was just sitting there having coffee with her roommate. Karolyn was expecting to catch us in the act, but I wasn't even there—I was playing tennis with Reuven Katz. But Karolyn was not to be denied. She just started planning more carefully—something I never did.

In the spring of 1979, Gio moved to Arizona where he got a job in the fitness business. I packed my gear and moved to the City of Brotherly Love as a newly minted Phillie. It didn't take long before Karolyn discovered that Carol had moved as well. I never tried to hide my relationship with Carol. I had made up my mind to get a divorce, but Karolyn was fighting to hold on to something that had already slipped away. I made arrangements for Carol to get a job as a bunny at the Playboy Casino in Atlantic City, which was just 45 minutes outside of Philadelphia. Carol shared an apartment with a girlfriend who eventually married my friend Hal Bodley, the Phillies beat writer. We'd all get together during the season and go out to dinner after the ball games. But after one particular Phillies game, Karolyn showed up by surprise, followed Carol back to her car, and punched her right in the mouth! Like I said, Karolyn was a lot like my mom—she could really pack a punch. But Carol didn't fight back. She wasn't the aggressive type. She just rolled up her car window and drove away.

After that confrontation, Karolyn moved back to Cincinnati and filed for divorce, which may have rattled a ballplayer with less conviction. But I have always thrived on conflict. It makes me stronger and helps me focus. I went 20-for-28 after Karolyn's lawyers served me with the papers. Teammates Mike Schmidt and Greg Luzinski were amazed by my performance. They asked me how I could perform under such stress. "Stress is facing a divorce when you don't want one," I replied. "I'm finally free from the distractions of a bad relationship."

When I arrived in Philadelphia, Mike Schmidt was the best player in baseball 3 days per week. By 1980, Mike Schmidt was the best player in baseball 7 days a week. I helped change his attitude. I stayed on his case until he believed that he was as good as he really was. The Phillies finished first in their division in each of the previous 3 years. But after I arrived, they dropped to fourth place. When a smart-ass reporter asked me what was the difference between first and fourth, I just stabbed him with a look. "Uh . . . 'bout three, asshole." He tried to insinuate that I was the cause for the drop in the standings but I wasn't. I played in 163 games, hit .331, got 208 hits, 40 doubles, led the league with 305 times on base, and struck-out just 32 times! Sound like I was a negative influence on the team?

In 1980, I played in one of the most exciting division championships in baseball history. Cy Young award winner "Lefty" Carlton shut down the Houston Astros 3–1 in the first game. Every game after that went into extra innings. I hit .400 in the playoffs and scored three runs in the final game against my old friend Joe Morgan who had been traded by the Reds. In the final game, we came from behind to beat Nolan Ryan for a 10th inning victory, which gave Philly their first pennant since the 1950 Whiz Kids. That dramatic victory put us in the World Series against George Brett and the Kansas City Royals.

We were up three games to two, one inning away from defeating the Royals and winning the World Series. The Philadelphia fans were going crazy. We were ahead 4–1 in the top of the ninth of the sixth game. With just one out, Frank White hit a pop-up toward our dugout. I was playing first base. But with bases loaded, I was playing back, not in, which meant it was the catcher's ball. Bob Boone drew a bead and got to the ball in a hurry. The ball came right down into Boone's catcher's mitt but his foot hit the top step of the dugout at the last second, which caused the ball to pop out of his glove . . . and into mine. I made the catch and killed the rally. With two outs, the Royals had no chance of winning. We killed their spirit. I slugged my mitt and gave the ball to our pitcher, Tug McGraw, who closed out the game by striking out Willie Wilson. Mike Schmidt won Series MVP honors by hitting .381 and two home runs. Bob Boone hit .412 and made some incredible plays behind the plate. Steve "Lefty" Carlton won two games and Tug McGraw threw smoke in relief. My catch became the "defining moment" in the World Series, as well as my career. "Pete Rose has a 12-year-old heart in a 38-year-old body," said Tug McGraw. Tug was right. I sure felt like a 12 year old. I played my hunches in the free agent market, landed with the right team, and got back on top of the baseball world! I was named *Sporting News'* "Baseball Player of the Decade," an honor previously bestowed on Stan Musial in the 1950s and Willie Mays in the 1960s. The *Sporting News* understood that I wasn't the most talented player of my era. But I had something that the fans liked. "He combined guts, determination, and stunning single-mindedness to make himself one of the game's biggest stars."

I continued to date Carol throughout my 4-year stay in Philadelphia. She moved from Atlantic City and got a job as a Philadelphia Eagles cheerleader which worked out great for both of us. She was gainfully employed, and I had another excuse to go to all the football games at Veterans Stadium. After my divorce was final, Carol joined me on many of my personal-appearance trips around the country. During a weekend visit to Virginia, the hotel concierge made the mistake of calling her "Mrs. Rose," which really struck a nerve. Carol was still a small town girl from Indiana who wasn't comfortable with big city morality. So, when the dust finally settled, Carol and I got married on April 11, 1984. I was playing for Montreal at the time and was in Cincinnati for a road game. We wanted to get hitched at home plate at Riverfront Stadium, but the Reds had a previous commitment with batting practice—go figure! So we settled for a private ceremony, which was held at Reuven Katz's house on the east side of town. Within a year, Carol gave birth to our son Tyler, who just happened to be born during halftime of a Monday Night Football game. I remember the night well—first, for obvious reasons, and second, because the Bengals were playing the Steelers, and I won my bet!

Besides making the transition from playing baseball to managing the Reds, the 1980s had another impact that changed my life—the sports memorabilia business. Wayne Gretzky and Bruce McNall of the Los Angeles Kings paid $451,000 for a mint-condition Honus Wagner baseball card. That's right—$451,000 for a baseball card! With that leading the way, the demand for sports memorabilia just started to skyrocket. The nostalgia craze was rolling full steam ahead, and I was happy to go along for the ride. Those same baseball cards that we bought as kids, the ones we used to clip on our bicycle spokes to make it sound like a motorcycle, were now worth a fortune. Ruth became Rembrandt, Cobb was Picasso— the older and more rare, the better. Former players like Willie Mays and Mickey Mantle were earning more money from public appearances than they earned from playing baseball! Can you imagine that someone would pay $50 to get an autograph from Willie Mays but only $10 to watch him hit a home run? The world had gone crazy with their obsession with sports heroes. The days of ballplayers working part-time jobs in the off-season were gone forever. Willie Mays was shocked when he discovered that his autographed Chesterfield cigarette ad was worth more than he was paid to film the actual commercial back in 1960!

Within a few years, another young man was rummaging around the attic of his grandmother's house and stumbled upon the baseball that Babe

Ruth hit for his first home run in Yankee Stadium. He sold the ball at auction for $110,000—jackpot! Who would have guessed that a baseball from 1920 would be worth as much as an Ivy League education 60 years later? Actor Charlie Sheen paid $93,500 for the ball that went through Bill Buckner's legs during the 1986 World Series. Another fan paid $280,000 for Eddie Murray's 500th home run ball. To top it all off, I was offered a healthy six figures for the black Mizuno bat I used to break Ty Cobb's record. Several of my friends told me to keep that bat as a souvenir.

Souvenir? Now, I don't know about you folks in the book-reading public, but if you could put $125,000 in the bank or hang a baseball bat on your wall, which would you choose? Hell, I already had bats. I had memories. I had the record. I had the photos and the videotape of the record. Why did I need the bat, too? After all, this was America . . . the land of opportunity . . . the birthplace of capitalism. Who was I to deprive some well-meaning fan of his constitutional right to buy a piece of baseball history? No, sir! Pete Rose would not be unpatriotic. I would put my wares on the open market to help keep the U.S. economy going strong! But don't worry—I decided *not* to sell that baseball bat, at least not right away. I held onto it . . . to see if the price might go up.

One of the first guys I met in the memorabilia business was a 16-year-old kid from Brooklyn named Mike Bertolini. He was standing on line to get my autograph during a card show in Pennsylvania. During the early 1980s, I signed autographs for $5 each. But the promoter would only allow two autographs per customer. Being a big Pete Rose fan, Bertolini bought 160 tickets at $5 each—$800 worth of autographs! But since the promoter insisted on keeping the line of customers moving, Mike had to go back to the end of the line 80 times. I laughed every time he came back around for another two autographs. But Mike was persistent. He told me that he could sell those autographs for $15 each—triple his investment. He'd tell a joke or ask me another question each time around. Finally,

Mike said that he felt like he knew me, which is the same reaction I got from a lot of the fans. You see, I've always been approachable, never standoffish. Whenever I did an autograph show, I made sure the fans got their money's worth. I never looked down on the common man because, hell, I *am* the common man!

I ran into Mike Bertolini again at another memorabilia show in Philadelphia during the off-season of 1984. He was standing in the lobby of my hotel, asking all the baseball players for their autographs. When he saw me, Mike struck up a conversation as if we were long-lost friends. Mike was energetic and street-smart, just like me. So we hit it off right away. I invited him to lunch and discovered that Mike came from the wrong side of the tracks. The more we talked, the more we laughed . . . and the more we laughed, the more we discovered that we had a lot in common. Except that Mikey was about 150 pounds overweight and 20 years younger. He might have been fat, but I was old!

About a year later, Mike invited me to a card show he put on in Los Angeles, just a few weeks before I broke Cobb's record. The turnout was amazing. I signed over 5,000 autographs, which set a one-day attendance record at that time. The fans were lined up around the block, and I refused to leave the hall until everyone got an autograph. I didn't finish until after midnight, when the police finally complained about curfew. That show gave Mike a real taste of success. But like me, Mike wasn't satisfied with just a little success. He wanted more. He had big plans for putting on special theme shows by renting convention centers for 3-day weekends with radio and television advertising. He had big ideas but no money and no contacts—something I had plenty of. For instance, if Mike Bertolini called Mickey Mantle, Mantle would not take his call. But if Pete Rose called Mickey Mantle to invite him to a card show, Mantle would come because he knew the show was legitimate. The same was true with Joe DiMaggio, Ted Williams, and Hank Aaron, or any of the other baseball stars that I knew personally. So Mike Bertolini and I decided to hook up and go into business. For instance, Mike would rent a convention hall in a place like Atlantic City. He'd make all the business arrangements, advertise, and set the itinerary. I would advance the money needed to secure the players and the venues. I would attend the show as a ballplayer, but I would also share in the profits.

Like most folks just starting out in business, we lost money. But not because of bad planning. Mike would buy 1,000 baseball bats from the Louisville Slugger factory at $25 per bat. Then he'd pay the ballplayers $50 to sign each bat. That's $75,000 in up-front costs. But he might only sell $45,000 worth of bats during one particular show, which meant he had a net loss of $30,000 on the bats. The same was true for photos, baseballs, and other memorabilia. But he always paid the players for every signature whether or not he sold all of their items. By the end of the show, he lost money but still had the leftover bats, balls, and photos. It was an ongoing venture because Mike kept the entire inventory to sell at future shows. I never got involved in the day-to-day operations, but I trusted Mike to stay on top of things. He was the businessman and I was the silent partner. Mikey was honest and loyal, traits I admired. And like most New Yorkers, Mikey knew a friend who could handle one of my other passions—sports action.

The other appealing aspect to memorabilia shows was cash. Just mention "cash" to any gambler and his eyes will light up, because gambling is a cash business, too. If I got paid $7,500 cash for a card show in Los Angeles, I'd have my stakes for a quick trip to Hollywood Park or Santa Anita to play the ponies. I wouldn't have to cash a personal check or draw on my salary for the funds. Since I never went to college, I never paid much attention to my finances. I paid lawyers and accountants to take care of all that stuff for me. They deposited my salary into an account, paid my living expenses, and invested as they saw fit. I owned an interest in three suc-

cessful restaurants and earned a steady income from commercial endorsements. I thought I was in great financial shape even though I was a
freewheeling spender. From 1984 through 1988, I earned well over $5
million. I drew a certain amount of money as an allowance, but I didn't
like to dip into my savings for gambling. The card shows provided me
with ready cash to use for recreational purposes—travel, dinners, and gifts,
not just gambling. Still, I was like a kid in a candy store, and through the
memorabilia business I was able to get my hands on a lot of fresh "candy."

By 1984, Tommy Gioiosa moved back into town and started working
out at Gold's Gym, which had just opened in Cincinnati. At 43 years of
age, I wanted to keep Father Time from kickin' my ass, and like every athlete my age, I refused to accept that I was slowing down. If I had been a
football player, my speed would have been an issue. Those guys have to
run full speed against younger players for the duration of the game. But a
baseball player only has to run in spurts, from base to base with plenty of
rest in between. My legs were as strong as ever, and my vision was 20/20.
But the baseball experts accused me of losing bat speed. So to stay on top
of my game, I started working out at the gym.

Through his contacts at Gold's, Gio made some inquiries and got in
touch with a local bookmaker, who agreed to take our action on football
and basketball games. Gio liked to gamble as much as I did. He just didn't
have the same means—at least not at first. If I bet two dimes, Gio would
bet a nickel. We usually bet on the same teams, which made the games
more fun to watch. If I won, he won. If I lost, he lost—a camaraderie thing.

Most real gamblers—guys who will bet a grand or more per game—
will always use a "runner" to call in their bets. The runner provides a buffer
between the gambler and the bookmaker in case someone turns up the
heat. He also handles the pickup and delivery—something I had no time
for. I knew that betting with a bookmaker was technically illegal. But my
brother-in-law was a cop, who informed me that they had never prosecuted

a case against a gambler in the history of the department. "Gambling was considered a victimless crime," he said. "I've never read where a gambler crossed over the center line at 90 mph and killed another gambler."

I preferred not to know the identity of the bookmaker at all or vice versa, but Gio could not get credit for a bet of two grand per game based on his income. He was probably earning only five or six hundred a week at the gym. So Gio informed his bookmaker, former assistant golf pro Ron Peters, that he was laying action for "Pete Rose." I would normally establish a "settle-up" figure of 30 grand to be paid on Tuesday—right after Monday Night Football. The settle-up figure was established for convenience because Peters lived 30 minutes away in Franklin, Ohio. Gio didn't want to drive back and forth every week for just a few grand. So normally, we'd wait until I either won or lost 30 before settling up. But Peters didn't want to wait. He wanted to settle up every Monday, regardless of the amount, which told me that Peters was inexperienced and small time. A gambler normally looks for a long-term relationship with a bookmaker—someone who can weather the ups and downs—someone who won't freak out if he wins or loses too much in any given week. I told Gio to make it clear that I traveled a lot and didn't expect to get paid every week if I won. I also didn't expect to hear any bitching and moaning if I lost while I was out of town. I didn't want to run to the bank and transfer money if I was in Houston or Dallas for 2 weeks. Gio explained the terms and Peters said he felt comfortable. So, I went along with the program. If I won during any given week, Gio would drive to Franklin for the pickup. If I lost, I'd give the cash to Gio and he'd wrap it up in a sock and make the dropoff at some pre-arranged site. At one point, Gio was supposed to toss the money into the back of someone's pickup truck as it was pulling into a gas station. Gio missed the truck and hit another car by mistake, which must have been pretty funny to everyone but Gio. He had to jump out of his car in the middle of a snowstorm before the $100 bills started blowing in the wind. Gio freaked out when he told me about the mishap. But I couldn't help but laugh. I didn't take it all that seriously. It was only a few grand, so I really wasn't worried. I bet on football the same way I bet on the ponies—for entertainment.

Needless to say, I trusted Gio. Hell, I practically raised him. But Gio had his own ideas about making a name for himself. He wanted to reap the benefits of success without actually doing the work, something I never understood. And being from Massachusetts, he had his own loyalties when it came to football. Gio always picked the Patriots over the Bengals, knowing that I could never bet against Cincinnati. So we started having some healthy competition in choosing our teams. You see, a wager is actually a competition. A bookmaker lays odds or gives points on the outcome of a particular sporting event. Let's say the Lakers are favored by six points over the Celtics. Any die-hard Celtics fan will want to *take* those six points as a matter of civic pride. He knows that in the name of Red Auerbach, the Celtics will destroy the Lakers—not just cover the point spread! At the same time, the die-hard Laker fan will *give* the six points in a heartbeat. He knows that his team can't lose with Jack Nicholson sitting courtside! An avid fan will lay $100 on the game just to stick it in the bookie's ear, which creates healthy competition. He's no longer just a fan. He's a competitor, trying to kick the bookie's ass. He's got a vested interest in the game. That's the difference between a gambler and a bookmaker. A bookmaker is in it for the money. A gambler is in it for the competition . . . the excitement . . . the action.

Gio and I did pretty well on football and basketball throughout the fall and winter. On any given week, I might have been down 10 or 15 grand with Gio's guy in Franklin, but I might have been up with my guy in New York, or Florida, or Dayton. You see, Gio wasn't the only runner I used to place my bets. Over the years, I met many bookmakers at the racetracks. These were honest, working-class guys who had wives and families—not the "Mafia" guys the press made them out to be. My guy in Florida was the maitre d' at the track restaurant, a guy I'd known for years. My guy in Dayton was a longtime family friend, a local fireman. So if I was down 15 to the guy in New York but up 5 to the guy in Florida, I was just minus 10 overall. Not earth-shattering money for a man in my tax bracket—it wasn't the same money I used for paying my mortgage or utility bills. It was "entertainment money"—the same money other folks spent on boats, cars, planes, or hunting and fishing.

The advantage to spreading the wagers around to different runners was one of convenience. I didn't want my runner to call Florida if I was living in Cincinnati. Likewise, during spring training I'd bet with the local guy in Florida. I could visit with him at the track, talk horses and speed figures, and have dinner. It was a personal relationship—not something dark and "foreboding" like it was portrayed in the news. Plus, if I ever went really cold and lost all of my bets—it was better to be down 15 to *three* different guys rather than down 45 to *one* guy. Like everyone else, bookies like to get paid when they win. They won't worry over 15 if the client is out of town or short on cash. They *will* worry over 45.

By the time spring training rolled around, my wagering focused on one last big quest of the year: March Madness. Growing up in Cincinnati, I learned to appreciate great basketball. I was exposed to some of the best college players in the country with the Kentucky, Indiana, and Ohio State teams. Back in the 1950s, my dad took me to every home game of the University of Cincinnati basketball team, and I got to watch one of the greatest players who ever played the game—Oscar Robertson. In the 1960s, I was a season ticket holder to the NBA's Cincinnati Royals, where the Big O *averaged* a triple-double for an entire NBA season—something nobody else has ever achieved. Over the years, I earned what you call a basketball "pedigree." I understood the game, so I knew how to bet the game. I'd pick teams that ran the fast break over teams that set up and waited for an open shot. I'd pick teams that played man-to-man over the zone defense. I'd pick teams with great coaches, like Bobby Knight, Dean Smith, and Al McGuire. I'd pick teams that featured star players who knew how to play within an organized system. But with all of that knowledge, experience, and passion, I'd still pick teams that lost. That's why they call it "March Madness"—because those kids drove me mad! Some young kid would come out of nowhere, steal the ball, and make a layup at the buzzer to win the game. Or some young star would call a time-out when none were left. But regardless of how much money I won or lost, I got a great deal of satisfaction from watching those young kids play. I got to the point where I could have sat in on the NBA draft and advised each team on their selections: "This kid has a great perimeter game but lacks the strength to go inside. That kid can post up and play in the paint. This kid has the total package." I may not have been an expert but I came damn close. One thing is for sure: If I was working for the Trailblazers in 1984, I would not have drafted Sam Bowie over Michael Jordan. Unlike horse racing, basketball is a sport where it's okay to pick the sure thing!

The end of March Madness meant the beginning of baseball. From that time forward, I was completely occupied with the business at hand, which in 1985 was breaking Cobb's career record for hits. The excitement I got from playing baseball was all I needed. Every move I made was recorded on national television. I had reached the top of my profession in a way that exceeded even my own dreams. Just months before the countdown to Cobb in the summer of 1985, the Miller Gallery in Hyde Park commissioned Andy Warhol to paint my portrait putting me into an exclusive club with the likes of Marilyn Monroe, Muhammad Ali, and Elvis. Then something strange happened after I broke that record. I had a letdown. I spent my entire life chasing records and, suddenly there was nothing left to chase. No more mountains to climb. I went through a period of withdrawal—a midlife crisis. But in order to beat the crisis, you first have to identify it. But I didn't identify anything that wasn't on my scorecard or racing form! In hindsight, I should have taken some time to reflect on my life—on where I'd been and where I was headed. If I had been a book reader, I could have read up on how other famous folks handled the "retirement" phases of their careers. I could have read about how the astronauts felt after they came back to earth from outer space. Some of those guys turned to drugs and alcohol because they couldn't cope with the letdown. But I didn't read books. So I never enlightened myself with the experience of other people. I could have called Dick Butkus and asked how he felt about retiring from the NFL after achieving god-like status as a player. I could have called Terry Bradshaw and asked how he felt about retiring after winning four Super Bowls. But I didn't find out how any of them dealt with retirement because I never actually talked to them. I never talked to anybody. It wasn't my style. Maybe I should have.

By the fall of 1985, Monday Night Football was a ritual that I never missed. I had reached a point where I thought they only played the game to give me a chance to get even from what I'd lost on Sunday! Go to any sports bar on Monday night and you'll see dozens of fans, who all have a wager on the game—even if it's only 50 bucks. It gives the viewers a reason to cheer or to bitch and moan. You'd be surprised by how many people will actually brag about losing. "That missed field goal cost me 50 bucks!"—not an uncommon phrase for a gambler. On the other hand, when you hear a guy bragging about winning—you know he's lying. Most gamblers lose. It's the nature of the beast.

By October of 1985, I went from cold to ice-cold. Every college and pro football team I picked either lost the game or failed to cover the point spread. Every dropped pass, missed field goal, and fumble came back to bite me in the ass. I reached the point where my guy in New York suggested that I start betting on hockey. I said, "Hockey! What the hell do I know about hockey?" He just laughed because obviously, during that stretch, I didn't know much about football either.

I got in kind of deep, so Gio arranged for one of his friends from the gym to front me a small loan to cover my losses with the local guy. I had been on a road trip and had to pay some large business expenses. Sometimes, it took as long as 2 weeks to transfer cash from an investment. So it was easier to shift cash among friends until I got flush. I repaid the loan 2 weeks later, but the loan was one of the first telltale signs. Like I said, I didn't like to dip into my savings for gambling. I didn't *like* to but I did— more often than I should have. Dipping into savings meant that I was getting in too deep, something I refused to admit at the time.

My annual salary from baseball was paid during the playing season. Outside of investments or personal appearances, I had no steady income throughout the off-season. So if I got in a tight spot, I could shift cash among friends until I made another score. My insurance agent, Steve Wolter, wanted to purchase the red Corvette I received from General Motors for breaking Cobb's record. So Gio arranged to have the car garaged until we completed the sale. At that time, I had a five-car garage, filled with three Porsches, an M-1 BMW, and a Rolls Royce—so I had no room for the Corvette. As it turned out, I must have run out of room for the black Mizuno bat, too. Wolter bought that as well.

Eventually, I busted out of my slump and won over 30 grand in one week. I was so happy to get back on top that I traveled with Gio personally to collect—a motive that was fueled by competition, not money. Gio and I drove up to Jonathan's Café, which was owned by Ron Peters. I had never actually met Peters, but as a gesture of good faith, I gave him an autographed baseball bat that he put on display in the restaurant. Peters didn't like coughing up all that dough and wanted a souvenir in return. I was happy to give it because like I said, I'd just kicked his ass on football. For that one week, I played my hunches and came out on top. I was a winner. Unfortunately, gambling and winning don't often go hand-in-hand. The NFL playoffs proved me right. Within a few weeks, I dropped back down. But I placed a string of interesting bets on the Super Bowl just to enjoy the action. I took the points, the over-and-under, and even bet that William "The Refrigerator" Perry would score a touchdown—a wager that actually paid off!

On February 5, 1986, I wrote three checks for 8 grand each to cover my losses on the NFL playoffs. Gio cashed each check to pay Peters, who insisted that all the checks be written for under 10 grand to avoid filling out a bank form, which would have to be reported to the authorities. From that point forward, my gambling cycle continued. The NFL turned into March Madness, which turned into the NBA playoffs, which always turned into the skids. Baseball season meant that it was time for me to put on my cleats and go to work. I always lived by one hard and fast rule: "You don't bet baseball." But for the first time in my life, I was no longer playing baseball.

I didn't realize it at the time, but I was pushing toward disaster. A part of me was still looking for ways to recapture the high I got from winning batting titles and World Series Championships. If I couldn't get the high from playing baseball, then I needed a substitute to keep from feeling depressed. I was experiencing what Sparky Anderson witnessed firsthand. "Peter is the only man I know who never—and I mean never—left home with any other intention but to win," said Sparky. "To know Peter, you must understand that he is not an "A" but a "double-A" type personality—not unlike General George Patton or Douglas MacArthur. Peter was absolutely driven. He didn't type those numbers into the record books, he earned them. I have never in my life seen a man who was tougher physically or mentally than Peter Edward Rose."

Sparky was right. I was driven—in gambling as well as in baseball. But for me, enough was never enough. I had huge appetites and I was always hungry. It wasn't that I was bored with the challenges of managing the Reds—I just didn't want the challenges to end!

According to the experts, gamblers experience something called "risk-craving" and "sensation-seeking" behavior. I can't speak for anyone else but those words sure describe how I felt when I placed my bets.

"Craving risk" might also explain why my Uncle Buddy put on that mask and hustled pool throughout the Midwest, despite being a legendary hitter who might have made a big splash in the majors. I never actually donned the mask, but in 1986 I started living in its shadow. I can't honestly remember the first time I bet on baseball. But I remember the first time I spoke openly about it. I was sitting in my living room, watching the 1986 playoffs between the Mets and the Astros. I had a group of friends over for the game—just like I'd done my whole life. Paul Janszen, a friend of Gio's from the gym, heard me talking about the score and asked me a question about gambling on baseball. Without even thinking about the consequences, I said, "Betting on the playoffs makes the games more exciting to watch!"

7

IN TOO DEEP

"It's like I have a shotgun in my mouth and my finger
on the trigger . . . and I like the taste of the gun metal."
ROBERT DOWNEY JR.,
award-winning actor, on his attraction to cocaine

As you look back over the history of our great country, you'll find that a lot of famous folks were involved in "questionable" activities. Athletes, entertainers, and politicians have all tried to keep their deep, dark secrets from leaking to the press for fear of losing the respect of an admiring public. Elvis, Rock Hudson, and John Belushi were just a few who didn't want their private lives revealed even though they had no intention of actually giving up their private passions. As the rumor goes, Prohibition didn't stop Joe Kennedy Sr. from hustling moonshine across the country. He figured that if people wanted to drink booze and were willing to pay for it, he'd jump right in and make a profit on the deal. He followed the simple rule of supply and demand. And apparently, he wasn't too concerned with whether or not his business venture was legal. It was profitable and enjoyable, which is probably what he had in mind. Common sense will tell you that he didn't run his boot-legging operation alone. He relied on trusted friends and runners—an inner circle. Hell, he might have had some partners on the payroll from the polit-ical world, which would have made him one helluva lot smarter than me. Come to think of it—that's probably why he never got caught! Maybe if I had enlisted the help of the mayor and the governor, my life would have turned out differently. The Roaring Twenties were filled with people just like Joe Kennedy, who wanted to enjoy everything life had to offer. My Uncle Buddy used to tell stories about the folks who hung out in the Speakeasies in New York and Chicago . . . folks who talked about the legends of the day—men who lived hard and played hard . . . men like Cobb, Speaker, and Ruth . . . men like Jack Dempsey, Red Grange, Jim Thorpe, and Damon Runyon.

I'm not trying to make excuses or shift the blame but for me, the 1980s version of the Speakeasy was the racetrack. They were filled with the most popular and colorful people from the era—men like George Steinbrenner, Don Zimmer, and Warren Giles. People like Will Farish, Bob Baffert, Seth Hancock, D. Wayne Lukas, and Virginia Kelley. It was hard to think that my gambling was wrong when most of my friends were doing the same thing. I can't begin to tell y'all how many other athletes, politicians, and respected businessmen were betting at the track or with the same or different bookmakers as me. Dozens of other players, coaches, and owners went to the racetrack during spring training . . . or wagered on football and basketball games during the off-season. Some of them bet as much or more than I did. One of my friends from the entertainment business routinely bet $50,000 per game on as many as 10 games per weekend—half a million dollars! He bet even more at the racetrack. He was also worth hundreds of millions, so he could easily afford the loss. In all our years together, nobody ever suggested that he had a gambling "problem." Everyone in our circle of friends had the same feeling: "It's his money . . . he can do whatever he wants with it!"

Paul Janszen started coming over to the house more often. Janszen was just the opposite of Gio. He was about six feet two and 260 pounds—strong quiet type. Gio was only five feet five but he was becoming loud and aggressive. Together they looked like Mutt and Jeff. Apparently, Gio was having some conflict with the owners of the gym over his abrasive personality. I didn't know it at the time, but the conflict involved more than personality. They had a disagreement over money, which supposedly involved drugs. So Janszen became Gio's new best friend and eventually mine, too. I started working out at the gym with Janszen because Gio's schedule was not as flexible. Janszen worked as a barrel salesman for his father's company, so he could name his own hours. I would train at different times and Janszen was always available—day or night. The more we trained, the more we hit it off. Afterward, he'd come by the house, help me with my quarter horses or play games with my son Tyler. Janszen, Gio, and Mike Bertolini would all hang out at my house during the weekends. We'd grill burgers and steaks on the barbecue and watch football games on television. I had three different sets hooked up to the satellite dish, so I could get any game that was being played—anywhere, anytime. Like I said, if I put my money on a game or race, I wanted to *watch* it or *listen* to it. Janszen fit in really well with the rest of the crowd. He was a no-nonsense guy who didn't drink or smoke. He was well-mannered . . . never cussed around the ladies or acted obnoxious like Gio. Later, I found out why Gio's personality was changing so drastically. But by then, it was already too late.

During the off-season, Gio and Janszen traveled with me to many of the memorabilia shows, which were hosted by Mike Bertolini. I would usually charter a private jet so everyone could go along for the fun. Janszen had a girlfriend, Danita, who became good friends with my wife, Carol. We'd all jump on the plane and enjoy the weekend trips together. The girls would go shopping while the guys would hang out at the different shows. I used to tease Carol and Danita because they'd usually spend more money on shopping than I made from the appearance fee of $7,500. I got some pleasure from turning my wife loose at the mall, which also gave me an education on the art of spending—as if I needed one. If statistics were kept on shopping, my wife would have batted 1,000. Truth is, she tried to get even with me for losing money on football games. She may have been trying to teach me a lesson. But Carol didn't understand that I got the same pleasure from gambling that she got from shopping. I didn't see any difference between the two hobbies—she did, which started to cause flak in our marriage. Still, those weekend trips were a lot of fun— well worth the time and money. Janszen took a keen interest in the sports memorabilia business and began to learn the ropes from Mike Bertolini. By that time, Mike was making a name for himself by promoting shows all over the country. In fact, I took everybody to one of Mike's shows in New York, where they got to meet Mickey Mantle—a real treat because everybody loved Mantle. He was one of the true legends of the game. Mick would laugh and talk with everybody. He never shied away from an autograph or a conversation. He appreciated the great life baseball had given him and wanted to give something back.

Like me, Mantle was a small-town kid who really enjoyed the fans. He was also thrilled with the financial boon in the sports memorabilia business, which enabled him to earn a living even though he was retired from baseball. Mantle, along with Willie Mays, was suspended by Commissioner Bowie Kuhn for their association with various casinos, which amounted to nothing more than playing golf and shaking hands with the high rollers. But according to Mr. Kuhn, they violated the "best interests of baseball." Mantle thought baseball was being completely unfair, since "public relations" was the only way a retired player could earn a living. Finally, Commissioner Pete Ueberroth agreed and overturned their suspensions in 1985.

The friendlier I became with Janszen, the more distant I became with Gio—something he resented. Carol tried to warn me that Gio was not trustworthy. She referred to him as a "snake in the grass." Carol heard rumors about the way Gio treated women . . . rumors she didn't like. But I've always been the type to give a guy the benefit of the doubt. If a guy was square with me, I usually ignored what other people said about him. But Janszen explained that Gio was using the phone at Gold's to call in the wagers and making a point to speak as loudly as possible so everyone in the gym could hear that he was betting for Pete Rose. Gio was also bragging about being a professional gambler. He wore a Rolex watch, drove an expensive sports car and carried a big wad of cash. Hell, I wore a Rolex, drove an expensive sports car, and carried a big wad of cash. Who was I to judge him? But Gio was also taking steroids, which made him more aggressive and less reliable—something that spelled trouble.

It's a good thing I wasn't a professional gambler, because during the next stretch, I went from ice-cold to Mr. Freeze. Between the playoffs, college and pro football, I hit an all-time low. The more I bet, the more I lost. The more I lost, the more I tried to double up to get back what I had already lost. During one 3-week stint, I wrote eleven $8,000 checks to my guy in New York. On top of the 88, I dropped another six figures to the other guys—far more than I ever should have allowed. I had to dip into my business account to pay the losses. So, before I go on, I know what you're thinking—"We all like to gamble, Pete. But why did you have to bet so damn much money?" I wish I could have just bet $100 a pop. But that didn't do it for me. I needed to have more riding on it.

"The *do it for me* Pete talks about is consistent with the *action-high* described by many gamblers," says Dr. Comings. "The action-high is caused by the release of dopamine into the pleasure center of the brain. This is called the *reward pathway*, which is present in all of us. Most people can be satisfied with normal rewards. But people with Pete's brain chemistry are not satisfied and must continue to push the envelope to get the stimulations they need. The release of dopamine into the bloodstream is extremely satisfying. Some gamblers even equate the experience with sexual orgasm, which explains why the impulse is nearly impossible to resist."

Truth is, I really didn't think that I was doing anything wrong at the time. I didn't see myself going into some addictive death-spiral. To my mind, I was just following the same competitive instincts I followed as a ballplayer. Sports taught me how to bounce back after a loss. If I was down 0–2 in the count, I didn't concede the strikeout. I dug in and looked for a good pitch to hit. If we were down 4–0 in the bottom of the ninth, I didn't concede the loss. I tried to rally the team for a comeback victory. If I was on a cold streak with the bookmaker, I didn't bitch and moan about my losses. I tried to pick some winners. I never quit anything in my life and I sure as hell wasn't going to start with a bookmaker! So, I did what every great hitter does when he goes into a slump. I got ready for the next pitch. I got back to basics. For me, basics in gambling meant "horse racing." In hindsight, maybe I should have done what Hutch did for me when I slumped in my first year with the Reds: sat on the bench.

Within a few weeks, I was back at Turfway Park where I had won big over the years. Jerry Carroll owned the track, and he gave me a private room where my guests and I could eat dinner and enjoy the races. At that time, I was a big celebrity in Cincinnati. I was hounded for autographs everywhere I went. I always loved the fans and gave freely of my time. But when I went to the track, I went for racing—not signing autographs. Jerry understood my need for privacy. Most nights, Jerry and his friends sat right along with me. But on this particular night, Jerry was out of town. Gio, Janszen, Arnie Metz, and I went over to play the ponies. We had a great dinner and studied the program. The Pick-Six was small on this particular night because there was no carryover from previous races. But I knew all the trainers and jockeys and had a good feel for the meet. You have to buy all of your Pick-Six tickets before the start of the first race. It varies from track to track but the Pick-Six is usually races three through nine or four through ten. You must pick the winner in all six races in order to win. Each horse has different odds, so the key is to pick at least one bullet horse—a sure-thing in each race. Each ticket is only $2, so your investment can be large or small—depending on how many horses you like. If you like just one horse in each race, then your total investment is only $2. But your odds of winning are limited. On this particular night, I liked several horses in each race and backed up my odds with extra combinations. I invested $2,000. I didn't bet any other part of the six races. I spent no extra money on trifectas or exactas—tickets I usually bought. Janszen bought in for a quarter-share, or $500, and then sold half of that to Gio. So I had only $250 invested in each race. Sure enough, our horse in the sixth race came from behind on the backstretch and nosed out the competition. We hit the Pick-Six for a $40,000 jackpot! We were all jumpin' and high-fivin' like we'd won the goddamn lottery. It was the same kind of excitement I got from winning baseball games—excitement that I missed since retiring from the active roster. My share was $30,000. Janszen and Gio won $5,000 each and I gave a few grand to Arnie Metz for helping me handicap the horses. After we settled down, Gio went to the window and cashed the tickets. The taxes were taken out immediately but Gio wanted to keep the stubs so he could deduct the full amount off his personal income taxes. I was never the type to submit losing tickets to my accountant for tax purposes. If I had been, I would have come out way ahead with the IRS. In order to claim those losses, you had to list your occupation as a "professional gambler,"— something Gio claimed to be. I was a professional baseball player. I gambled for diversion, relaxation, and pleasure—not tax deductions. But that experience taught me a lesson about Gio. He was a manipulator. He liked to scheme. That was Gio's first big racetrack success, which probably went to his head. I had won over a dozen Pick-Sixes over the years, so I was used to the excitement. Gio wasn't. Two weeks later, while I was out of town, Gio went back to Turfway. He got drunk and lost all of his winnings. He caused a big ruckus and started disturbing the stewards in the next booth, which forced the owner to close down my room. The stewards are a group of former jockeys who watch each race to catch possible fouls. They are the only folks at the track who are not allowed to gamble. But Gio thought he was above it all . . . thought he deserved to be treated like a celebrity just because he was my friend. He forgot that it was my room—not his. Jerry Carroll told me that Gio's insulting behavior had gotten way out of control and that he didn't want "that asshole causing any more trouble." After that, I started to cut my ties with Gio—something I should have done months earlier.

Later, I discovered that Gio was betting against me on football—taking the opposite teams I selected, which would have produced big winnings during my cold streak. He was also trying to hit the middle—playing different point spreads to win both ends of the same bet. Worse yet, Gio was giving me a different point spread than the spread he got from Peters, which meant Gio collected the money on bets that I should have won! Gio even persuaded Peters to give him 10 percent of my losses as an inducement for keeping my business. If there is one thing a gambler hates more than losing, it's being cheated by his runner.

Before I left for spring training, Gio claimed that I was down 34 to his guy in Franklin. I can't honestly remember if I was really down that much or just pissed off that Gio beat me with the phony point spreads. At least half of that money could have been won through fraud. But Gio said that if I didn't pay up, someone would burn down my house or break my kid's legs. I didn't believe the threats were real. But Gio had ballooned up to 230 pounds from the steroids and was acting like a gorilla. If I called the police, my gambling activity would be exposed—something I couldn't afford. So while in Florida, I called my accountant and told him to issue a check for $34,000. That was the end of my betting with Gio and Peters—or so I thought.

Over the next few months, Janszen and his girlfriend, Danita, became good friends. In fact, Janszen went out of his way to do things around my house . . . like mowing the lawn and trimming the trees. They spent the Christmas holidays with us, and I invited them to spend spring training with my family and me in Tampa. 1987 was going to be a good year for the Reds. We had come off consecutive second-place finishes in 1985 and 1986 and were ready to make a move. I was looking for strong hitting from Eric Davis, Kal Daniels, Buddy Bell, and Barry Larkin. If our pitching staff stayed healthy, I thought we had a chance at winning our division. Early sessions of spring training started at 10:30 in the morning and lasted until 2:30 in the afternoon. As soon as practice ended, all the players split for their favorite form of recreation. A third of the players went straight to the golf course. A third went to the beach. The other third went to the race-track. As soon as I finished with my manager's meetings, I'd head over to Tampa Bay Downs with Janszen. The ponies started running at 1:00, so I'd get there in time for the last few races. While at the track, I'd usually see a group of the other owners and managers—guys like Joe Torre, Bill Giles, Jim Leyland, and George Steinbrenner. We'd talk about players and prospects . . . outrageous salaries—anything of interest.

While at the track, I introduced Janszen to Stevie Chevashore, one of the regulars at my booth who ran my bets to the track window. Stevie also had a friend in New York named Val—short for "valet parking," a job he held at a local restaurant. Val also worked for a local bookmaker. Stevie and Janszen made a connection and began booking my action on basketball through Val. Why? Because I was betting more money than the local guy could handle.

Once the exhibition baseball games started, my schedule got busy. We'd practice from 10:30 until 2:00, then start playing the games at 2:30, which didn't end until 5:00 or 6:00. I no longer had time to go to the racetrack un-less our game was rained out. The dog track, which was open for evening races, provided the only other source of local sports entertainment—except for the NBA or March Madness, which happened to be in full force. So Jan-szen started calling in our bets with Stevie, who in turn called Val in New York. Since he was calling out of state, Stevie established a few code words and numbers to simplify the process and to avoid detection. They never mentioned money or used the word "bet" just in case the phones were tapped. We agreed on a settle-up figure of 50 because sending funds to New York was more difficult than driving back and forth to Franklin, Ohio. Like Gio, Janszen would piggyback onto my bets with whatever money he could afford. If I bet two dimes, Janszen would bet a nickel. He stayed within his means—at least in the beginning. In some ways, I had the best of both worlds. After a full day of managing baseball, I enjoyed a full night of watching basketball or dog racing. It was "sports smorgasbord," which sat-isfied my appetite for "action." In previous years, my sports gambling ended with March Madness. In 1987, March ended—the "Madness" didn't. Ask any gambler, and he'll tell you the line gets crossed easily. If you're in the throes of it, if you're down to your book, your natural reaction isn't to stop gambling. That might be what someone who doesn't have my personality quirks might do. But me? Well let's just say I'm not a quitter.

Stevie arranged for Janszen to call Val in New York directly. Stevie was only a runner, so he became an unnecessary link in the chain. Janszen started running all of my sports action, which was taking on a new energy. He continued to work around the house and help out with the horses. But he was spending more time at my house than I was. He even had a key to the front door. I'd look at the sports page in the morning and give my fa-vorites to Janszen, who would call them into New York. After spring training, I was only down 10 or 15 from all of my losses on basketball—not a large amount when spread over 2 months. But Janszen just shook his head at the futility. Even when I won 5 outta 10 games, I still lost money because of the 10 percent vigorish. On other days, I'd pick 8 out of 10 winners but 7 outta 8 failed to cover the point spread. So I lost again.

Finally, the temptation got too strong and I began betting regularly on the sport I knew best—baseball. This wasn't a no-account playoff bet on a couple of teams I had nothing to do with. I was betting on baseball while I was managing a major league ball club in the regular season. But in all honesty, I no longer recognized the difference between one sport and another. I just looked at the games and thought, "I'll take a dime on the Lakers . . . a dime on the Sixers . . . a dime on the Buckeyes . . . and a dime on the Reds."

I didn't even consider the consequences.

"Sometimes gamblers just forget the boundaries," says Dr. Comings. "It is very consistent with impulse disorders and ADHD for Pete to just not be able to distinguish between sports when it came time to place his bets. He just may not have been able to draw the line. On the other hand, he may have done it on purpose for the added thrill . . . because he knew it was illegal. It's much like politicians and powerful dictators. If a person does an illegal act and gets away with it again and again, he discovers that no one makes him accountable. He may have thought, 'I know about this rule but no one will ever dare call me on it.' "

◆ ◆ ◆

Carol was very busy at home with my son Tyler, who was only 3 years old. She had grown tired of all the traveling. The major league schedule has 162 games, which can be grueling to most folks. I happened to thrive on the schedule. I got stronger as the season went on. Janszen went along with me on a few of our road trips. He was still learning the ropes of the memorabilia business and making contacts with various promoters. He was also giving weight-lifting tips to a few of our power hitters. At six feet two and 250 pounds, Janszen fit right in with the players. He never did anything to raise suspicions. He was a real gentleman—at least in the beginning. If I was out of town, Janszen would call me in the afternoon or evening and give me the money line. But, for me, the thrill wasn't about the odds. I got involved because I was rooting for my teams—no, *believing* in my teams. I bet the Reds to win every time. I bet the Phillies to win even though they were huge underdogs and on a losing streak. It wasn't the smart way to bet. But it was my gut feeling . . . and I always bet with my gut. I never—ever— bet against my teams. If I had, I'd be doubting everything I believed in. And, hell, to my way of thinking, we were going to win every night. You can't be a competitor and think otherwise.

Janszen maintained his New York connection from April until mid-May but was having some trouble collecting when we won. At one point, I was down 31 and Janszen was down 9 when I left for a road trip to Montreal. We were still 10 short of the settle-up figure, but the guy in New York told Janszen he wanted some stew. The whole purpose of a settle-up figure was to prevent a petty squabble from week to week. I didn't place any bets that night because I was on the airplane for a three-game trip. But Janszen called to place his own bets and got into a big argument with Val for welshing on the settle-up figure. I didn't know it at the time but supposedly Janszen sent him some money just to end the dispute. The next day, I called Janszen and placed my new bets. I won eight out of nine games, which wiped out my losses and put me plus-10 for the week. Janszen called back the next day and told me that he never got the bets down—that Val wouldn't take the action. At that point I was furious. Janszen fell for one of the oldest tricks in the book. The bookmaker needed our money to pay his losses to other clients. If the situation had been reversed, the guy in New York would *not* have paid us! He would have told us to stick to the settle-up figure, which was 50—not 49—not 40—but 50!

It's the rules of the game—three strikes and you're out. The umpire won't give you four strikes just because you're in a slump. But Janszen caved in to the pressure. The guy in New York claimed that he was still owed 10. But I was plus-10 from my new winnings. It wasn't my fault the bookmaker suddenly claimed he didn't take the action—or that Janszen suddenly claimed he didn't get the bets placed in time. Either way, I had no way of knowing who was telling the truth. I told Janszen to forget the guy in New York. I refused to deal with him after that fiasco. He wasn't worth the trouble. Certain bookmakers have a sarcastic expression: "We're gonna knock this guy out," which means they want to bleed you until you're broke. But a gambler never wants to "knock out" his bookie because then he'll have to take his action someplace else. A gambler wants a smart bookmaker who will stack up the action on both ends so that he will always win from the vig. If your bookmaker is inexperienced or likes to gamble himself, he might take all the action one way, which can leave him short on funds, which is probably what happened with the guy in New York.

Either way, I was pissed off. I should have read the handwriting on the wall. But I wasn't thinking straight. I went back to Ron Peters in Franklin, Ohio. Only this time, Peters refused to take the action because he claimed that I still owed him 34 from the previous spring—the same 34 that I gave to Gio—the same $34,000 check that Gio cashed and kept for himself!

But Peters had won big money on football and basketball with me in the past and was eager to get back in business. Finally, as a gesture of good faith, Janszen showed Peters a copy of my canceled check for the $34,000. Peters grinned when he saw the check. He suspected all along that Gio kept the money for himself. Peters acknowledged that I had paid the debt and resumed taking my sports action.

I won 10 during the first week and then I went on a roll. Every game I picked turned up aces. Peters complained to Janszen that he was "getting murdered on baseball by Pete Rose." He claimed I was "hotter than a 10-peckered billy goat." There was just one problem. Peters had no intention of paying his losses. He told Janszen that I still owed him the 34 despite the fact that he agreed the debt was already paid. As soon as I hit 40, Peters stopped paying even though he was still taking the action. If I had been losing, Peters would have been crying for his money every week. Instead, he pleaded poverty—just like the guy in New York. He complained to Janszen that his wife had left him and ran off with over $200,000 in cash. But Janszen didn't believe his excuses. He did a little investigating and discovered that Peters had a bad reputation for stiffing other people at his country club. At that point, I stopped betting sports altogether. Hell, I had no choice. I ran out of bookies! But by stiffing a client, Peters committed a cardinal sin—a sin that Janszen never forgot.

In the meantime, the guy in New York was not finished with Janszen. He kept calling and asking for the 10 he thought he was still owed. He even brought Stevie back into the mix, thinking Stevie could persuade Janszen to pay up on the dispute. Janszen got tired of the harassment and changed his phone number. Then, someone made a phone call to Janszen's mother, threatening his life. Janszen went berserk. Nobody wants their mother exposed to a small-time gambling dispute. It was a sleazy threat from sleazy people. Janszen called Stevie and the guy in New York and told them both that if he ever got another harassing phone call, he was going straight to the FBI. At that point, the conflict ended—or so I thought.

Throughout the off-season, I attended card shows with a local entrepreneur named Charles Sotto. Charles earned a degree in Economics from the University of Cincinnati and was a very reputable young promoter, whose work ethic I admired. As it turned out, Sotto's wife was a speech therapist, whose talents also came in handy. My son Tyler was only 3 years old at the time and was having some trouble pronouncing his words. Mrs. Sotto came over to my house and spent time working with Tyler, which really gave him a boost in confidence. As a way of saying thanks for helping my son, I went out of my way to establish contacts for Sotto in the memorabilia business. I introduced him to Randy Thyberg, a Los Angeles based promoter, who put on West Coast shows, which drew big crowds. I even invited the Sottos along on the private jet and arranged for tables where they could sell memorabilia. At the same time, Janszen started his own company called Premier Sports, which dealt primarily in Pete Rose bats, balls, and photos. Janszen started to get really friendly with Sotto and suggested they partner up on a few memorabilia shows. At first, I thought it was a good idea. The relationship was good for them . . . good for business . . . and good for me. They were planning a big show for October in Louisville right around the time of the big races at Churchill Downs. The show had to be postponed but that didn't stop me from going to the races.

Just before the races, I received a phone call from my good friend Mike Battaglia—the track announcer at Churchill Downs. Mike and his father, John, are two of the most knowledgeable and respected horse handicappers in the country. They really know their stuff. Mike had been calling the races throughout the season and had some great hunches on the ponies. Mike invited me to sit with him in his private box . . . try to hit the Pick-Six, which started out at over a half million dollars. I called Mike Zicka, who owned a charter service and asked to use a private helicopter for a quick trip to Louisville. Mike arranged for Bob, his top pilot, to make the flight. Bob had flown in Vietnam and was a very experienced pilot—one I'd used for years. He was also a very good friend. We picked up my friend Arnie Metz and boarded the chopper bound for Louisville. After 12 years as the Reds groundskeeper, Arnie was what you'd call an "earth" person—he hated to fly. Whenever I traveled by private plane, I had a running gag with all my friends. Just before takeoff, I'd ask them the same question. "How do you feel about being referred to as 'other passengers'? "Whattaya mean?" they'd ask. "Well, if this sumbitch goes down, tomorrow's headlines will read: 'Baseball legend Pete Rose and *other passengers* were killed in a tragic crash.'"

Most of my friends laughed at the gag, but Arnie didn't appreciate my sense of humor. He got really nervous. And y'all know what happens when a feller gets nervous. After takeoff, we circled over Riverfront Stadium and then headed west along the Ohio River. After just a few minutes, Arnie turned white as a ghost and closed his eyes. So I gave the prearranged signal to Bob, who waited until it was safe, and then dropped the chopper into a 90-degree vertical drop toward the river. I grabbed Arnie by the arm and screamed, "Oh my god, Arnie, we're outta fuel. I think we're goin' down!" Arnie was scared half to death. He started screaming and praying until I just busted a gut laughing. The expression on Arnie's face was priceless. He looked like he was having a heart attack! Finally, Arnie realized that we were just having some fun at his expense. After Bob brought the chopper under control, Arnie started cussin' a blue streak. Then he took off his sweater and wrapped it around his waist for the rest of the night. I can't honestly remember if Arnie really pissed his pants, but that sweater never left his waist for the rest of the night. I'd never admit it, but I was just as scared as Arnie. I was just more prepared for the thrill.

When I got back to Cincinnati, I told Janszen about the helicopter prank and about how we just missed out on the big Pick-Six. He laughed at the stories but I could tell he was upset that I didn't invite him along. Janszen had been a constant companion for over a year. But since I was no longer gambling with him, I didn't need to see him on a daily basis. I invited him along to the card shows and promoted his memorabilia business. But Janszen couldn't accept the fact that I had other friends and other responsibilities.

Just before the holidays, Janszen came over to my house with 1,500 baseballs. He told me that he had a friend in Chicago who wanted to give the baseballs to all his employees as Christmas gifts. I signed the baseballs along with 25 bats and a few hundred color photos. Janszen gave me a $5,000 deposit check against the $25,000 I would normally earn for all those items, but the check bounced. It wasn't like I needed the money so I didn't worry about it.

At about that time, Janszen traded in his Corvette for a Blazer and put his Rolex watch into a safe. Janszen was very proud of that watch because I sold it to him at a big discount. But he claimed he didn't want to draw attention to himself. I told him that if he worked hard for his money, he should be proud of his success. But Janszen wanted to keep a low profile. At that point, I started to put two and two together but didn't come up with four. I should have been more suspicious. But as a gambler, I looked at him from a different perspective—clouded judgment. During the one year that I'd been friends with Janszen, he never discussed any outside activities or did anything suspicious in front of me. But let's face it, I wasn't exactly squeaky clean. I didn't want my gambling activity exposed to the public. So trust and loyalty had to be a two-way street.

Just before spring training, Janszen and I drove to Cleveland for a personal appearance. I took another woman along for the trip—an error in judgment in what had been a full year of bad judgment. When I arrived in Cleveland, Carol was waiting for me. I suspected that Janszen called Carol and gave her the tip. But at that point, it didn't really matter. All hell broke loose. Carol was furious. She felt betrayed—and rightly so. But that wasn't all. She blamed me for bringing a bad element into our lives—people who hung on my success without paying their own way. She saw Janszen and Gio for what they were—sycophants. "I want these people out of our lives, Pete," she said. "They're users! They're not interested in you—they just want to be a part of your success." Carol was right. But it wasn't just my choice of friends—it was me. Whether it was a 90-degree vertical drop, chasing women, or gambling, I was pushing the boundaries in every aspect of my life. "Chaos" would not have been too strong a word.

During spring training of 1988 I got a call from my lawyer, Reuven Katz, who said that Janszen paid him a visit and requested money. He said that Janszen had gotten himself into trouble and needed a lawyer. Janszen told Reuven that back in 1985 he had sold steroids and had also been involved in some small-time cocaine deals. Janszen explained that he never discussed his drug or steroid involvement with me because he was afraid it would jeopardize our friendship. Janszen was right. I may have been a hard-core gambler but I would never get involved with drugs or steroids. Janszen wanted $30,000 to help pay his legal fees but I didn't feel comfortable with loaning 30 because I didn't think Janszen could repay the money. Instead, I agreed to loan him $10,000. Reuven also recommended several good attorneys.

When I returned from spring training, I helped Sotto with his card show—the one I committed to in Louisville back in October. I arranged for Willie McGee from the St. Louis Cardinals to attend and I even waived my standard appearance fee of $7,500 as a gesture of good faith. During the show, Janszen tried to renew our friendship. But I had to distance myself from him—something he resented.

After the show, Janszen called me on several occasions to get back on my good side. But I never returned his calls. A few days later, Janszen sent his girlfriend, Danita, over to my house with some baseball bats that he wanted me to sign for his memorabilia collection. Janszen was desperate for money to pay his legal fees and was pulling out all the stops. But Carol got into a big argument with Danita and threw her out of the house. After that, Janszen went berserk. He called Charlotte Jacobs, one of our closest friends, and made threats against my wife and kids.

"Janszen called me right away," said Charlotte. "He said he was going to shoot Carol and blow her brains out for every tear Danita shed for getting pushed out of Pete's house! Later, Janszen said he tried to call Carol to explain his feelings but that Carol wouldn't talk with him. Then, Janszen threatened to blow up Carol's car. During yet another phone call, Janszen wanted me to arrange a meeting with Carol. He said that he missed Tyler and wanted to see him again."

"I don't know anything about steroids," said Charles Sotto. "But if they make you paranoid, erratic, and aggressive, then Janszen sure fit the description. He was unstable and had major mood swings. After I found out that Janszen stole my customer mailing list, I ceased doing business with him. But still, he called me on several occasions asking me to set up a meeting with Pete so he could get back on Pete's good side. Janszen called Jeff Ruby, Mike Bertolini, and Charlotte Jacobs—everybody. He wanted desperately to be a part of Pete's life. But Pete wouldn't have anything to do with him after he threatened his wife and kids. At one point, Janszen made a point of telling me that he was working as an informant for the FBI . . . that he was going to wear a wire and set up Ron Peters on a drug charge. He even threatened me with an IRS investigation if I told anyone about his plans. I was a completely legitimate businessman, so I had nothing to fear from the government. But Janszen scared me to death. He was volunteering this information as if he was proud of himself. He knew that I was close friends with Pete, yet Janszen told me, 'We're gonna fry that sonofabitch . . . wait and see!' At that point, I called Pete and warned him to be careful. 'Janszen is a vindictive person,' I said. 'When he feels hurt—he'll strike back!' "

"Pete and I got into our biggest fights over his selection of friends," said Carol. "I knew that Gio and Janszen were both snakes. Every time Janszen came by the house, I got the feeling he was casing out the place. Danita called me late one night in a panic. She'd locked herself in the bathroom. I could hear Janszen screaming in the background and banging on the door. He was threatening to kill her. Danita wanted me to call the police. She had the door barricaded. She was crying hysterically, screaming that Janszen was going to kill her. This happened on more than one occasion. I told Pete not to trust these people . . . they were users. But he just didn't listen."

In January of 1989, my attorney, Reuven Katz, received another letter from Janszen requesting more money. Reuven, who handles pensions, contracts, and tax matters, felt like he needed some outside help. He called Roger Makley, a former federal prosecutor from Dayton, who had significant experience in criminal cases. Roger examined Janszen's letter and listened to my story concerning our relationship over the previous year and a half. Roger advised me not to fall for Janszen's tricks. "If you pay him one dime," said Makley, "you'll be paying for the rest of your life. It'll never stop because he will always keep coming back. It is borderline extortion." At that point, I followed my lawyer's advice. But I still had a major dilemma. Janszen knew that I had bet on baseball through him and through other bookmakers. If that went public, I could get suspended from baseball. I wanted to settle my situation with Janszen as quietly as possible. He's already in trouble with the Feds. But if I go to the cops with his threats, the stuff about my gambling gets leaked to baseball and to the public. I wanted to get rid of Janszen and stay in baseball. In his letter, Janszen threatened to go to court if I didn't come up with some money. He was bluffing. He went to the Commissioner of Baseball instead.

At the time, I had a plausible excuse. "I'm guilty of one thing in this whole mess," I said. "I was a horseshit selector of friends." I was being honest. But I was also shifting the blame onto other people. Truth is, I used Janszen and Gio the same way they used me. I got what I thought were reliable people to place my bets with bookmakers. They got access to a celebrity lifestyle they never earned—a lifestyle they envied when it was taken away. I'm certainly not proud of my actions or my associations. And looking back on it now, I still can't believe I let things get so out of control. But it's like that old saying, "When you lay down with dogs, you get up with fleas." Hell, I was scratching all over.

8

BUSTED

"I did not have sex with that woman—Ms. Lewinsky!"
—*BILL CLINTON*

Now don't get me wrong. I'm not pointing my finger at Bill Clinton's finger-wagging performance on national television. I believed him when he proclaimed his innocence. Hell, I understood his dilemma. He did what every young man does when he gets caught with his hands in the cookie jar—he denied it! It's called "plausible deniability," or so I'm told. But plausible deniability is a very effective expression used by educated people to keep from admitting to an embarrassing if not illegal situation. You see, Bill Clinton was not supposed to chase women—as if being president of the United States somehow excluded him from the pleasures enjoyed by the rest of the male population. It wasn't until they found the sperm on her dress that he changed his tune. After the DNA evidence was revealed, Mr. Clinton admitted to having an "inappropriate relationship," which wasn't legally defined as sex because "that depends on what the definition of *IS* is." The stand-up comics had a field day with that one. "Washington crossed the Delaware, Lincoln freed the slaves, and Clinton proclaimed that blow jobs were no longer an act of sex!"

I like Bill Clinton. He was a confident and charismatic leader. He worked his whole life to become president and he wasn't going to be taken down over an "indiscretion" that didn't affect his job performance. He was a scrapper—just like me. His mother, Virginia Kelley, was one of the greatest ladies I ever met—a major asset to the world of horse racing. She attended the races at Oaklawn almost every day. And her son, the president, supported her passion for racing despite the scandal that some of his political opponents tried to create. Bill Clinton had the same passion for ladies that his mother had for racing. I can't fault either one. In fact, Mr. Clinton was much like another great president—John F. Kennedy. Except that in Kennedy's era, the press didn't report the affairs. They looked the other way. But the Republican Party didn't look the other way. They spent $40 million to expose Mr. Clinton's cover-up. They hired a lawyer named Kenneth Starr to turn up the heat—a level of scrutiny that I would soon become familiar with. You see, major league baseball had its own version of Starr. His name was John Dowd.

On February 21, 1989, two days after the start of spring training, I was summoned to New York to meet with Commissioner Peter Ueberroth and his soon-to-be successor, Bart Giamatti. I suspected that Janszen had followed through with his threats to squeal to the commissioner. But I had no idea how much Mr. Ueberroth knew or what he might have believed. In fact, I was hoping the whole matter could be resolved quickly, so I could get back to spring training. I flew to New York and met with my attorneys, Reuven Katz and Robert Pitcairn. They advised me to keep a low profile. They suggested that we listen to the commissioner review the evidence and then meet afterward to discuss the "appropriate strategy." Our legal system is based on the principle of innocent until

proven guilty. Since the burden of proof was on the prosecution, my attorneys suggested that we weigh all the evidence before making any rash
decisions. For all they knew, the case would boil down to Janszen's word
against mine. I wasn't thinking so much about fighting baseball as
standing up against Janszen—the guy who threatened to blow my wife's
brains out and cripple my son. During the previous month, Janszen
pled guilty to one count of federal tax evasion for selling steroids. I
knew he was being investigated from the letters he sent to Reuven
Katz, but I didn't know how damaging that investigation would prove
to be. But Janszen turned stool pigeon—the worst kind of scum. As
soon as the Feds turned up the heat, Janszen flipped like a goddamn
burger. In return for his cooperation, Janszen avoided prison. He was
sentenced to just 6 months in a halfway house—a fraction of the punishment given to his cohorts at Gold's Gym. My attorneys didn't think
Janszen would make a credible witness. Based on the lies he told in the
past, I had to agree.

After arriving, we waited for 45 minutes in the reception area just outside the commissioner's office on Park Avenue. By making me wait, the
commissioner was sending a message. The nature of the meeting was serious. While waiting, I paced back and forth and looked at photos of Hall
of Famers like Babe Ruth, Hank Aaron, Ty Cobb, Roberto Clemente, and
Willie Mays. I thought about their great accomplishments and wondered
when I would take my place among them. Then, as I walked into the commissioner's office, my impulsive sense of humor took over. I pointed to the
photos on the wall and asked, "Why ain't I up there?" Everyone laughed.
It eased the tension and took my mind off the business at hand. I wasn't
even eligible for the Hall of Fame but everyone knew that I had the cre-
dentials. In a subtle way, I was probably reminding them of who I was—
Pete Rose, baseball's all-time Hit King. But on this particular day, they
weren't interested in my records.

146

YOUNG PETE
Six-year-old Pete, the apple of his dad's eye

BUDDY AND BIG PETE ROSE

Left to right: Pete's Uncle Buddy Bloebaum, who was also the legendary pool shark known as "The Masked Marvel." Pete's father, Harry Francis "Big Pete" Rose, who played amateur football for 23 years.

**BIG PETE ROSE
AT SCHULTES' FISH HOUSE,
DECEMBER 1944**
*The same wall that young Pete
used as a throwing target*

ROSIE
*Pete's mom, Rosie, visiting her
grandchildren in the 1970s*

1970S CHRISTMAS WITH THE ROSES
*Left to right: Sisters Caryl and
Jackie, Pete, brother Dave, and
mom "Rosie" in front. Pete couldn't
help but tease Rosie—that was
the nature of their relationship.*

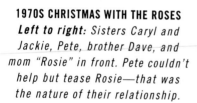

Jackie Schwier

FOLLOWING IN DAD'S FOOTSTEPS

As a 120-pound high school freshman, young Pete
makes a diving tackle against rival Elder High School

PROMISING ROOKIE
*Pete Rose with Reds
scout Slugger Blomski*

APRIL 8, 1963
*Pete's first at-bat
against the Pittsburgh
Pirates. His first at-bat
resulted in a walk!*

GENERAL OFFICES
307 VINE STREET

CROSLEY FIELD
FINDLAY AT WESTERN AVENUE

Founded 1869 – The First Professional Base Ball Club in America

THE CINCINNATI BASEBALL CLUB CO.

NATIONAL LEAGUE

REPLY TO:

Dear Pete

Old Blomski hasen't forgotten about you. I have been waiting until you got your feet on the ground. I talked to your Dad after he got back from Erie. He said that you were a little down in the dumps. Breaking into Pro Ball is not a bed of roses you have to take the bitter with the sweet.

Dont get the idea that the manager is down on you he has a job to do at the present time the club isn't going to good. to him every body looks bad, His job depends on the showing of the club. Dont expect a pat on the back in Pro ball when you have a good night it is your job. you are getting payed to do a job, If he keeps you on third do the best job that you can. play any place thy and keep in the lineup

GENERAL OFFICES
307 VINE STREET

Founded 1869 – The First Professional Base Ball Club in America

CROSLEY FIELD
FINDLAY AT WESTERN AVENUE

THE CINCINNATI BASEBALL CLUB CO.
NATIONAL LEAGUE

REPLY TO:

If they only have one catcher let him know that you can get behind the dish. By all means keep hustling dont let a hitting slump interfear with your fielding just keep taking a level swing and you will get your share of hits. Reno asked your Dad if you always hit is a crouch maybe you are to low try standing up a little with your back leg bent just a little and take the short step and every time at bat think that you are going to knock the pitcher down and swing the bat dont punch at the ball, Pete play any place and hang in there, We will work on your weakness this fall, So dont worry about base hits you know in your mind that You are a fair hitter so just keep swinging and sooner or later they will drop in,

as ever
Slugger Blomski

Letters courtesy of Jackie Schwier

SLUGGER BLOMSKI
Letter written to Pete by Cincinnati Reds' scout Slugger Blomski, after a visit with Pete's dad in Erie, Pennsylvania. Pete was in his first year in the minors, playing for the Geneva Redlegs in the NewYork/Penn League. At five feet seven and 145 pounds, Pete was not doing well and was "down in the dumps." Slugger reminded Pete that he was a "fair hitter."

ALL-STAR
*Pete Rose as an established
Major League star
with the Cincinnati Reds*

TEAMMATES
*Pete Rose with two-time
MVP Johnny Bench*

THREE-TIME BATTING CHAMPION
Pete Rose in the heydey of the Big Red Machine.

SEPTEMBER 11, 1985

*Pete hugs his son, Pete Rose Jr., after breaking Ty Cobb's record
for career hits. Longtime friend and coach Tommy Helms looks on.*

WINTER 1985
Pete holding Tyler in the trophy room, Indian Hill estate

HIT KING HITS 60
Pete Rose celebrates his 60th birthday with his family. Left to right: Fawn Rose, daughter from his first marriage; Pete Rose; Cara Shea, daughter; Tyler Rose, son; Carol Rose, wife

SEPTEMBER 23, 2002
*Pete's last game,
Cinergy Field.
This photograph was
taken moments before Pete
appeared on the field.
The steps are in the back
of the dugout from the
clubhouse. This was his
first appearance at
Cinergy since
he was banned in 1989.*

SENIOR NIGHT
*Left to right: Pete Rose; Tyler
Rose, son; Carol Rose, wife;
Cara Shea, daughter. As a
6'4" starting guard on his
high school basketball team,
Tyler Rose celebrates with his
dad, mom, and sister.*

Charles Sotto

I sat before Peter Ueberroth, Bart Giamatti, and Deputy Commissioner Fay Vincent, and I faced the biggest decision of my life—one that would affect my past as well as my future. Mr. Ueberroth explained that he heard disturbing reports about my gambling habits and wanted to give me a chance to clear the air. He asked me if I had been making any illegal bets. I said that I bet on the 1989 Super Bowl and lost $2,000 because I picked the wrong team. Mr. Ueberroth was a true sports fan. He smiled and nodded as if he understood. Then, someone asked me about the Pick-Six. It was reported in the newspapers a month earlier that I hit the Pick-Six at Turfway Park for over $265,000. Racetrack gambling is perfectly legal, so I didn't think the Pick-Six was any of their business. I was also trying to protect my friend, Jerry Carroll, who owned the racetrack. Jerry partnered with me on the winning ticket and didn't want any negative publicity. He did nothing wrong in buying his tickets but sometimes people will get suspicious when the owner hits a big jackpot at his own track. So in protecting Jerry, I denied having any part in winning the Pick-Six. I told a white lie. Basically, the commissioner said that he wasn't interested in football or the racetrack. He wanted to know if I bet on baseball. I made my decision. I said, "No, sir. I did not bet on baseball."

So before I go on, I know what you're thinking: "Why didn't you just tell the truth, Pete . . . admit that you had a problem?" It's a fair question— one that I've asked myself many times over the past 14 years. I wish I had an easy answer but I don't. It's what my writer calls the "human condition"—behavior that everyone understands but can't quite explain. If the Commissioner had presented evidence or given any indication of his position, I might have handled things differently. But I really didn't believe I had a problem. I knew that I broke the letter of the law. But I didn't think that I broke the "spirit" of the law, which was designed to prevent corruption. During the times I gambled as a manager, I never took an unfair advantage. I never bet more or less based on injuries or inside information. I never allowed my wagers to influence my baseball decisions. So in my mind, I wasn't corrupt. Granted, it was a thin distinction but it was one that I believed at the time. Still, I was backed into a corner. If I had been an alcoholic or a drug addict, Baseball would have suspended me for 6 weeks and paid for my rehabilitation. The Players Union had very clear language to deal with those particular "transgressions." But I didn't drink or use drugs. I gambled. And not just on horses, football, and basketball—I broke the cardinal sin. Baseball has a hard-and-fast punishment for breaking Rule #21. It's nailed to the clubhouse door at every ballpark in the country— *"Any player, umpire, or club or league official or employee, who shall bet any sum whatsoever upon any baseball game in connection with which the bettor has a duty to perform shall be declared permanently ineligible."* The distinction between drugs, booze, and gambling told me that Baseball was interested in punishment—not treatment. I should have had the opportunity to get help but baseball had no fancy rehab for gamblers like they do for drug addicts. If I had admitted my guilt, it would have been the same as putting my head on the chopping block—lifetime ban. Death penalty. I spent my entire life on the baseball fields of America and I was not going to give up my profession without first seeing some hard evidence. I just kept telling myself that "permanently" is a long goddamn time. Right or wrong, the punishment didn't fit the crime—so I denied the crime.

I didn't know it at the time, but Baseball had already begun its investigation. During the summer of 1988, federal agents were investigating rumors of drug traffic at the Gold's Gym where I trained. From what I heard, the managers operated a small-time drug ring using Gio as their "mule." Apparently, the government had little interest in my gambling activity. But they had a big interest in stopping a local drug ring. My name must have popped up in the agent's report because I worked out with Gio and Janszen—two of their main suspects. Kevin Hallinan was Baseball's director of security at that time. Mr. Hallinan got tipped off to the situation and put one of his investigators on the case. But his investigator ran into a dead end because Janszen, the government's chief witness, was on the lam. The Feds turned Janszen into an informant. He squealed to save his own ass. They were using Janszen to catch his friends, who were involved in the same crimes Janszen himself had committed. He taped phone conversations, wore hidden microphones, and lured his friends into buying drugs. Hell, Janszen even secretly taped people that the FBI didn't *ask* him to tape! He was a man on a mission. Charles Sotto was right— Janszen was a vindictive person.

As soon as I returned to spring training, the media questioned me about my secret visit to New York. Mr. Ueberroth was quoted in the press as saying, "We asked Pete Rose to come to New York. We didn't order him. There's nothing ominous and there won't be any follow-through." The commissioner told a white lie—the same white lie I told him about the Pick-Six. It was no big deal. So I told the press exactly what I was instructed to say: "The new commissioner wanted to ask me a few questions about baseball matters . . . to help him get off on the right foot." Truth is, the press didn't believe the commissioner or me. They smelled a coverup.

Meanwhile, baseball's "no follow-through" had already begun. Two days after my meeting, John Dowd went over to the halfway house in Cincinnati and interviewed Janszen. Dowd was the Washington, D.C., lawyer who was hired by Baseball to conduct the investigation. Dowd worked in the Justice Department during the Jimmy Carter administration and spent most of his career prosecuting cases against organized crime. Dowd had a reputation for being a really ambitious feller—a power hitter. He had big ideas about making a name for himself on the Pete Rose case. Shortly after Dowd questioned Janszen, I was asked to give fingerprints and handwriting samples. But when my attorneys asked what the samples would be compared to, Dowd refused to answer, which warned me about the one-sided nature of the events that followed. Obviously, Janszen had given John Dowd one helluva story—a story that would soon rock the sports world. Dowd's investigation was technically called an "administrative procedure," which meant that I had little or no rights. Under Baseball rules, I had to cooperate fully, which I agreed to do. But my attorneys were not allowed to be present as Dowd questioned my accusers. We were denied the right of cross-examination, which would have protected my legal rights and exposed some half-truths, lies, and slander before they found their way into the media. But I had no choice. I was under Baseball's jurisdiction—not the courts. The hunt was on. If it had been just gambling, I don't know if it would have gone so far, but I was mixed up with a whole crew who were criminals as well as gamblers. I don't doubt that Dowd smelled blood.

I didn't know it at the time, but the indictments in the government's drug and tax cases were already in. Most of the guys that Janszen trapped were either already in jail or just days away from sentencing. So they were all eager to cash in on their story. Peters, the bookmaker from Franklin, Ohio, was the first canary to sing. He agreed to plead guilty to one count of drug trafficking and one count of filing false tax information. His lawyer approached *Sports Illustrated* and offered to sell his story for an "undisclosed sum of money." I'm not sure how the whole thing went down but I was told that *Sports Illustrated* refused to pay him a dime. Apparently, the magazine had already talked with Janszen. So Peters sang for free—or so I thought. He just figured out a better way to get himself greased.

With the rumor mill grinding daily, Baseball had no choice but to announce that it was investigating me for "serious allegations." The cat was officially out of the bag. Everyone suspected those allegations concerned gambling. But they didn't know the details or the extent. *Sports Illustrated*, which had been investigating the case for weeks, was the first to break the story, with a one-page article written by Craig Neff called "The Rose Probe." The story was filled with speculation about my gambling activity but lacked any real proof. I was linked with Peters, Janszen, and Gio but the writer made a point to mention their criminal activity, hurting their credibility. The article gave me cause for concern but I was in no way desperate. I was more concerned with what they could *prove*—not what they *alleged*. I had weathered through some pretty nasty media storms in my day and figured this one would be no different. But within hours, over 50 reporters descended on the Reds spring training camp in Plant City, Florida. Although they had me surrounded, I did my best to maintain composure. After 26 years in the big leagues, three World Championships, and more than a dozen television commercials, I had learned a thing or two about a thing or two. I could handle the media. I followed my instincts and responded with humor. I sat in the dugout and casually fielded questions about the allegations. I even joked around with the reporters and said, "If I were a betting man, I'd bet that I did not bet on baseball." I suggested that the circuslike atmosphere created by the media would help prepare my team for the World Series. I turned a negative into a positive. But the story wasn't going to disappear with a few offhand remarks. The second day produced twice the number of reporters, who hounded me everywhere I went. This time I was testier. When pressed on the subject of betting on baseball, I snapped back, "Innocent until proven guilty." I even threatened potential lawsuits if the reporters didn't verify their sources before going to print. I was drawing the battle lines. That night, I met with my friend and lawyer, Reuven Katz. Katz had been a father figure to me ever since my dad passed away. He handled all of my finances and business ventures and provided me with some much needed moral support. If I had been a player, my conflict would have been handled through a grievance procedure as provided by the collective bargaining agreement. But since I was a manager, I had no other resources. I had to provide and pay for my own defense. Reuven told me to relax and concentrate on managing the Reds. He understood the stakes and assured me that he would do everything in his power to protect my legal rights. But the media was relentless. They printed allegations that I had been forced to sell all of my record-setting memorabilia to pay off huge gambling debts. They raised issues from my divorce, paternity suit, and even printed quotes from my kids, which were from 10 years in the past. Every controversial thing I ever did was being reported as if it happened yesterday! But I remained defiant. I gave the impression that I was still in charge. But the guy who appeared on the Wheatie's box and had met five different presidents was feeling the strain. On the inside, I felt like a piece of meat.

On Opening Day, I returned to Riverfront Stadium, where I was met with standing ovations and banners, which read "Free Pete," and "You bet we back Pete." The response gave me goose bumps. Most of the fans were on my side. I was the local boy who made good. My roots ran deep into the community, where my headfirst style of play became a trademark not just for me but for the city itself. They knew what I did for the city of Cincinnati and they weren't going to turn their back on one of their own. They refused to believe the rumors, which were mostly coming out of the New York media—considered "enemy territory" in the Midwest. Just before game time, Johnny Bench paid me a visit to offer his support. He asked if there was anything he could do for me. I said, "Yeah, give me $500,000 and see if you can get rid of about 50 kilos!" Johnny laughed at my sarcastic remark, which put the media speculation about my criminal activity into context. He even made a comment about how well I was holding up under the pressure. During the heyday of the Big Red Machine, we were the best baseball had to offer—the team of the decade. His visit brought back great memories—same memories the fans appreciated. Most folks in Cincinnati understood that gambling was a big part of our culture. Horseracing, lottery, black jack, and bingo were all considered healthy forms of entertainment. Since I never tried to hide my passion for gambling, most folks just accepted me for who I was. I appreciated their confidence and support. But I had mixed emotions. If the fans *believed* I was innocent, then by God, I had to *be* innocent.

We beat the Dodgers 6-4 on Paul O'Neill's 4-for-4 performance. But that was my only highlight on Opening Day. I also earned my 15th cover of *Sports Illustrated*. But this cover was not like any of the previous fourteen. The photo and six-page article depicted me as a man under siege. It was the hottest story of the year—filled with much more than speculation. The article provided detailed information about my gambling activity, lucrative memorabilia business, and association with convicted felons and even implied that I was under an IRS investigation for tax violations. The story was the magazine's equivalent to a grand slam—it touched all the bases. I was accused of betting on baseball and owing hundreds of thousands to bookmakers. I was portrayed as a "compulsive gambler," which made me cringe. Most celebrities know that there is a hint of truth in even the most outrageous articles. This one was no different. But after the reporters added their slant, even the truth turned into half-truths, which turned into exaggeration, which fueled the rumor mill. The media felt obligated to air or publish every accusation regardless of how hurtful or far-fetched. They smelled blood in the water and dove into the feeding frenzy with a vengeance. For the next 6 months, all the major networks had their TV crews trained on my every move. They camped out at the stadium and they camped out at my house. They were on a 24-hour "Pete Rose watch."

One photo showed me talking on the dugout telephone. The accompanying story insinuated that I was calling a bookmaker. Everyone in baseball knows that the dugout telephone is only hooked up to the bullpen—not to the outside. But the writer never bothered to check before printing his "exclusive story." Maybe he didn't care. Another accusation had me giving hand signals to bookmakers, who were supposedly sitting in the stands during a time when the stadium scoreboard was being repaired. That report would have made me laugh if it hadn't been so stupid. Can you imagine a major league manager giving hand signals to someone in the stands? As if such gestures wouldn't look obvious if not totally ridiculous? Hell, if I had been that desperate to hear some baseball scores, I would have just walked into my office between innings and called the goddamn Sportsline! But the truth didn't stop the rumors from spreading. They picked up momentum like a snowball rolling downhill. Former player and broadcaster Tony Kubek came into my office during a rain delay in Philadelphia and told me that he just heard a story that he wouldn't touch with a 10-foot pole. He said that Hal McCoy of the *Dayton Daily News* just told him that I told McCoy that I once bet $250,000 on the 1988 World Series between the Dodgers and the A's. New York writer Jack Lang heard the rumor and discussed it openly in the pressroom, which meant that every writer in the country would eventually hear the story. When I asked Lang why he talked about the rumor without first asking me if it was true, which it wasn't, he claimed McCoy was a "reliable source." Outside of Las Vegas, I know of no place in the world where a person can place a bet for $250,000. Even in Las Vegas, you have to walk into the casino with the cash and physically give it to the sports book, which would wake up everyone in the world. Like I said, I might have been thoughtless but I wasn't stupid. When I got back to Cincinnati after the road trip, I confronted McCoy with the accusation. Of course, he denied ever saying anything to anyone. But to this day, both Jack Lang and Tony Kubek swear that McCoy told them the story was true.

Another rumor had me owing hundreds of thousands of dollars to Mafia bookmakers. Although my ex-wife denied it, she was quoted as joking that she once got a newspaper filled with dead fish, which was her sarcastic reply to a question about my alleged debts to bookmakers. Apparently, some reporter decided the story was true and added his own slant. He assumed that since Mike Bertolini was an Italian and from New York, he must automatically be connected to the Mafia. Hell, even Ron Peters laughed at that one. He said that he couldn't imagine that any bookmaker in the world would let a client run a tab for hundreds of thousands of dollars—*especially* the Mafia!

As the outrageous stories continued, the media scrutiny grew tighter. ABC and CBS television cameras followed me everywhere I went. Bob Jamieson and Laura Sauer became regulars in my office. They even started to come into the clubhouse before the games. Finally, Jim Ferguson, our publicity director, threw a fit. He yelled at the reporters and asked, "If Dan Rather was being investigated, would you barge into his office while he was working?" But the reporters were oblivious. Sauer and Jamison were both smart journalists. They had a hot story and were milking it for all it was worth. They were waiting to get the live reaction as soon as Baseball made its decision . . . or as soon as I cracked under the pressure—which wasn't going to happen. I got so pissed off that I wanted to give a press conference to answer the allegations. But my attorneys gave me a personal gag order. They felt like anything I said would be misquoted or used against me in Baseball's ongoing investigation. I had associated with known gamblers and made illegal bets through bookmakers and that was enough to get me kicked out of baseball. Any admission to that fact could have gotten me suspended right away, which is not what I wanted. I wanted to stay on the job—managing the Reds. My attorneys insisted that we wait for "due process," which was my best chance to get a fair settlement. So I continued to answer "No comment" to every gambling question, which didn't play too well with the national media. The whole scene was getting ugly. Fortunately, the Cincinnati fans understood my side of the controversy and remained loyal. They were smart enough to read between the lines. People called into the local talk shows voicing their support. They felt like I was being "framed by a host of convicted felons." Fan mail started pouring in with encouraging statements. Local nurses called into the radio talk shows to brag about my visits to local hospitals, where I signed autographs for the kids in wheelchairs. Under normal circumstances, I would object to such reports because I always insisted that my charity work be kept private. I didn't want to appear like I was grandstanding. But if ever I needed some good publicity—it was then. Every newspaper article and photo had me looking like a man on life support—gasping for breath. It was the beginning of the most depressing and embarrassing time of my life. It was the same attention I received just 4 years earlier when I was chasing Cobb's record. But this time the attention was all negative. The media, which had been an ally throughout my career, had suddenly turned on me. Didn't they understand that I was Pete Rose—three-time World Champion? What about all those hits, runs, and headfirst slides? What about Fosse, Harrelson, and the frog-hop catch I made out of Boone's glove? Didn't all the great memories account for something? Couldn't they write something nice? They were uncovering the private, destructive side of my personality and reporting it to the whole world. I resented it. Hell, I denied it! The media was on the trail of the biggest scandal in baseball history. They had every right to dig for the truth. But that didn't make the digging any less painful.

On April 1, Bart Giamatti took over as Commissioner of Baseball. He was a Renaissance literature scholar and the former president of Yale University. I never went to college, although I once joked that "I almost bought one." The commissioner and I couldn't have been more different. He wrote poetry and talked about the "theory" of baseball. I cussed like a sailor and played the game the way it was meant to be played—nothing "theoretical" about me. The Players Association viewed Mr. Giamatti as an Ivy League "intellectual" and questioned his ability to relate to the re-

ality of the game. I viewed him as a strict authoritarian. Just months before, when he was National League president, Mr. Giamatti hit me with
a 30-day suspension and a $10,000 fine for pushing an umpire—the
biggest penalty ever imposed against a manager for a rule violation. His
decision brought heavy criticism from the former executive director of the
Major League Player's Association Marvin Miller, who thought Mr. Giamatti was making a mockery of "due process." Baseball listened to the umpire, who just happened to be gay, and without even hearing from me,
dished out my suspension. Hell, I didn't push him because he was gay. I
pushed him because he made a horseshit call. If I had been a player, I
could have filed a grievance with the union. But since I was a manager,
I had no such protection. I had to take my punishment—like it or not.
Thirty days for pushing an umpire? Should have been 5 days max! Obviously, I didn't expect Mr. Giamatti to be lenient with my gambling, but I
was hoping that he would be fair. As soon as Mr. Giamatti took office, he
got rid of all the employees that were loyal to Peter Ueberroth—a
"streamlining" effort that ruffled some feathers and raised a warning flag
of what was in store for me. Despite our differences, Mr. Giamatti and I
had one thing in common. We both loved baseball with a passion. He was
the new kid on the block and I was the best ambassador baseball had. I felt
like I had the advantage. But the rules were stacked in his favor.

From his first day in office, Mr. Giamatti was consumed with the Pete
Rose investigation—not the kind of duties he wanted. Between the fans,
media, and baseball purists, the commissioner was under enormous pressure to deal with my case fairly—no whitewash for a star player. On the
other hand, I was Charlie Hustle—baseball legend. I would not go down
without a fight. In some ways, he was "damned if you do and damned if
you don't." I can't justify all of his decisions. But I believe that he was
doing his best under difficult circumstances. He just wasn't ready for the
onslaught of media attention and public debate. At times, I think the

pressure affected his judgment—just as it affected mine. Throughout the investigation, Mr. Giamatti or someone in his office leaked information to the press—information that served the investigation, not justice. At one point, Mr. Giamatti even gave an exclusive interview to the *New York Times*, which exposed issues that should have been kept confidential. Hell, the investigation wasn't even completed and I got the impression that he had already made up his mind.

Within a few days after Mr. Giamatti took office, federal court documents were released from the Ron Peters drug case. The documents said that a Cincinnati resident known as G-1, which supposedly referred to me, bet through Janszen "an average of $2,000 per game on as many as four to eight games a day, approximately 4 days per week," during May 1987. Those reports were fairly accurate. They supposedly came from betting records that were seized from Peters' house during the government's investigation. But Peters would later testify that he shredded or burned all of his betting records. So I can't vouch for their credibility. Neither the records nor the G-1 codename actually proved any connection to me because Peters testified that he had dozens of "other clients." But they made for tantalizing headlines, feeding the public's huge appetite for the case. Meanwhile, evidence from Janszen's testimony to John Dowd—testimony that was supposed to be kept confidential—was being leaked to the press. The *Cleveland Plain Dealer* reported that Janszen claimed he placed bets for me on baseball and that Dowd's investigators were busy checking phone records to verify his accusation. Fortunately, the paper also noted that Janszen could not furnish any proof of my betting and that he certainly "had an ax to grind" over an alleged debt. Almost simultaneously, Gio was indicted on charges of tax evasion and conspiracy to distribute cocaine. Fry and Stenger, the co-owners of Gold's Gym, where I worked out, were already serving 8 years on drug charges. Even though the police cleared me from any drug-related activity, my life was starting to look like an episode of *The Untouchables*—guilt by association. I was waiting for Elliot Ness to show up and read me my rights. Hell, if it hadn't been for Wade Boggs and Steve Garvey, I might not have been bumped from the headlines. Boggs, the Boston Red Sox All-Star third baseman, was taking a lot of heat over Margo Adams, who traveled with him on road trips. Everyone knew about the affair but Boggs' wife. Dodger great Steve Garvey, who had a reputation as "Mr. Clean," was reported as having one child outside of his marriage and another one on the way. His wife was also a tad bit surprised to hear the news. The stand-up comics had a field day with all of us—"What do Pete Rose and Steve Garvey have in common with the Breeders' Cup?—Rose bet on it and Garvey won the damn thing!" We were the "Bill Clinton" of our era. Other allegations had me selling my three World Series rings to pay off bookmakers. To answer the charges, I sent all three rings to be displayed at my local bank in Cincinnati. I reminded the press that the bat and ball from my 4,256th hit were also on display at Sorrento's restaurant—owned by my friend Willie DeLuca. I did everything in my power to fend off the accusations. I was in what politicians call "damage control." But as evidence from the federal case started mounting, the pundits were putting nails in my coffin.

"Pete knew that he made some serious mistakes, but the personal attacks really hurt him," says Carol Rose. "Pete would get so pissed off that he would stand up and scream at the television and call Janszen an f'-ing liar! The camera trucks were all parked outside on our front lawn. Pete wanted to go outside to talk to the reporters. But Reuven Katz told him not to say anything to the media, which only made matters worse. The entire ordeal was really stressful—not just for Pete but for the whole family. Tyler was only 5 years old and he was already feeling the pressure. I was pregnant with Cara at the time and Pete was worried that something bad might happen. It made us all sick to our stomachs. Most of the time, Pete would just get angry at all the reports, which served as his form of therapy. Anger was a great motivator for him. Pete knew only one way to deal with adversity—fight. It all stemmed from his childhood because that's how everyone in his family handled conflict—they fought. Fighting just came natural to Pete. But then one day, Pete got real quiet. He just went into his room . . . and cried. I thought about going in and trying to talk with him. But he would have just shut down. Pete never learned to open up with those kinds of feelings. So I stayed in the hallway and gave him his space. I didn't know the truth at the time, but I could tell that he was devastated."

On April 20, I arrived back home from a long road trip. I flew on the red-eye but only got about an hour and a half of sleep. I was exhausted. The media scrutiny was less intense on the road because nobody knew where I parked my car or ate my meals. I was able to find some peace and quiet but not as much as I needed. As soon as I got back home, the media circus continued, and it was really taking its toll. But this was the day my lawyers arranged for my deposition with John Dowd. We would meet in the basement of a church in Dayton, Ohio—guaranteed privacy from the media. After 2 months of the investigation, I was anxious to see the extent of Dowd's evidence. I had never actually met Mr. Dowd but I sure heard a lot about him. His name appeared in the newspapers almost as often as mine. He spoke with the media and seemed quite pleased with being a celebrity. I might have been in a more cooperative mood, but earlier in the day, my lawyers got wind of evidence that changed the scope of the entire case. In return for his Ron Peters testimony against me, Dowd promised to write a letter requesting leniency for him in his drug and tax case. Like I said, Peters didn't sing for free. He found something more important than money—freedom. Dowd wrote the letter but Bart Giamatti, the Commissioner of Baseball, signed it to make it official. The letter was sent to federal judge Carl Rubin, who would be sentencing Peters in just a few days. The letter praised the "significant and truthful cooperation" of Mr.

Peters and stated that the Commissioner found Ron Peters' testimony to be "candid, forthright, and truthful." Unbeknownst to Dowd, Judge Rubin was a close friend of my lawyer, Reuven Katz. Judge Rubin was furious when he read the letter. He called Katz and told him that he just received a "very disturbing" piece of evidence. Judge Rubin wondered what the hell the commissioner was thinking by "vouching for the credibility of a drug dealer?" I'm no lawyer but even I could figure that one out. If Bart Giamatti believed Peters' testimony to be "honest and forthright" even before he listened to me—then Mr. Giamatti had already made up his mind. In legal terms—the letter was "proof of bias."

I joined my trial lawyers Makley and Pitcairn and Mr. Dowd and his team of lawyers along with the head of Baseball's security in the basement of the church. After I was sworn in, Mr. Dowd began asking his questions. In light of Dowd's letter, Mr. Makley asked "for the record" if the proceeding was going to be "fair and impartial." Mr. Dowd assured us that it was. He wasn't aware that we had already heard all about the letter. The lawyers were squaring off for a game of "legal chess." I tried to be cooperative but Dowd began by asking questions about my associations with people who had knowledge of the sale of certain memorabilia items. Mr. Dowd knew that I was being investigated for possible tax violations. Any admission I made regarding the unreported sale of memorabilia, income from card shows, or gambling winnings could be leaked to Dowd's friends in the Justice Department and used against me. My lawyers got the "distinct impression that Dowd's questions represented a clever but veiled threat"—if he couldn't get me on gambling charges, by God, he'd get me on tax evasion. But according to Baseball, I had no rights against self-incrimination. Any time that I hesitated with an answer, Dowd threatened to report to the commissioner that I was being "uncooperative," which could bring immediate sanctions and penalties. Talk about "damned if you do and damned if you don't." I felt like I was testifying with a goddamn sword hanging over my head! Instead of backing down, I blocked out all distractions and played Dowd's chess game just like I played baseball—to win. Dowd was after my scalp, so I made him dance for his dinner. He was going to have to prove his case—not have it handed to him on a silver platter.

After about an hour, Dowd asked me about betting on football, which I freely admitted. But for a lawyer who spent his career fighting organized crime, Dowd didn't seem to know too much about gambling. He asked me about how and when I placed my football bets . . . "Before kickoff?" I grinned and said, "I wish it was the other way, John. I wish they could kick off first. That would be nice." My lawyers both cracked a smile, but Mr. Dowd didn't relate to the humor. He kept right on digging into matters that were really none of his business. He asked confusing questions that referred to several different years at a time. Then I realized that I was answering yes to a question I thought referred to 1987 but in reality was 1986. Dowd had cleverly slipped in a whole different year, thinking I would answer "yes" when I actually meant "no." But Mr. Makley caught the mistake, stopped the questioning, and asked the stenographer to read back the question. When my suspicions were proved correct, Mr. Makley said, "You're asking wide-ranging questions, John, which are going to cause confusion on the record . . . and if that is what you want, that's fine." But Mr. Dowd didn't seem to care about the confusion. He was a man on a mission. The legal maneuvering continued throughout the evening and then resumed the next day. After every question that concerned one of my friends, Mr. Dowd asked if that person had ever been in the baseball clubhouse. Right away, I realized where Dowd was going. At the very least, I had associated with "known gamblers"—a violation of Rule #21. So I admitted to placing illegal bets on football and basketball through Gio. The confession was enough to get me suspended from baseball for 1 year. I had turned over all of my banking statements, canceled checks, and phone records so I knew that Mr. Dowd could prove my gambling activity to a certain extent. But I denied ever making bets with Janszen or Bertolini, who were affiliated with me in legitimate business interests. Both guys traveled with me on road trips when I had an autograph show in the area. Janszen even made some calls to bookmakers from the hotel phone while I was at the ballpark. But any gambling connection with him was purely circumstantial—nothing Dowd could prove in a court of law.

After my deposition, Judge Rubin went public with his objections to the commissioner's "ill-advised letter requesting leniency for Peters." He questioned the manner in which Baseball was handling the investigation, suggesting that it was dragging on way too long. Folks in the media speculated that since Baseball had no power to subpoena witnesses and no "smoking gun" to prove the allegations, they might be stalling until the government's tax case was filed in court. In which case, I would get grilled and Baseball would be let off the hook. Judge Rubin criticized the media for biased reporting. He said I had been "tried, convicted, and executed" in the press. He believed there was evidence of a "vendetta" against me.

At that point, Reuven Katz asked Bart Giamatti to excuse himself as the "decision-maker in my case." He believed that it was impossible for me to get a "fair and impartial hearing." Public sentiment had shifted in my favor. Some people even wrote letters calling for Mr. Giamatti's resignation. But Mr. Giamatti refused to budge. He claimed that he had not "prejudged" my case. The commissioner made it clear that he would not—under any circumstances—relinquish his authority to hear the charges against me and to take any disciplinary action if necessary.

On May 9, Dowd submitted a 225-page summary of his report to the commissioner. Two days later, Mr. Giamatti scheduled a hearing for May 25 to give me an opportunity to answer the charges. We asked for and received an extension until June 26 to study the evidence and prepare our defense. Within minutes of reading the report, my lawyers found what they called "outrageous examples of inappropriate and biased conclusions, inaccuracies, half-truths, slander, and hearsay evidence." In short, the report had more goddamn holes than Swiss cheese.

Of the evidence Dowd claimed was "most significant" were three "betting sheets" Janszen claimed that he stole from my house. Janszen was telling the truth about having access to my house. Hell, he had a key to my front door. But I never kept betting sheets. I kept track of my wins and losses with a bottom-total—nothing more than a balance sheet, which I kept in a ledger. I threw away or burned the papers after each week. Janszen handled a great deal of my autograph business, so he knew my signature and my handwriting. Dr. Evelyn Walker, a friend of Carol's from Atlanta, was visiting once and saw Janszen forging my name on several bats for his own memorabilia business. When she questioned him about the signature, Janszen just smiled and claimed that he was "helping me out." Truth is, he was helping himself. Janszen's "betting sheets" were forgeries. But what really stood out in my mind was Janszen's excuse for stealing the "betting sheets" in the first place. He testified that he wanted some "insurance" in case I failed to pay up on the so-called debt—a debt he never mentioned until after it happened. The betting slips he claims were mine had games from April 9 through 11 of 1987. If Janszen was telling the truth, how could he have been looking for "insurance" on a debt that hadn't even occurred yet? He didn't send the money to New York until the middle of May—5 weeks later! No jury in the country would believe that Janszen could predict the future . . . or that an experienced gambler like me would leave "betting sheets" lying around the house for 5 weeks. Also, I was still on good terms with Janszen until the following February. Why would he need "insurance" against a friend, who paid for thousands of dollars worth of his travel, supported his lucrative memorabilia business, and exposed him to a lifestyle he didn't want to lose? In a slang expression used by the cops, something was hinky.

Dowd mentioned in his report that I was Ron Peters only baseball customer in 1987. If Dowd really believed that—then I have some ocean front property in Montana that I'd like to sell him. No bookmaker can afford to stay in business with only one customer. But the biggest blunder in the entire report came from Dowd himself. He claimed that the testimony of Peters and Janszen had been "voluntary and forthright." Dowd said that neither of them "has anything to gain for his voluntary act of cooperation with this investigation." Nothing to gain, my ass! Both Peters and Janszen cut deals to get a lighter sentence. They had a helluva lot to gain. Janszen avoided the Crowbar Inn altogether and Peters received only 2 out of a possible 23-year prison sentence on his drug and tax charges.

During the next several days, I met with my legal team of Katz, Pitcairn, Makley, and Stachler to listen to their strategy. They believed that the Dowd report was an "impossible burden of proof for the prosecution—one that would never be admissible in an administrative procedure or in a court of law." But Mr. Giamatti was not bound by the law. He was given broad and sweeping powers to operate within the "best interests of Baseball"—granted by the generosity of the United States Congress and its antitrust exemption. Due process is guaranteed in business, government, and private matters—just not in Baseball. Due process provides for the right to confront your accusers, the right to a fair and impartial hearing, the right to present witnesses on your behalf, and the right to *not be deprived of your livelihood*. Now don't get me wrong, I've never been the type of feller who stands on the soapbox preaching about injustice. I knew that I made some major mistakes. I wasn't trying to prove my innocence— I was trying to keep my head off the chopping block. But if Baseball could run to the courts the moment its livelihood was threatened—so could I. I had a Constitutional right to a fair and impartial hearing, where the punishment fit the crime. I was fighting for my career . . . for my livelihood. Right or wrong, I was fighting for *survival*—a basic human instinct!

So, on June 19, we filed a lawsuit against Commissioner Giamatti and Major League Baseball to halt the June 26 hearing. We petitioned the court to have a judge—not the commissioner, make the ruling on my case. My lawyers appeared before federal judge Norbert A. Nadel in the Common Pleas Court of Hamilton County and argued our position. John Dowd was the only witness to take the stand for Baseball. He vigorously defended the merits of his investigation but admitted having regrets over persuading the commissioner to sign the "ill-advised" letter. "I wish I had signed it," he said. "We probably wouldn't be here today." We called only three witnesses to my defense, my lawyer, Robert Pitcairn, George Palmer, a former state appeals court judge, and Sam Dash, the former chief counsel to the committee that investigated Watergate. All three testified that Mr. Dowd's report was one-sided. Mr. Dash was the most vocal in my defense. "Dowd's report was not the work of a professional investigator," he said. "If I had been given a report like that by one of my deputies, I would have fired him. Pete Rose has been put into an impossible situation. I can't think of another case in this country where a man has been asked to prove his innocence. In my opinion, Mr. Giamatti cannot serve as an impartial arbiter."

On Sunday, June 25, I was sitting in front of the TV set in my office at Riverfront Stadium. I was waiting for the start of our 1 o'clock game against the Dodgers. I was also waiting to hear the ruling from Judge Norbert Nadel, who would be appearing live from the courtroom within minutes. Rumors were spreading that I would be fired or suspended if I lost the court decision. I felt like a gunslinger before the big showdown. I was understandably tense. Fans gathered outside the stadium, listening on their handheld radios. Others gathered outside the courtroom carrying signs and banners. One gentleman, dressed up like Uncle Sam, held a sign that read, "High Noon! Don't Hang Pete!" It was a major media event. The commissioner issued a 5 o'clock deadline for the next day to make his decision on my case. So the judge's ruling came right down to the wire. I figured that I had a 50-50 chance of winning but I was not optimistic. Then, I was hit with the surprise of my life. Judge Norbert Nadel appeared before the live TV cameras and issued a temporary restraining order preventing me from being disciplined by Major League Baseball for at least 14 days. The judge ruled that by calling the testimony of a convicted drug and tax offender "candid, forthright, and truthful," the Commissioner of Baseball had "disqualified himself as an impartial adjudicator." "To allow the commissioner to continue with his hearing would be futile, illusory, and the outcome a foregone conclusion," he said. After the judge made his ruling, one lady stood up in the courtroom and said, "God bless him!" People in Cincinnati were dancing in the streets. From inside my office, I heard the stadium crowd erupting in cheers. The fans even hung a banner in the bleachers, which read, "Pete-1, Bart-0, Thanks, Norb." Stadium security removed the banner under the steady stream of booing. Needless to say, I was relieved. But I was not boastful. If anything, I was humbled. Jim Ferguson, the Reds publicity director, stopped by to offer his congratulations and ask that I appear with Marty Brennaman on the Reds' local radio show. I told Marty that I was just happy to see that I would have the chance to take my case to the next level. I knew that if I could get a punishment that fit the crime—the fight would have been worthwhile. But I was not out of the woods. Baseball filed for an immediate appeal. Mr. Giamatti stated that he would "fight the decision tooth and nail." He believed that Baseball, not the courts, had ultimate authority to carry out justice over its players. But 3 days later, the appellate judges refused to lift the temporary restraining order. They agreed with the lower court's decision—Commissioner Giamatti would not be conducting his hearing on me. The decision was a major victory for our team. It proved that my lawyers were making an important legal argument—*Due Process* v. *The Best Interests of Baseball.*

9

THE LONG HOT SUMMER

"I realized that I saw everything in life as a challenge—
a challenge I expected—no, had to win."
—PETE ROSE

I got a kick-ass feeling from stepping onto the baseball field that I can't even begin to describe. It had life and energy—like a pot of boiling water on the stove. It felt so good that I never wanted the game to end. During the summer of 1989, I rediscovered that misplaced feeling—my love for the game. From the time they threw out the first pitch until the last out, I forgot all about the chaos in my life. I forgot that I was involved in a fierce legal battle, a major publicity crisis, and a potential lifetime ban. I even forgot that I was spending hundreds of thousands of dollars on lawyers and investigators. Those 3 hours of baseball each day provided my only escape, my sanctuary from the pain and scrutiny. The TV cameras were still focused on my every move. But the reporters were no longer asking questions or making accusations. It was like they all disappeared. I knew in my heart that I was facing my last days. So I enjoyed the excitement of every game. I paid attention to all the little details—details I ignored for too long. The air smelled differently. So did the hot dogs and beer. Even the roar of the crowd took on a different meaning. When I shook an umpire's hand, I looked him in the eye and listened to what he had to say. I grinned when I heard the "crack" of the bat or the "pop" of the glove. I winced when a hitter got fooled on a breaking ball for strike three. I even talked to a struggling pitcher differently. I wondered if maybe he still had a little something left in his arm before I yanked him off the mound. I treated every game as if it might be my last. I thought back to my days as that scrappy little kid who played baseball with his dad on hot summer days. The whole experience caused me to take a good hard look at my life. I got angry with myself for jeopardizing a career that I loved so much. Most folks know that I'm not a warm-and-fuzzy guy. I'm not "given to matters of introspection." I fought my battles in the trenches, where sensitivity was a worthless human emotion. But my life was crashing down around me and it was time to face the demons. Of course, facing them privately was different from admitting to them publicly. I asked myself some serious questions, like: "What the hell was I thinking?" "How could I have let things get so out of control?" I lost my dignity, the respect of my peers, and I was on the verge of losing a million-dollar-a-year job—all because of gambling. I couldn't believe that I had gotten myself into such a mess. It was like being in a bad dream. Hell, it was a goddamn nightmare!

I made another discovery about myself during the solitude of those baseball games. I realized that I saw everything in life as a challenge—a challenge I expected—no, *had* to win. If you tell me that I can't hit or throw, I'll prove you wrong. If you tell me that I can't field or run, I'll prove you wrong. If you tell me that I can't, I'll damn sure prove that I can! My attitude paid off big time on the baseball field. But in my personal life, I didn't separate the battles I could win from the battles that weren't worth fighting. I spent 24 years building a baseball career that other players could only dream of. And I put it all at risk over the thrill of the "risk" itself. I spent thousands of hours in the batting cage. I took hundreds of grounders and fly balls each day in an effort to master my craft. I was known for a diligent work ethic that was unequaled among my peers. Nobody worked harder or took the game more seriously than Pete Rose—nobody. Yet after knowing Janszen for only 7 months, I trusted him to place bets on the game I loved. How could I be so disciplined in one aspect of my life and so reckless in the other? I thought back to the times when friends and family tried to warn me that my gambling was getting out of control. Why did I ignore their advice? How could I have been so arrogant? I was bothered by the very thought that something might be wrong with me. So I dismissed the thought altogether. You think I gamble too much. I'd think, well fuck you. I'll prove to you that I can get away with it! After all, I was Pete Rose—baseball's all-time Hit King. I had more records than anybody on the damn planet. Nothing could possibly be wrong with someone who achieved that much success— nothing! I couldn't handle the conflict, so I denied the conflict. I kept telling myself that I wasn't a bad person, that I just did some bad things. Yes, I was a hard-core gambler. But I didn't scheme and manipulate. I wasn't an ass-hole, like other guys. I didn't sell drugs—like Gio. I didn't threaten to kill someone's wife and kids—like Janszen. I didn't squeal to save my own ass— like Peters. After all, it was *my money*. If I wanted to gamble, it was my own damn business! Throughout my life, if I did something wrong, whether it was making an error or cheating on my wife—I took responsibility. I didn't dwell on guilt or negativity and I never hid from the truth. With Pete Rose, "what you see is what you get." But this truth was different. Admitting that I bet on baseball meant accepting the death penalty—something I refused to accept. Unlike baseball, the courtroom game didn't end after nine innings. It dragged on for months and months. And I couldn't use my bat and glove to win the damn thing. I had to rely on the advice of my lawyers, whose rules and language I didn't understand. I was dying a slow death. But

I was too proud to let anyone see the pain. At one point, I got so frustrated that I went to Marge Schott and asked if I could show up at the stadium just minutes before the game to avoid the media. But that was never an option. It would send the wrong message to the players and the fans. The manager had to be front and center, taking full responsibility for his actions and his team. So I continued to fight with everything I had left . . . which wasn't much. As soon as the baseball games ended and the intense media pressure resumed, I snapped back into the posture of a man in charge. After all, I had a baseball team to run.

From the beginning of spring training, I had just one goal—bump one spot in the standings. The Reds had finished in second place the previous 4 years in a row and 1989 was going to be our year. I was tired of knocking on the pennant door. It was time to beat the damn thing down! Team owner Marge Schott felt the same way. She was tired of being a "brides-maid and never a bride." She had just returned from Rome, where she met with Pope John Paul II. She gave him a souvenir Reds jacket for good luck and a shot at "divine intervention." She was hoping the Pope would dash a little holy water in our direction. I'm not a particularly religious man but I was willing to take all the help I could get. But since the Pope couldn't hit, field, or pitch, I didn't put too much stock in the strategy.

Reds General Manager, Murray Cook, and I spent the off-season trying to shore up the roster. I wanted to bring in free agent Mike Schmidt but he re-signed with the Phillies. Instead, we traded Nick Esasky and Rob Murphy to Boston for Todd Benzinger and Jeff Sellers. Ted Williams told me that Benzinger was the best young hitter he'd seen in years. So we gave up two star players to get him. To make up for the loss of Murphy, we picked up reliever Kent Tekulve and a strong starter in Rick Mahler. Mahler was a workhorse who could give us seven or eight strong innings. Danny Jackson, Tom Browning, and Jose Rijo were my veteran starters— the best rotation in baseball. We also had the best left-handed reliever in

171

the game—John Franco. Rob Dibble threw in the high nineties and was just as good. We had a team of smart young players who believed in themselves. Browning had thrown a perfect game, Larkin was the best shortstop in baseball, and Sabo had won the Rookie of the Year award. Jackson was coming off a 23-8 record and Davis won the Golden Glove. He also hit 26 dingers and had 21 game-winning RBI. Most folks thought we had the league's best outfield in Paul O'Neill, Kal Daniels, and Eric Davis. If everyone stayed healthy, I thought we could win it all. Things were looking great until we got hit with a rash of untimely injuries. Davis pulled his hamstring, Daniels had knee surgery, and my ace, Danny Jackson, went on the DL with a sore shoulder. Hell, if it hadn't been for bad luck, we would have had no luck at all. My outfielders started less than 30 games together due to injuries. Among all of our starters, we lost over 220 games to the disabled list, which hurt our chances for a run at the pennant. We were still in first place through the middle of June. But by the end of the season, the injuries were too much to overcome. We dropped to fifth place—our worst finish since I took over as manager.

Throughout that stretch, folks in the media blamed our poor performance on distractions caused by baseball's ongoing investigation. I can't honestly say that my players were not affected by the scandal. But I can say that none of them ever complained about it. From the beginning, I told the guys to concentrate on baseball and let me handle the rest. Since my gambling had nothing to do with the players, I asked them to avoid any questions about my case. They all understood. Baseball players have their own code of honor: "What is said in the locker room—stays in the locker room." Trust and loyalty. They took the attitude that what went on between the lines was far more important than what went on behind them.

It was the beginning of a new era, where million-dollar salaries created resentment between reporters and players. The players had all grown sour because of the sensational coverage and viewed the media with mixed emotions—totally different from when I played in the 1960s and 1970s. If a player showed up for a charitable event, it was reported in small print near the obituary column. If a player got into an argument with his wife, it was front-page headlines. He was labeled a "wife-beater" and ordered to seek therapy. The press lived by the motto "If it bleeds, it leads," which caused the players to feel exploited. They felt like they were living under a microscope where every move was blown out of proportion just to attract readers and viewers. As a result, the players treated the media like adversaries. And the media responded by probing into every controversial detail as if they had graduated from the "Jim Gray School of Broadcasting." So I handled the investigation the same way I handled the media during my 44-game hitting streak in 1978. The ultimate goal was winning games—not personal records. So I ushered the press away from the clubhouse, to where I could field questions without causing distractions. In 1978, I talked about my chances of catching DiMaggio without interfering with our chances of winning the pennant. I didn't want Bench or Morgan to be annoyed by all the media attention. In return, the players appreciated the show of respect and pulled for me to break the record. I followed the same tactic in 1989 and got the same result. Tom Browning, a great competitor, was one of the first to voice his opinion. "Pete's never allowed the investigation to affect the ball club or the way he runs it," Tom said. "Baseball is Pete's number one priority and I admire the way he's dealt with the pressure. He's one of the few guys who could deal with it. We're pulling for him. We hope everything will work out." Eric Davis was never shy about expressing his feelings either. "We're all relaxed because nobody bothers us," said Eric. "Everybody bothers Pete." It got to the point where the less I said—the more other people stood up on my behalf. After losing three straight one-run games in Atlanta, Braves manager Bobby Cox talked about how lucky they were to win against a talented Reds team. When asked whether Baseball's investigation had any effect on our team,

Bobby just laughed. "The controversy didn't seem to bother Pete or his players," he said. "Hell, Pete Rose has nerves of steel."

But even if there had been team dissension, we would have used it to our advantage. Athletes have their own kind of tunnel vision, which allows them to block out distractions and focus on the game. Reporters who think a clubhouse has to be harmonious to be successful just don't understand the competitive nature of a ballplayer. Reporters speculate on events that might tear apart team chemistry without realizing the chemistry is strengthened by conflict. I've seen teams where everyone got along just fine and finished in the cellar. The players were too "comfortable" with each other. I've seen other teams where guys hated each other's guts and won it all. In fact, every team I ever played on had some kind of conflict, which fed the competitive drive. Nothing motivates a player like conflict. A clubhouse, like the rest of the world, is diverse. Not everybody gets along. Some players drink too much, which offends the teetotaler. Others cuss and chase women, which offends the born-again Christian. I tell all my players the same thing: "You don't have to like each other to play winning baseball." You just have to respect each other while you're on the field. If your best friend strikes out with runners in scoring position, you damn well better get up in his face. If your worst enemy hits the game winning RBI, you better be the first to congratulate him. The Jeff Kent-Barry Bonds shoving match proves my point. The two could barely look at each other without fighting. The San Francisco Giants rode their conflict all the way to the World Series. The Oakland A's of the early 1970s were known for their conflict with Charlie O. Finley. But they won three straight World Series titles. I believe dissension, when harnessed just right, can strengthen team chemistry. Baseball is an aggressive game played by aggressive men. Most athletes thrive on aggression. It's part of the game and it's part of life. I tell all my players to take advantage of every situation and turn it into something positive. If you're feeling jealous because the star player is getting paid big bucks—good! Jealousy is a strong motivator. Turn it into something that can help you negotiate a better contract for yourself. If you're feeling hurt because you're riding the bench—good! Hurt is a strong motivator. Turn it into something that can earn a starting position on the team. If a player comes to me looking for sympathy and understanding, he's barking up the wrong tree, which is probably why it was impossible for me to reach out to anyone else during my own crisis. I had no experience with "sympathy and understanding." So I expected none. I ran a ball club—not a church social. If a player wanted to join the Boy Scouts, he could go play for the Dodgers. If he wanted to kick ass, he could come play for the Reds. Throughout the investigation, the media tried to imply that distractions were tearing our team apart. Hell, the ass-kickers I had in Cincinnati rallied around me and formed a close bond.

Two days before my victory in Judge Nadel's courtroom, John Dowd went public with some allegation that proved, in my mind at least, just how biased this probe was. Dowd stated that his investigation turned up betting slips in my handwriting, which proved that I bet on Reds games. His evidence proved no such thing. Fortunately my legal team of Katz, Pitcairn, Stachler, and Makley had done their homework. They found expert witnesses who took a more realistic approach to the flimsy evidence in the Dowd Report. Robert Massie, a handwriting expert who worked with the sheriff's department in Montgomery County, was the first to come forward. Mr. Massie was very experienced and well respected in the law enforcement community. He served as a consultant for many years with the Miami Valley Regional Crime Lab, the Secret Service, and the FBI. Without going into all the details, which have been discussed over and over in numerous publications, I'll just cut to the chase. Mr. Massie examined the original betting sheets, which were printed—not written. Printed letters are harder to identify than written letters. But the papers had all been treated with a chemical used for analyzing fingerprints—ninhydrin. The chemical "warps and discolors" the paper, which caused the "ink impressions to bleed so much that the line quality of the handwriting could not be completely identified." Mr. Massie claimed that it was impossible for any expert in handwriting to determine the author of those betting slips. Dowd's fingerprint evidence was even hokier. Ralph Nickoson was a Certified Latent Print Examiner who worked for the Dayton Police Department for over 20 years. He examined all three of the betting slips and found only one identifiable print that belonged to me. He stated that all three sheets of paper were "suspiciously lacking in smudges, ridge detail, and other indications of being handled." Common sense will tell you that if I sat down to write all of those games on three different sheets of paper, my prints would be all over the damn things. The explanation was obvious. Janszen worked with me for hours at a time while I signed autographs. He handled a lot of my paperwork. He probably handed me a sheet of paper, which I looked at for a moment and then handed it back. Afterward, he forged the handwriting to use as evidence against me. But Janszen screwed up on that, too. In writing down the teams and games, Janszen got his information wrong. He listed one game—Dodgers against the Cardinals—when they weren't even scheduled to play! He made another blunder when he listed the Expos at the Reds. The real game was actually played a day earlier but in Montreal. Does anyone believe that I would bet on a game and not even know who the home team was? Mike Bertolini, who spent more time with me than anybody during that time, laughed when he saw the alleged betting sheets. "I saw firsthand how Pete kept track of his bets," said Mike. "It was nothing like what Janszen produced. His sheets were phonier than a three-dollar bill."

Hell, even Dowd's own polygraph examiner said that Janszen lied. Of course, we didn't know it at the time because Dowd conveniently left that particular information off his report. I reckon he didn't want to be bothered by insignificant details like the truth. When questioned later by Mr. Makley, Mr. Dowd rationalized the failed lie detector test by saying that the examiner said something that "upset Janszen." When Mr. Makley asked just what it was that upset Janszen, Mr. Dowd couldn't answer—only to say that he brought in another examiner. Hell, I understood his dilemma. We can't have the perjured testimony of a convicted felon questioned because he just happened to be upset, can we? So rather than accept that Janszen lied, Mr. Dowd brought in another examiner until he got the results he wanted. Bottom line—Mr. Dowd couldn't prove his case. It was filled with half-truths, lies, and circumstantial evidence—evidence that would not hold up against cross-examination in a court of law. But at that point I was becoming more and more interested in the court of public opinion.

At the same time, the *Plain Dealer* in Cleveland filed a suit to have the Dowd Report opened to the public. The Ohio State Supreme Court ruled in their favor, saying the public had a right to hear the evidence. The 225-page summary to John Dowd's report was released to the media. It was a devastating blow. Within days, I earned my 16th cover of *Sports Illustrated*. But again, not for the reasons I wanted. The article was titled "The Case Against Pete Rose," and presented explicit testimony from Ron Peters on how he took my bets on baseball from Janszen. Even though the evidence was circumstantial, it painted a pretty strong picture from "overwhelming corroboration from interviews, telephone records, and taped phone conversations . . ." At the very least, I looked guilty of associating with some very shady people and of being pretty damn shady myself. The *Cincinnati Enquirer* and other newspapers and magazines ran articles calling for my resignation. I was accused of "dragging baseball through the mud" and of holding the game "hostage." The Pete Rose media watch had suddenly turned into a "death watch." But then something strange happened. As media speculation pointed to my guilt and eventual demise, an overwhelming number of people came to my defense. Rob Dibble was one of the first to express his opinion. "How can you take somebody out of the game who is Baseball? It's his money. What he does outside of the white lines is his business!"

Local anchorman at WLWT-TV, Jerry Springer was also very vocal in my defense. Jerry had firsthand experience with scandal. While serving on the Cincinnati City Council, he became a repeat customer of a local prostitute and paid for her services with personal checks. But Jerry never backed down from controversy. He admitted his mistake, resigned from the council, and was later elected mayor by a landslide! As an anchorman, Jerry became famous for his Emmy-winning nightly commentaries. "I remember what Pete's done for this town and for baseball, and for every kid who wore a 14 on his jersey, slid headfirst into second at the local school-yard pickup game, and who saw in Pete that you didn't have to be born with superior skills to make it in this world, that sheer hustle and determination and trying your best all the time was the real ticket to the top," said Springer. Bob Trumpy, former Cincinnat Bengals player, hosted a sports talk show on WLW radio. Bob was also a good friend, who kept the rally alive with the public. One local caller, Larry Dennedy, said: "Pete Rose is a homegrown hero. He probably has a disease, but to me, he's still a Hall of Famer. I don't care if he killed his mother-in-law, I'd still vote for him." Writer Lonnie Wheeler, in a special to the *New York Times*, quoted a local bus driver named Sandy True, who was not as sympathetic. "As a player, I thought he was dynamite," said Sandy. "As a guy, I think he's an arrogant, egotistical creep." But when asked if I should be in the Hall of Fame, Sandy said: "Oh yes, absolutely."

During that time, I received a phone call from my son, Pete Rose Jr., who was 19 years-old and playing for the Baltimore Orioles Class-A farm team in Erie, Pennsylvania. His manager, Bobby Tolan—my former team-mate, gave Petey a few days off to deal with the stress that was building over my situation. Petey was going through a tough time with hecklers in the minor league ballparks. One stadium played Kenny Roger's "The Gambler" on their sound system every time he stepped to the plate. Petey was also taking a lot of heat from the media, who hounded him everywhere he went. They kept asking questions that he couldn't answer—goading him into talking about a scandal that didn't concern him. But Petey never complained. He was a stud—a tough-assed kid. But his batting average dropped from .300 to .258 during the year and Bobby Tolan was concerned. Petey just asked me how I was holding up and if there was anything he could do to help. I told him that there were more positives than negatives to being Pete Rose Jr. I told him to forget about what was happening to me and to concentrate on baseball. I gave him the same advice I gave to all my players: "If you're feeling distracted—good! Turn it into something positive. Learn to focus on the business at hand!" While Petey was growing up, I always told him that "You gotta take the good with the bad." Petey learned to be tough because that's what I demanded of him . . . the same thing my dad demanded of me.

At the same time, my daughter Fawn was graduating from Thomas Moore College in Cincinnati. She spent her first 3 years at Ohio State but transferred to get her degree in premed psychology. We were playing a three-game series in St. Louis at the time, so I chartered a private plane and flew in for the ceremony. Fawn was the first college graduate in my family and I didn't want to miss her graduation. My relationship with Fawn had been strained over the years due to my commitment to baseball and my highly publicized divorce from her mother. I wish the visit could have been under happier circumstances. And looking back now, I might have had more to say to my kids on a personal level. But like I said, I had no experience with sympathy and understanding . . . so I had none to offer.

On July 3, the federal judges in Cincinnati sent my case against baseball to John Holschuh, the U.S. District Judge in Columbus, Ohio, and the next step in the judicial review process. Judge Holschuh announced that he would need at least 2 weeks to decide whether or not he even had jurisdiction in the case. On July 31, Judge Holschuh ruled that my case should be held in federal—not state court. At that point, I was very disappointed. I had already received a favorable ruling in state court and was hoping to keep the matter close to home. According to my attorneys, our lawsuit did not have any legal issues of a federal nature. But on August 17, the U.S. Court of Appeals refused to hear our appeal on the "issue of jurisdiction." Instead, they set August 18 as the date for my hearing on the preliminary injunction. There was just one problem. The case would take months to prosecute. My lawyers informed me that nobody had ever challenged baseball in the federal courts and won. In recent history, Charles O. Finley, George Steinbrenner, and Ted Turner all tried and either lost or withdrew their suits. Finley, the owner of the A's, sued Commissioner Bowie Kuhn in 1976 over his attempt to sell off three of his star players. Finley lost. In 1977, Ted Turner, owner of the Braves sued Mr. Kuhn over his fine and suspension for tampering with another team's player. Turner lost. In 1983, Mr. Steinbrenner, owner of the Yankees, sued Mr. Kuhn over the repercussions of the statements he made over the George Brett pine-tar incident. After being hit with a $250,000 fine and a $50,000 bill for baseball's legal fees, Mr. Steinbrenner withdrew his suit. The owners were all faced with the same dilemma. Baseball, by virtue of its anti-trust exemption, had absolute power to decide each case based on whatever was in "the best interests of baseball"—God-like power. The owner's lawyers all argued that even though the Major League Agreement granted complete authority to the commissioner—giving any one person that kind of unrestricted authority was perhaps illegal because it denied the basic principles of "due process." Despite the strength of the owner's argument, the judge in each case ruled that baseball had "ultimate authority." Other sports like basketball and football had procedures to appoint an independent third party to hear cases like mine. Julius Erving used such a procedure to void his contract with the ABA and jump to the NBA. Baseball could have agreed to the same type of arbitration procedure months earlier. Both sides would have been bound by the decision of an arbitrator, who would have doled out a punishment that fit the crime. But the commissioner had made clear that he was not going to relinquish "ultimate authority" under any circumstances.

At that point, neither baseball nor I wanted to continue the fight. The ordeal was taking its toll on everyone concerned. The commissioner approached my lawyers and offered a settlement—12 years suspension. I said, "No thanks." Within a few hours, he came back with another offer—6 years. I still said "No." I thought I had leverage. Baseball did not want to go to court with the Dowd Report. You can't win a case, which is based on manufactured and circumstantial evidence. On the third try, baseball hit the jackpot. The commissioner offered a suspension with the right to apply for reinstatement after 1 year. He also agreed to a stipulation that made no formal finding that I bet on baseball. Mr. Giamatti even gave my lawyer a personal assurance that he had an open mind on reinstatement . . . that he was not committed to 6 or 12 years, like he first offered. The settlement looked like a win-win situation. My lawyers explained that even if we went to court and won, we would have done no better than what was offered by the commissioner. Based on what I admitted in my deposition, the commissioner would have put me on the permanently ineligible list for at least one year anyway. Continuing with a court battle would not have prevented that from happening. We honestly saw the settlement as a positive ending to a bad situation.

I managed my last baseball game on August 21, a night game at Wrigley Field. We beat the Cubs, 6–5. I stepped onto the field and shook hands with the best closer in baseball—John Franco. After I shook hands with all the other players, I took one last look at the ivy on that old brick wall and turned in my spikes. I honestly didn't feel that bad. I was more relieved than anything. I figured I'd be away from the game for at least 1 year. But after what I'd done—1 year was fitting punishment. One year would give me time to regroup, take stock of my life, and get back on the right track. That night, I got a call from home that my wife, Carol, had

181

gone into early labor. I got on the earliest flight and went straight to the hospital. I witnessed the birth of my daughter Cara Shea, cut the cord, and counted 10 fingers and 10 toes. I was thrilled. They say that babies bring hope and joy into a family. They were right. My wife and son were as happy as I've ever seen them. Carol was also relieved that my personal ordeal was over. Perhaps our life could get back to normal. The afternoon of Cara Shea's birth, I flew to Minnesota to appear on the Cable Value Network shopping show. I took a lot of heat for appearing on the program. People thought that I looked desperate . . . "hawking my wares" while on the verge of collapse. I signed my contract to do the show way back in June. I had no idea the timing would coincide with my settlement with baseball or the birth of my daughter. Still, I set a CVN record, selling over $1.2 million in merchandise in just over 4 hours. I also earned $100,000—much needed money for an unemployed baseball manager who just spent over a million dollars in legal fees!

On August 24, Bart Giamatti held a press conference at the Hilton New York and announced that I had agreed to be placed on the permanently ineligible list in accordance with Major League Rule #21. The settlement stated ". . . The commissioner will not make any formal findings or determinations on any matter including without limitation the allegation that Peter Edward Rose bet on any Major League Baseball game." The settlement also stated: "Neither the commissioner nor Peter Edward Rose shall be prevented by this agreement from making any public statement relating to this matter so long as no such public statement *contradicts* the terms of this agreement and resolution." Shortly after the commissioner announced the settlement, he fielded questions from the media. When asked about his personal opinion, Mr. Giamatti replied that based upon reading the Dowd Report, he believed that I did bet on baseball. My lawyers and I were slack-jawed. We felt like we had been slapped in the face. Within hours after signing the agreement, which made "no finding," the commissioner reneged on his own terms! I asked my lawyer Roger Makley how Mr. Giamatti could get away with such a flagrant violation. Mr. Makley was just as shocked as I was. He said, "Don't worry, Pete. Within a few days, he'll have to answer to the media and the public on why he said those words." Hours later, I held my own press conference at Riverfront Stadium. I could sense a huge sadness in the room . . . like I was attending a funeral. I apologized to the fans and to the media for making some bad mistakes. But my spirit was not broken. The commissioner's statement provided me with plenty of resolve. Right or wrong—I felt betrayed. Everyone talked about my "morality" but what about his? It was wrong for me to lie but okay for the commissioner? I spent over a million dollars in legal fees and investigators. I fought through baseball's worst scandal ever. And at the end of the day, I came away with the exact settlement I would have received if I had confessed in the beginning— Lifetime Ban, "The Death Penalty." But I got something they would not have given me without a fight—an agreement that made no finding that I bet on baseball. An agreement I believed would allow me to return to the game I loved and eventually be inducted into the Hall of Fame. As it turned out, the agreement wasn't worth the paper it was written on.

Nine days after signing the agreement, Bart Giamatti died of a massive heart attack. Howard Cosell and others in the media accused me of "killing" the commissioner. I appreciate hype as much as the next guy. But Mr. Giamatti smoked three packs of cigarettes per day and was 50 pounds overweight. I had nothing to do with the health problems that caused his untimely death. But that didn't stop the pundits from blaming me anyway. From everything I read in the papers, Mr. Giamatti claimed to be at "peace" with his decision on my lifetime ban. With all due respect, the 6-month ordeal was far more stressful on me and my family than it was on Mr. Giamatti. He wasn't facing a lifetime ban. I was. He didn't spend his life savings on legal fees. I did. But in a strange and sad way, he paid a far greater price—something I wouldn't wish on anybody.

Perhaps things would have been different if Mr. Giamatti hadn't died. I might have taken legal issue with his public remarks. I might have gotten a fair hearing on reinstatement after a year's suspension as we had all agreed. But it didn't happen that way, and the time for bitterness has long since passed.

The next few days were the worst of my life. Although I put up a good front, my life was in shambles. I tried to convince myself that everything was okay. But for the first time in my life, I was out of baseball . . . and running out of options. It took awhile for the shock to settle in but eventually I felt disgraced. Some gamblers bottom out when they lose their money. I bottomed out when I lost baseball. In an article written by Murray Chass of the *New York Times*, George Steinbrenner expressed his personal feelings. "I consider Pete Rose a friend. But he's a gambling addict and needs help," said George. "He has a real problem and he needs help with that problem. The way he gambles and the amounts he probably gambles, I happen to know. I've seen him at the track on numerous occasions. I believe you have to treat gambling the same way you treat alcoholism or drug abuse. It's a sickness. He's got to admit it and face up to it. I care for Pete Rose and for what happens to him." Mr. Steinbrenner wasn't the only friend to express that feeling. But I honestly didn't believe I had a "problem" . . . definitely not a "sickness." Then my lawyer Reuven Katz gave it to me straight. "If you don't seek help," he said, "I can't continue to represent you as a client." Reuven's statement hit me pretty hard. Ever since losing my father, Reuven had been a trusted friend—my go-to guy. And after losing everything else, I didn't want to lose him, too. So as difficult as it was, I went to a psychiatrist—James Hilliard, M.D., from the University of Cincinnati. Under the circumstances, Dr. Hilliard was very understanding. He watched the television broadcasts and read the newspapers during my 6-month-long ordeal. He saw a full-blown account of my alleged gambling activity. But Dr. Hilliard wasn't interested in newspaper accounts. He wanted to hear firsthand what I thought about my gambling situation. My first instinct was to convince the shrink that I didn't have a problem—"Pete Rose logic." I explained that I gambled for excitement . . . pleasure . . . and competition. "I wasn't interested in winning money," I said. "I enjoyed the action." I grew up in a community where sports and gambling went hand-in-hand. And the men who I watched gamble, were among the finest on the planet—honest, hard-working family men, who were all good athletes. I saw problem gamblers as degenerates who held no status in life, people who gambled every day until they lost everything. I reminded him that I didn't drink, smoke, or use drugs, and that sometimes I went months at a time without gambling at all. In my mind, I still didn't fit the profile of the typical "problem" gambler. But Dr. Hilliard was very patient. He didn't want to pressure me into saying anything I didn't really believe. He wanted me to find my own way. During our first few sessions, Dr. Hilliard listened while I talked about my sports gambling. As I began to open up, he said something that hit home. "Problem gambling has more to do with the frequency of betting and the amount bet relative to the resources and the damage it inflicts on personal and family life." And then I started to think about my habits. Slowly but surely, it began to sink in. I began to realize that maybe I had a problem after all. Gambling wasn't really about winning "money." It was about "craving the risk," something I was pretty damn good at. I gambled past the point of being able to control it. I slid right past inappropriate gambling and right into gambling with my career—a bet I lost!

After just three sessions with Dr. Hilliard, I realized that I denied having a problem for a long time. And because of my success in baseball, my family and friends let me get away with it. But let's face it. Can you imagine anything more "damaging" than being banned from your profession for life? After finally admitting that I had a problem, Dr. Hilliard congratulated me on taking the "first step" toward recovery. Then, he suggested ongoing counseling with other gamblers, who sit around in a group environment and share their experiences. During the next few weeks I attended Gamblers Anonymous in an effort to learn more about my condition. But those sessions were not as helpful as the private sessions with Dr. Hilliard. I sat and listen to people who told stories about hocking their wife's wedding ring . . . committing armed robbery . . . people who were suicidal . . . who couldn't wait to get out of bed in the morning to gamble. Many of them had serious personal problems that went way beyond gambling. It wasn't the most uplifting environment but I took the sessions seriously and tried to make the best of an awkward situation. But I've never been the type to sit around with a group of strangers and spill my guts. "Hi, my name is Pete and I'm an addict"—not my style! Besides, several of the group members were more interested in hearing baseball stories than my gambling activity!

Within a few weeks, I left Cincinnati for a prearranged book and publicity tour. My agent and lawyer suggested that since I received so much negative publicity during the investigation, why not talk about the progress with my therapy? Under normal circumstances, I probably would have chosen to wait before going public. I was still in the early stages of recovery. But I felt pretty good about my progress and decided to give it a try. I appeared on the *Phil Donahue Show*—my first public appearance since my lifetime ban. Mr. Donahue read an opening statement in which I admitted to having a gambling disorder. Afterward, I appeared on stage to a much-appreciated standing ovation. I spoke honestly about my gambling problem. "I can't gamble on anything anymore because I can't control it," I said. "I've come to learn that compulsive gambling makes you less than honest about your life. Sometimes, I didn't remember what the real story was anymore. But once I admitted I had a problem, I was on the road to recovery." When fans from the audience asked about my plans for returning to baseball, I replied, "I'm not sure I want to. I want to be reinstated for one reason and one reason only. I want to go to the Hall of Fame."—an honest statement that earned another standing ovation from the crowd. When Mr. Donahue brought up all the negative publicity during the investigation, I just grinned. "I knew it was only a matter of time before I was partly responsible for the Lindbergh baby," I replied—a response that brought down the house. Still the appearance was not a cakewalk by any means. Mr. Donahue talked about evidence from the Dowd Report and questioned whether he believed in my innocence. I understood his position but remained steadfast with my own. I knew that there were people out there who believed everything they read or heard about me. I also knew I couldn't change their minds. At that point, I was only interested in turning my life around—not opening old wounds. I put the "betting issue" to bed when I signed my agreement with Major League Baseball. "No finding" means "No finding." Period! I wasn't going to renege on an agreement that I fought so hard to get.

But as fate would have it, I wouldn't get off that easy. The fallout from the government's investigation of Janszen, Gio, and Peters continued to rain down on me. I was still being investigated by the grand jury for possible tax violations—an ongoing legal problem that threatened everything left in my life, including my therapy sessions with Dr. Hilliard. Within weeks, I was charged with 22 counts of filing false tax information. My lawyers and I continued to fight and won on 20 of the 22 counts. But on April 20, 1990, I pled guilty to two counts of filing false income tax reports by failing to report income. I paid $2.2 million in taxes between 1985 and 1987, which were the years in question. But the Internal Revenue Service said that I owed them $2.362 million. They said that I failed to report over $350,000, which came from gambling, autograph shows, and sports memorabilia sales. In addition to the $162,000 in back taxes, I paid another $154,000 in penalties and interest. But that wasn't enough. The federal judge in Cincinnati determined that I committed a crime by "underdeclaring" my income and insisted on prison time. To add insult to injury, I was fined another $50,000 to pay the cost of my own incarceration. Now, ain't that a bitch? "Hey Pete, we're sending you to jail, and by the way, it will only cost you another fifty grand!" One of the biggest misconceptions about my sentencing is that people think I went to prison for betting on baseball. I didn't. It's not against the law to bet on baseball. It's against baseball rules to bet on baseball. But some people believe that I went to prison because the authorities couldn't prove that I bet on baseball.

When it comes to card shows and autograph signings, all the ballplayers took cash—Mantle, Mays, Killebrew—all of 'em. You fly in for one day, do your signings, get paid in cash, and then leave. I accepted a check one time, for 17 grand in Houston, and it bounced like a goddamn basketball. That's the kind of people I was dealing with in the card show business. So, when a promoter asked me whether I wanted cash or a check—whattaya think I said? So, before I go on, I know what you're thinking: "Hey Pete, didn't your attorney tell you that the money had to be reported on your taxes?" He probably did. But I didn't listen. I was real headstrong in those days. But do you think the promoters who ratted me out were telling the truth? If the IRS cracks down on a promoter, do you think he won't cover his own ass? He'll say he paid Pete Rose 25 grand for that card show in Houston. But all he really paid me was 15. If he overstates what he paid me, then it doesn't look like he was cheating on his taxes. It looks like I did! And since it's a cash business, there was just no way to trace it. That's why I was better off with a plea bargain. Even if 20 of the 22 counts of tax evasion are bogus, the judge will still throw the book at you for the 2 that are legitimate. For instance, 16 of the counts involved Pick-Sixes, where the taxes were taken out at the track at the time the tickets were cashed. On two of those tickets, I was partnered up with Jerry Carroll, who owned the racetrack at Turfway. Jerry was a millionaire many times over, so he wasn't concerned with paying the taxes. He just didn't want the negative publicity of winning a Pick-Six at his own track. As a baseball player and local celebrity, I didn't want to be dragged into the papers either. So my friend, Arnie Metz, cashed the winning tickets and paid the taxes—$80,000 out of a total jackpot of $266,000. I had no idea that all of us had to sign the ticket. So that was an honest mistake on my part. But can someone please tell me how the IRS got "cheated" after they already took $80,000 of our winnings? It wasn't like they would get more money if Jerry and I signed the ticket!

"The charges against Pete were legitimate but not criminal," says attorney Roger Makley. "Upon reconstruction of his income records, Pete should have paid his taxes and fines like everyone else and been allowed to get on with his life. In all my years as a prosecutor, I never saw the government file charges unless the net tax fall was at least 20 percent. Pete's total obligation was less than 5 percent. After totaling his income from gambling, the government agreed that Pete was a "net loser." But in order to offset the winnings, they insisted that the losses be declared. Bottom line—if the IRS wanted to make an example of Pete Rose, it succeeded. After Pete was sentenced, athletes and entertainers from all over the country amended their tax returns to declare cash from public appearances. Baseball stars like Duke Snider and Willie McCovey even made apologies. But to the best of public knowledge, none have gone to jail."

I was wrong to do what I did. But I'm probably the only person in America to go to jail for under-paying his taxes by four percent. The experts said that I wasn't going to prison for "under-paying" taxes. I was going to prison for "failing to report material information on my tax return"—a charge that had never before resulted in a criminal prosecution. But in order to keep things on the fair and balanced side, I'll let you hear what federal judge, S. Arthur Spiegel had to say in his pre-sentencing speech:

> *We must recognize that there are two people here, Pete Rose, the living legend, the all-time hit leader, and the idol of millions; and Pete Rose, the individual, who appears today convicted of two counts of cheating on his taxes. Today we are not dealing with the legend. History*

and the tincture of time will decide his place among the all-time greats of baseball. With regard to Pete Rose, the individual, he has broken the law, admitted his guilt, and stands ready to pay the penalty. Under our system of law and sense of fairness, when he has completed his sentence, he will have paid his debt to society and should be accepted by society as rehabilitated. Only time will tell whether he is to be restored to his position of honor for his accomplishments on the ball fields of America.

I'm still not sure where the judge got the idea of "two people." If there had been another Pete Rose in the courtroom, I would've sent *that* sumbitch to jail and just gone about my business. But since my case with baseball had been settled without a public hanging, the judge was under a lot of pressure to get his "pound of flesh."

A few days after my sentencing, I heard a quote from my mom who said, "If Big Pete were still alive, none of this would have ever happened." As you know, it's not healthy to argue with your mother, especially one like Rosie. My dad was the only man I ever idolized—the only man I ever listened to. I'm sure Dad would have read me the riot act for associating with the kind of sleazeballs I had fallen in with. Dad would have seen what I couldn't—or wouldn't—that folks like Gio, Janszen, and Peters were not to be trusted. But Dad passed away 18 years earlier and with him, according to Rosie, went the "rudder for steering my life." Those words are a little too poetic for my understanding but they do contain some truth. You see, it was easy to blame my misfortune on the premature death of my dad . . . or on hanging out with low-lifers . . . or on feeling depressed after I retired from the active roster . . . or on the fact that John Dowd didn't play fair. Or, hell, maybe the Pope just turned out to be a Yankee fan!

There was some truth in all of the excuses. But shifting the blame didn't change the blame. The responsibility rested squarely on my shoulders. I just wasn't ready to accept it.

10

MY PRISON WITH BARS

*"I've listened to every detail of every case from every
inmate in this prison and from what I've been told,
I'm the only sumbitch in here who is actually guilty."*
—*PETE ROSE*

I waited in the holding area for what felt like days. From time to time, a few prison guards walked by to get a glimpse. I'm sure they thought they were being casual about it but they couldn't help but gawk at the sight of Charlie Hustle in lockdown. One guard grinned when he saw me. Another just shook his head, pretending to be disgusted. Either way, I knew I was in for a rough time. Eventually, I was escorted to the infirmary where I was strip-searched and given a physical by the prison doctor. Then, I was given a set of green army fatigues to wear, along with a commissary card and an identification number, which I had to memorize and recite on demand. Hell, I never thought I'd be wearing anything other than number 14 on my back. To keep things in perspective, I tried to pretend that I was a rookie all over again with a different set of rules to abide by. Instead of chalk lines and umpires, I had to deal with barbed wire and prison guards. You see, umpires take a lot of heat from players, managers, and fans. But they've got a tough job and they're just trying to do the best they can. So, I decided to treat the guards just like umpires which I did even after I found out what sadistic bastards they were. The guards didn't want to hear me bitching and moaning about the strike zone . . . or creating all these little barbs because this runner was "safe" or that runner was "out." I figured my days in the joint would go a helluva lot easier if I just learned to cooperate. It's like they say: "You gotta get along to go along," which was pretty much the same advice that I got from my dad just before my rookie year. "Do your job, obey the rules, and don't complain," said dad.

At one point, I met with Pete Hall, my workday foreman, who gave me the standard prison "orientation" speech. Pete Hall had worked for the prison for years. He was about 50 years old, tall, and rugged, so he'd already been around the block with and without his bicycle. He knew how to run his outfit and he didn't take shit from nobody. In fact, he kind of reminded me of Fred Hutchinson, my first manager with the Reds. They were both no-nonsense guys, who expected everyone to be on time and do their job without bitching about the circumstances. Anyway, Mr. Hall explained that I would be treated just like every other prisoner with no special privileges for being a sports star. He explained that I would be housed in a barracks on level one—a minimum-security facility and assigned a daytime job working at the main prison. Marion, at that time, was the only level-six prison in the country. It held federal inmates from levels two through six, which was designated by the threat they posed to the rest of the prison population. For instance, the real bad guys—guys who were serving life sentences, the John Gotti types—were all kept on level six. Most of the lower level prisoners, who had already served between 3 and 10 years, were rewarded with better privileges based on good behavior, but they were still kept behind bars.

Mr. Hall continued with his speech by explaining my daily routine. Wake-up call Monday through Friday, would be at 5:30 A.M., after which

I would shower and report to the mess hall for breakfast. After breakfast, I would report to the Sally gate, just outside the main prison, where I would submit to a body search by the prison guards. Upon passing that body search, I would be escorted through a metal detector, into the main prison, where I would submit to another body search before being escorted to my weekday job. Then, I would submit to another body search before eating lunch. The same procedure would be repeated in reverse after lunch and again at the end of the work shift. All totaled, that's six body searches per day, which didn't include something else called *Count*. Whenever we heard the blast of an air horn, all inmates would fall in line against the nearest wall and call out our name and number.

I recognized the officer's speech for what it was. I'd heard tirades from baseball managers like Fred Hutchinson and Sparky Anderson throughout my playing career. They were all designed to get a player's attention for the good of the team. In 1963, Fred Hutchinson threw a bucket of baseballs through a glass window to get our attention. But this speech was different. The whole prison process was intended to humiliate, not inspire. The body searches . . . the Count . . . the prison doctor sticking his finger up your ass. That's what prison is all about: humiliation and control.

The main prison was supported by a workforce from the lower level inmates, who were assigned jobs based on their individual skills. Some guys worked in maintenance, woodshop, or laundry, while other trained inmates got jobs in the electrical or plumbing departments. When it came time to discuss my job assignment, Mr. Hall asked me if I had any special skills. "Well, sir," I replied. "I'm pretty good with a fastball down and away." Until that time, Mr. Hall had been pretty serious but my answer made even him crack a smile. "So I've heard," he said. "Why don't we put you in the welding department? It'll be a good place for you to start." Now, I wasn't looking to get off on the wrong foot but I didn't know shit about welding and I sure as hell wasn't about to get my hands burned from doing something dangerous. So I asked Mr. Hall to reconsider my job assignment. I reckon he was one step ahead of me because he just looked me square in the eye. "Pete," he said, "your presence here is going to cause a lot of problems. And I don't like problems. The welding department is about as far away from the general population as I can put you—which is going to be best for both of us." "But what about my hands?" I asked. "I can't be working around acetylene torches and tanks." "Don't worry, Pete," he said. "We have plenty of trained welders. But no one to sweep the floors, which is what I had in mind, given your experience with those baseball bats." Now, most folks would have been a little bit humbled by that comment—maybe even pissed off. But not Pete Rose. After all, I'm the only player in major league history to play in the All-Star game at five different positions. In fact, I'm the only guy to play in over 500 games at five different positions, which should tell y'all something about my ability to adapt to change for the good of the team. Even though I began my career as an infielder, I won all of my Golden Gloves and batting titles while playing in the outfield. I'd learned that it paid to be flexible—especially when you've got no choice. So by God, if prison guard Pete Hall needed convict Pete Rose to sweep floors . . . then I'd be the best goddamn floor-sweeper in prison history. Yes, sir, I was actually starting to feel pretty good until Mr. Hall gave me one extra warning that stuck firmly in my mind: "Be careful and don't get into any fights, Pete," he said. "Because if you get caught fighting, we'll put you over in the main prison on a level three or four, where you'll have to worry about where you take a shower." You can just imagine the impact that statement had on me. I had visions of those guys in the movies—guys who got sentenced to 6 months and wound up serving 6 years! I was planning on serving my 5 months as quietly as possible. The idea that things might get worse didn't sit too well. In fact, that warning reminded me of a story about Al "The Bull" Ferrara, who used to play for the Dodgers. The Bull went to Japan on a baseball barnstorming tour and took what he thought was a beautiful young Asian girl out to dinner. I reckon the Bull had one too many drinks because he started kissing and squeezing and got himself all excited. But when he reached under the girl's dress, he came up with a hand full of the wrong sexual equipment! When I asked the Bull what he did after that, he said, "Hell, Pete, I'd already spent $200 on dinner. I had to get something for my money, so I just went on with it." "Went on with it?!!!" Now, I'm not accusing the Bull of anything. He might've been telling that story just to draw some laughs—which he did because I was laughing my ass off. But anybody who knows anything about me—*knows* that I was a switch-batter, not a switch-hitter. And just the thought of being passed around the cell-block by some leather-vested sonsabitches—hell, let's just say that from that moment on I didn't care how bad I got treated. You could bet the farm that Pete Rose would *not* be fighting in prison!

As I was led across the compound, I received a bunch of stares and whispers from the other inmates. But I had been a public figure for 30 years and I was used to that sort of thing. What I wasn't used to was the action that followed. The first blast from that goddamn air horn really caught me by surprise. So I lined up against the barracks wall with the other prisoners . . . waited for my turn . . . and called out my name and number: "Rose, 01832-061!"

I found out later that the 061 at the end of my number meant that I was from Cincinnati. Three different digits meant Memphis, St. Louis, or Chicago. The numbers gave the guards a system for keeping track of the prison population. So, if you ever forgot your number, you'd screw up the guard's Count—something you didn't want to do because . . . well, I'll talk about that later in my book.

The first night was the worst. I had plenty of time to reflect on my situation. I was lying on a scrawny little prison cot with plenty of time to think. I had been kicked out of baseball and I was serving time in federal prison. It was the lowest point of my life. I started thinking about how things got so bad . . . and then all of a sudden, I just stopped worrying. I've never been one to dwell on the past and I figured any negative thinking would only hurt my chances for survival. So, I thought to myself, "I don't belong here. The punishment didn't fit the crime." I didn't feel that bad about the taxes because I didn't think I was really that guilty, but I was here to be made an example of. So I sucked it up and began to prepare myself for 5 months on the "humiliation" diet. I know it may sound strange but one of the first things that hit home was waking up in the middle of the night and not being able to go downstairs to get an Alka-Seltzer—a convenience not allowed in prison but one that I took for granted.

I didn't sleep much those first three nights, but not because of my conscience. I didn't sleep because they gave me a bunk right next to the shit house. All of the newcomers had to sleep in temporary quarters, where the lights were left on all night. But, hell, the lights weren't what bothered me— it was the sound of all those toilets flushing that kept me awake. Remember what I said about "humiliation and control?" Well, there is nothing more humiliating than trying to sleep while listening to a bunch of convicts farting in the next room. I'd spent 30 years of my life inside of dugouts and locker rooms. I've smelled more than my share of rank farts—which reminds me of a time we were playing against the Pirates up at Three Rivers Stadium. I came up to bat in the leadoff position in the top of the third inning. I was watching the pitcher throw warm-ups to his catcher, Manny Sanguillen. Then, I saw the umpire, Shag Crawford, all doubled up like he was in terrible pain. I said, "What's the matter, Shag, you sick?" Shag just winced. "Hell, no, I'm not sick," said Shag. "Sanguillen had another batch of Dominican tacos and he's blowing the worst goddamn farts I've ever smelled." Sure enough, I stepped into the box and as I waited for the pitch, Sanguillen just let one rip. The stank damn near knocked me to my knees. The ball was about a foot outside, but Shag raised his right hand and screamed, "STRIKE ONE!" I stabbed Shag with a look and said, "Are you fuckin' crazy?" But Shag lifted up his face mask and said, "I hope you brought your swingin' bat, Pete, because if Sanguillen keeps farting, every goddamn pitch is gonna be a strike!" Shag was right. The whole game only lasted an hour and forty minutes—the fastest in major league history. That was the only time in my life that I was in a hurry to get out of the batter's box, which should give y'all a vivid picture of how I felt about the stink that was coming through prison walls. Now, I'm not an early riser. I'm a "wake up at the crack o' noon" kind of guy. But I was shaved, showered and 5 minutes early when I heard the blast of that air horn at 5:30 the next morning.

I put on my army fatigues and walked over to the main gate, where I waited along with the other inmates. Each one of us had to raise our hands in the air and call out our prison number while the guards frisked us down. Then, we were led one by one inside the main prison where we had to submit to another body search before reporting to the mess hall. Entering through the gates, which were covered in barbed wire, was a real eye-opener. It gave me an eerie feeling that I'll never forget. It was like walking into a dark cave with no other weapon but a switch and not knowing whether the grizzly bear was asleep or awake.

We had to eat our lunch with the rest of the prison's main population— a daily reminder of where you *didn't* want to be. As I sat down for my first meal, the thing that hit me was the caliber of company I was in. Most of the level-one guys—or "campers" as we were called—were in for drug deals, extortion, passing bad checks, or theft. A few of them were informants like Janszen and Peters—guys who squealed on their friends to save their own asses. I was the only guy in there for tax evasion. But the guys on the higher levels were the really nasty guys—guys you didn't want to mess with. So, I just looked around for a quiet corner, sat down, and stared at my plate. Now, I'm not what you call a connoisseur of fine foods. I'm basically a steak-and-potatoes kind of guy. But I realized right away why I didn't see any fat people in prison. That chow was the worst goddamn food I ever tasted in my life—processed eggs, stale toast, and black coffee. But I just kept my thoughts to myself, which is what you're supposed to do in prison. After chow, I lined up for another humiliating body search and then got escorted to the welding department, all the way in the back of the main prison . . . near level six. As I mentioned, the level-six guys were in for rape, murder, and armed robbery—charming stuff like that. They had three guards for every one prisoner on their cellblock. So security was real tight. We weren't allowed contact with those guys, not that we wanted any! And since they were serving life sentences, about the best that they could hope for is to some day get reduced to a lower level where they could sit and talk and touch. The level-six guys were only allowed one hour of sunlight per day. So all they did was read and work out . . . read and work out . . . read and work out. There were rows of thick bars separating us, but I could just barely see them from where I started sweeping the floors. But these were not the type of guys you wanted to meet. John Walker Jr. was serving life for selling Navy secrets to the Soviet Union. Edwin Wilson was serving 50 years for running guns for Ghadafi. On my way back to the mess hall, I had to wait for several minutes for the electronic bars to open, which gave the lifers some time to stare at me and express their opinions. Since I had made the headlines just about every day during the previous year, all of the guys had read about me and had become "experts" on my gambling case. One inmate raised his fist and called out: "Hey, Charlie, you got hustled. Right on, man!" Jeff Fort, who was linked to El Rukins and the United Nations bombing attack, had a different opinion. He yelled out something sarcastic but I couldn't really hear what he said. Another convict tried to put me in my place when he yelled out, "Hey, Rose. You fucked up. Look at you now!" I expected to get ridiculed by those guys, so I can't really say that those things bothered me too much. I never paid much attention to the advice of others, and I wasn't about to start listening to the wisdom from guys in prison. But Carlos Lehder, who ran one of the biggest drug cartels in

Colombia, said nothing at all. He just stared at me and kept his opinions to himself. He was serving 130 years so he was cold-blooded.

By the third day, I had experienced another setback. Some low-life had stolen my commissary card. I reckon he thought it would make a nice souvenir because he damn sure couldn't use a card that had my picture on it. Not unless he was looking for a stupid way to get caught. Since we weren't allowed to have money in prison, I had no way of paying for my incidentals. But the loss turned into a gain. At that time, a fellow inmate approached me. "Mr. Rose," he said. "I'm Billy Haas. But you can call me Catfish. I'm the manager of the prison softball team and I'd like you to try out for second base." As you can well imagine, I felt honored to be offered a "tryout" for the prison softball team. So I looked at him real friendly-like and said, "Are you fuckin' crazy?" He got embarrassed and apologized because he really didn't mean any disrespect. Hell, I told him that I wasn't insulted. I just couldn't play softball because I had knee surgery just 2 weeks before coming to prison. Catfish got relieved, started laughing, and used his own commissary card to pay for my toothbrush and other personal supplies. Catfish confessed that the barracks had been buzzing with the rumor that Pete Rose was coming to Marion and that he and all the other guys were excited to meet me. "What other guys?" I asked. "You'll see," he replied. About an hour later, I was escorted from my bunk behind the shit house to my new quarters in an army barracks, where Catfish introduced me to his best friend, Billy Guide. As veterans on the detective squad, both Guide and Catfish earned impressive reputations by busting some of Chicago's toughest drug dealers. Then, as members of the "Marquette Ten," an undercover taskforce both got convicted for conspiracy to distribute cocaine. Both guys claimed to be innocent. And I believed them. After what I'd been through with John Dowd, I was ready to believe any conspiracy theory that came my way. Guide and Catfish had already served 6 years of their 20-year sentences and offered to show me the ropes to make life a little easier. About an hour later, I received a new commissary card. So, I figured it couldn't hurt to make friends with somebody who had a little clout. Guide was a tough-ass kid from the south side of Chicago, who grew up on the wrong side of the tracks. Like me, he earned his bones by relying on street smarts, guts, and determination. So, we hit it off right away. Guide worked in the recreation department and offered to help get me gym privileges so I could rehab my knee. Besides being manager of the softball team, Catfish worked in the landscaping department and took care of the lawns and shrubbery. He even did some work on the warden's private home. So, if push came to shove, he could get off the prison compound for a few hours with a friend on the motor pool. Then, I got introduced to another ex-cop—Larry Brady. Brady was not part of the Marquette Ten, but he was convicted of conspiracy just the same. Brady had already served 20 years of a 30-year sentence. He had a beautiful home in Chicago . . . and another home in Arizona . . . and another in Colombia . . . and a nice Learjet to travel back and forth to all three. When I asked how he got caught, Brady said, "Somebody squealed on me." "Who?" I asked. "About a hundred different people," he said. Hell, by that time, I was starting to feel a little better. In just a few short hours, I had gone from Stalag 17 to an episode of "Hogan's Heroes." I just couldn't wait to meet Colonel Klink!

But any good feelings I had in the joint disappeared pretty quickly. It didn't take long before I found out why they called our entrance to the main prison the "Sally" port. As I mentioned, the guards had the right to randomly search any prisoner at any time, day or night. So one of the redneck boys decided to put me to the test. As I lined up to pass through the metal detector, I was called out and ordered to submit. I had no idea what they might be looking for. A plastic knife or fork was about the only thing I could've had in my possession. But hell, I didn't make a big deal about it. I just shrugged my shoulders and stripped down naked. I figured that if I acted like it didn't bother me—they'd leave me alone. "The way Pete handled himself with that first strip-search was impressive," said Guide. "If he had bitched and complained about it, or shown any weakness at all, those guards would've strip-searched him every day—just to humiliate him. But Pete stood there like he couldn't care less—a real man's man." You gotta understand—these guards weren't the sharpest tools in the shed. Most of them were high school dropouts, who had nothing else going on in their lives. St. Louis, Memphis, and Chicago— all the big nightspots—were several hours away. Since they were starved for entertainment, the only way the hacks got their rocks off was by tormenting the inmates. So, I just put my clothes back on, passed through the metal detector, and went about my business as if nothing had happened. I think, though, I overheard a few sarcastic remarks about what a nice ass I had.

By 4 o'clock in the afternoon, I was finished with my work shift. All of the inmates had to remain standing until the end of evening Count before reporting for supper. But during supper, we all started to unwind a little bit. Guide and I would usually sit and talk about racehorses and beautiful women but not too much about the beautiful women. We didn't talk about the women because I found out pretty quickly that it was a sore subject. I was only in for 5 months, so the thought of my wife being with another man was never an issue. Now, I might've felt different if I was in for 5 or 10 years like the other guys. One of the other ex-cops claimed he got set up because his wife was having an affair with the chief of police. You can just imagine the kind of tormenting thoughts he had about his wife. So we pretty much avoided that subject altogether. Catfish was a die-hard Cubs fan, which made him a prime target for humiliation. Y'all know how I feel about the Cubs. I reckon I rubbed that in his face about once a day. But Catfish once had a tryout with a minor league club, so all he wanted to talk about was baseball. He kept bugging the shit outta me about playing on the softball team until finally I agreed to help coach—which was the only way I could shut him up. But the one thing that *everyone* wanted to talk about was the details of their "unique" criminal case. Everybody wanted to tell me about how they got busted . . . about how they were set up or ratted out. I heard all about conspiracies and fraud and blackmail . . . and about how every judge and every lawyer in the system was on the take. I heard so much legal terminology that I think I could have passed the goddamn bar exam. I listened to every detail of every case from every inmate in that prison. And from what they told me—I was the only sumbitch in there who was actually guilty.

After a few days, I started to settle in to my new routine. Guide and Catfish tried to keep things light by pulling pranks. After 30 years in a baseball locker room, they figured that I knew every prank in the book. But I was never a prankster in my playing days. Pranksters were for teams that lose. I didn't like team clowns because I thought they were trying to cover up for a lack of talent. That's why I respected Kirk Gibson for running off the field after one of the Dodgers put that goddamn shoe polish on his cap. Gibby was pissed off and he let everyone know about it. Kirk Gibson didn't come to Los Angeles for pranks—he came to play baseball, which is a big reason why the Dodgers won the World Series that year. But even if I had wanted to pull some pranks in prison, I had no access to the props. I had no matches to set a guy's foot on fire . . . no whipped cream for a pie in the face . . . no shampoo for the perpetual suds trick . . . no Atomic Balm for a jockstrap. So Guide had to get really creative in order to make me laugh. On occasion, he tried to short-sheet my bed but I caught him every time. He knew that I had done my basic training at Fort Knox, Kentucky. I was a perfectionist when it came to certain details, like keeping my bunk and footlocker in meticulous order. Every morning, I'd tuck my sheets and have my bed made before anyone else in the barracks. Then, one day, I folded my blanket and the damn thing wrinkled back up. I folded it again and it wrinkled right back up again. I kept on folding . . . and it kept on wrinkling until finally, I heard the guys bustin' a gut from across the barracks. Guide had gotten some sewing thread from the commissary and had rigged my blanket to a pulley. He was hiding in the corner, holding that string in his hands, while Catfish and Brady were trying to block my view. They couldn't help but laugh when they saw the frustrated look on my face every time that blanket wrinkled back up. They went to a lot of trouble to play that little prank, which helped to keep us all from going crazy. Go figure. I was serving just 5 months. Those guys were gonna be in prison for one-third of their lives but they were going out of their way to keep me from getting depressed. That's what you call a "solid"—a gesture of friendship.

Weekends are special to just about everybody. As a kid, Saturday mornings meant waking up and waiting for my dad in the front seat of his car, busting a gut to get out to the field where we'd play ball until long after the sun went down. On those days when I wasn't playing ball, I'd be at the racetrack with Dad, Dud Zimmer, and Ed Brinkman Sr.—three of the greatest guys who ever walked the planet. Then, as I got older, Saturday mornings still meant heading out to the ballpark . . . or over to the racetrack with friends. I reckon you might call me "a creature of habit." But my first Saturday morning in prison was hardly memorable. I never slept late because the sound of that goddamn air horn kept everybody off-guard. Hell, I slept in a barracks with 24 other men—nobody ever slept late. After making my bunk and avoiding my stale breakfast, I went along with Guide, Catfish, and Brady, who invited me to the lounge room to watch a college football game. Watching college football is one of my favorite hobbies. So I figured that I might get a reprieve from the daily routine of body searches, air horns, and Count. TV privileges were reserved for inmates with good conduct records or for those who had performed well on their workday jobs. Since all of the guys enjoyed sports, there was never an argument over which channel to watch. That lounge TV was always turned to sports, which provided an easy way for me to strike up a conversation with my newfound peers. The guys would either ask me what I thought about a certain play or they would tell me why I was wrong. Yes sir, I found out quickly that when it comes to sports, everyone is an expert. It didn't matter how much actual experience

I had on the playing field—those guys knew more than me. If they said a referee made a horseshit call—I agreed. If they said a quarterback couldn't throw—I agreed. If they said a receiver couldn't catch—I agreed. Finally, Catfish looked over at me and said, "You played pro ball for 24 years, Pete. Why don't you put those assholes in their place?" "Hell, they're all criminals," I said. "I don't want them pissed off at me. You never know what they might do." Anyway, I was sitting there watching a football game and this guy comes over and starts playing the guitar . . . singing me this song. Then, he asks for my autograph, and I'm thinking the whole thing is kind of funny. But Guide got defensive and reminded me that autographs were considered "contraband." If I signed anything whatsoever, I could get sent to solitary confinement for insubordination. Then, Guide asked the guy what the hell he was doing with a guitar. I didn't think too much of it at the time but Guide got really suspicious about the whole thing and started to make a stink. Then, a guard came over and told us that everything was okay. As it turned out, the head of prison Fire & Safety—I think his name was Steve Tussey—decided to bring in a band to provide some weekend entertainment for the inmates. Now, I was more interested in the football game than the entertainment but that singer just kept on walking in front of me . . . playing that damn guitar. "One of the first things that hit me about Pete is that he was very naïve," said Guide. "I could see right away how people could take advantage of him. He had been a baseball player his entire life and this was the first time he had been outside of his protective environment. I didn't expect him to be as suspicious as me—I was an undercover cop. But I had already served 6 years and I'd never once seen a band inside the joint." As it turned out, Guide was right to be suspicious. That singer had a hidden camera inside his guitar. A few days later, the pictures showed up in the tabloids with captions that said Pete Rose was having a great time in prison . . . just lounging around . . . watching TV all day long. Go figure. I'd been in the joint for a week. I'd slept next to the shit house . . . been pushed, prodded, and strip-searched, yet the tabloids made it sound like I was in a "country club."

I never did find out who was responsible for arranging that "special entertainment." But I heard the warden was really pissed off that his security got breached. I'm sure a few of the hacks got their asses chewed out. I also heard the tabloids paid $20,000 for those photos. So how much did the guitar player pay to bribe his contact on the inside . . . four or five grand? The whole experience changed my attitude about which inmates were guilty and which ones might have been innocent. I had been "set up" and didn't even know it. All of a sudden, the concept of judges and lawyers being "on the take" didn't sound so far-fetched. If someone in the prison system was willing to "look the other way" for a small time payoff— imagine what a judge might do for a million dollars? That is why I believed Guide and Catfish might have been innocent. They were both good guys, who didn't seem capable of committing those crimes.

As it turned out, Sunday morning was no better than Saturday. We began our day by submitting to a strip-search just outside the barracks. This was early fall, so the weather wasn't too cold. But I knew that in December, standing out there buck naked in the snow, would be no picnic. The guards read all of our mail and monitored all of our phone calls. So there was no such thing as privacy—anywhere, anytime. But Sunday was visitation day and there was a new kind of energy in the air. By 9 o'clock in the morning, the families started pulling into the compound. Every visitor got searched coming in and searched going out. Then, after passing through security, the families were allowed into the visitation room. The men were allowed one kiss from their wives but no conjugal visits. I saw the happy look on Guide's face when his teenage son ran up and gave him a hug. The whole thing really cheered me up. The most difficult thing about prison was being away from your family. So getting the opportunity to see them on weekends really eased the pain. I watched as over a dozen kids started playing tag behind the barracks and I started thinking that it might be okay for Carol to bring my son Tyler for a visit. As I mentioned, money was really tight at that time. I had to sell just about everything I owned to pay off my debts and legal fees. And since Cincinnati was no longer a welcome place for the Rose family, Carol and the kids moved into a two-bedroom "cracker box" apartment in Plant City, Florida—an area where I had spent time during spring training. Then, I got an idea. Two years before, a sportswriter friend of mine had fallen on hard times. I loaned him $20,000 to help him pay—talk about ironic—his back taxes! So I waited in line for the prison phone and made a collect call to my wife. After smoothing out all the rough details and convincing Carol that jail was a "piece of cake," I suggested that she phone my sportswriter friend and call in the marker. My family needed the money for living expenses, and with 20 grand, they could afford a weekend trip to Marion. I was starting to feel a little better until I got back to the visitation area. Remember what I said about good feelings not lasting very long in prison? Well, I saw something that really turned my stomach—something totally uncalled for. As soon as all of the families got settled in, the guards set off that goddamn airhorn, which signaled the Count. Right there in front of their wives and kids, each inmate had to fall in line and call out his name and number. I reckon one of the inmates forgot his number, which screwed up the guard's Count—something you didn't want to do. They made him submit to a strip search. I'd never seen anything so embarrassing in my whole life. I lost a lot of respect for the guards because they didn't have to signal Count on visitation day. Hell, I could understand if we were hardened criminals on level five or six but we were "campers" for chrissakes. There was no need for it. They only did it to humiliate the prisoners in front of their families, which pretty much killed any idea I had about bringing my family in for a visit. I figured I would have to go cold turkey for the full 5 months because there was no way that I'd let the bastards humiliate me in front of my kids. They could take my freedom, but, by God, they weren't gonna take my dignity.

11

LESSONS

"Watching my son leave the prison compound
was the hardest thing I ever had to do. It was the only
time in my life that I ever felt helpless."
—PETE ROSE

Having bad knees might not have been the only reason I avoided playing on the prison softball team. I thought if I started playin' ball again, it might bring back some memories that I wasn't ready to deal with. I can't begin to tell y'all how painful it was to get kicked outta baseball. And, since prison was *not* the kind of place to let down your guard and spill your guts, I kept all my feelings to myself . . . just like I'd done my whole life. Hell, I didn't know any other way. I had no problem expressing myself playing baseball or through humor, anger, sex, and gambling. But any other emotions felt unnatural. It wasn't like I never *felt* the emotions—I just never learned how to *express* them in a way that was acceptable to most civilized folks. I spent over 40 years on baseball fields, where sensitivity was a worthless emotion—a weakness. And one thing I had no time for

207

was weakness. But since Catfish had done me a "solid" with the commissary card, I wanted to return the favor and give him a hand with the team. After completing my 8-hour work shift, standing for the evening Count, and looking at my stale supper, I moseyed on over to the practice field and took a gander at how Catfish ran his squad. Right away, I could see how his finely tuned managerial skills were hard at work. Eddie "the Embezzler" coached first base, where he could steal the other team's hand signals. Bob "the Paper Hanger" was one helluva feller. He kept the scorebook, so he could kite an extra run during a tight game. Danny "the Dealer" was on the mound and just like clockwork, Harry "the Informant" kept disrupting team chemistry by shooting off his goddamn mouth. If Burt Reynolds had shown up, we could've filmed the sequel to *The Longest Yard*—softball style. Truth is, those guys were all out there having fun and most of them took the game pretty seriously. I was surprised by how talented they were. For just 2 hours, twice a week, they got a chance to forget about the drudgery of prison life. So I decided to join in and hit some infield practice while Catfish worked with the pitchers. I hit grounders, threw it around the horn, and hit another round for turning two. Strangely enough, the feel of that bat in my hands gave me a much-needed boost, which I hadn't felt in a long time. Looking around the field, I noticed that the shortstop was either stabbing at the ball or dogging it on every other play. His name was Marco—a tough-ass kid, who had been shot five or six times during a robbery attempt. He missed so many grounders that I thought the ball was bouncing right through the bullet holes in his chest! Hell, I probably would've said something encouraging to Marco but like I said, he was a criminal and I didn't want to get him pissed off at me. Marco was a stand-up guy and a good athlete. He probably would've appreciated a tip. But I've never been the type to preach at my players—not my style. When I managed the Reds, I kept things pretty simple. Get 'em on, get 'em over, and get 'em in—basic hardball strategy.

I figured that if a player couldn't get excited about playing major league baseball, then he was already beyond my help. The first thing I told all my hitters was this: "You only gotta be successful 3 outta 10 times. You're not going to be successful 4 outta 10 times—we already know that. It ain't that goddamn hard, so just go out and do your job." I used three techniques while managing the Reds: If a player needed a kick in the pants—I gave him a kick in the pants. If he needed to be left alone—I left him alone. If he needed encouragement—I gave him encouragement. Each player had to be treated in a way that he best responded or else I'd be hurting my own cause. I had just two rules: Be on time and play hard. Sparky Anderson, on the other hand, wouldn't hesitate to jump all over a player if he thought he needed a kick in the pants. When it came to motivation, Sparky had a ton of colorful stories to get a player's attention. If Sparky had seen Marco muffing them grounders, he would've stopped practice, got all up in his face, and said something like this: *You're stabbin' at that ball like it was a goddamn T-bone steak! What do you do when you see a girl with a great set of tits? You don't just run right up and grab 'em! You gotta caress those puppies and bring 'em into your body real slow and easy-like . . . let 'em come to you like nature intended. Hell, you gotta treat that baseball the same way . . . just like it was your Momma's fine jewelry!*

I knew if I mentioned tits and jewelry to a bunch of convicts, I might start a prison riot. So I decided *not* to take a page from Sparky's playbook—even though the guys would've enjoyed the theatrics. Besides, I wasn't out there for teaching. Catfish was the manager and I didn't want to steal his thunder. It was his team when I got there and it would be his team when I left. The last thing the guys needed was to have some hotshot blow into prison, give them some razzle-dazzle, and then after 5 months, leave them high and dry. So I just kept a low profile and tried to enjoy an evening of softball. In fact, if my knees hadn't been so bad, I probably would've jumped into the lineup and played a few innings. Hell,

I would've played the entire game and hoped for extra innings. There has never been anything in my entire life that I enjoyed more than playing baseball, which is why I kept playing until the age of 45. And even then, I didn't step down quietly. I've just never been much of a spectator. I have trouble watching other people do what I preferred to be doing myself. But given my circumstances in prison, I was pretty upbeat and encouraging. From time to time, I'd offer a tip or take a personal interest in a player, which seemed to boost team morale and irritate the guards at the same time. The guards had their own softball team, which played against the inmates. So they weren't too thrilled by the idea of Pete Rose helping the opposition. Given my feelings toward the guards, I was only too eager to offer my assistance to the home team. For instance, Bobby Hampton, another tough-ass kid, was having some trouble during batting practice. I wasn't gonna mention anything because it was none of my damn business. But he asked for my advice. So I took a look. Hell, I recognized the problem right away—kid had a hitch in his swing. "Where you from?" I asked. "St. Louis," said Bobby. "Figures," I replied. "Another convict from the Show-Me State who never got showed!" Catfish started to snicker but I wasn't joking. I was trying to make a point. I asked Bobby if he had ever seen Stan Musial swing the bat. But Bobby said that he never went to the St. Louis Cardinals games because his old man was never around much. Right away, I knew I was hitting on a touchy subject. So, I just backed off and continued my conversation until I could determine how best to help him. One of the first things every manager learns is that the players don't really listen. They'll look at you in the eye but they don't actually hear what you're saying. I talked to Bobby about his family . . . and his neighborhood . . . about his girlfriend . . . and about how he got busted . . . until finally he seemed at ease and in the right mind-set to receive a tip from a total stranger. "Try keeping your inside elbow closer to your hip," I said. "It'll keep your bat in the strike zone as you swing." Sure enough, Bobby stepped up to the plate and drilled the next few pitches deep into the gap. Then I offered one more piece of incentive: "Beautiful girls don't fuck the .200 hitters," I said. "They fuck the stars." Bobby just grinned and dug into that batter's box like he was Hank Aaron. He started rippin' the balls all over the field. "Watching Pete interact with those players was really something special," said Guide. "After all, how many people can say they'd been tutored on the art of hitting a fastball by Charlie Hustle? I could tell right away why Pete was a good baseball manager—he just had a way with the players. I knew that Pete was hiding a lot of pain. But we all followed a strict code in prison, which meant you didn't talk about the past. So those few hours on the field really seemed to cheer him up."

About 2 months later, the warden sponsored a two-man hitting contest and Bobby asked me to be his partner. My knees had gotten much stronger by then, so I agreed to team up with him. The contest was set up to where each team got a certain number of points for home runs and base hits. Bobby and I were both hitting ropes that day and we won the contest by a huge margin. I felt pretty good about winning something again . . . and I probably learned a little something along the way. When Bobby started talking about his family background, I realized just how lucky I was. Sure, I was in jail the same as Bobby but I was in for "failing to report income," a charge that should've been settled out of court. I had no prior criminal record. Outside of a few speeding tickets, I had never even been to court, except for my divorce, which isn't illegal. And except for the time when the IRS contested my tax deduction for buying new Jeeps for all the Reds coaches, which I won. But most of my fellow inmates got started in a life of crime because they came from broken homes—something I couldn't relate to. I couldn't help but think that those convicts could've had a better life had they been nudged in the right direction early on. I know this may sound a little preachy, but a good kick in the ass from a parent can go a long way toward preventing a life of crime.

My next few weeks in the joint went just like the first. The same 5:30 wake-up call, same humiliating body searches, and the same weekday job. The only thing I had to look forward to was the evening activities, which were reserved for inmates with good conduct records. If you broke the rules, you'd get a "shot" or a mark against your record. If you got too many "shots," you'd get shipped over to the main prison or put in "the hole"—solitary confinement. Needless to say, I tried my best to walk the straight and narrow. But the guards didn't make it easy because they were always looking to bust us on some nit-picky thing. Since Guide was in charge of the recreation department, I was able to get into the gym on a regular basis to exercise my knees. One of my best memories as a kid was watching my dad play basketball at Christ Church. As soon as I built up a little strength, I started to shoot hoops and play some one-on-one. I'm not going to pretend that things went smoothly because they didn't. In prison, the blacks out-numbered the whites 3-to-1. There was a lot of racial tension. The black guys hung out with the black guys. The white guys hung out with the white guys and the Jews hung out with—well, like I said, there were no Jews in prison because they ate all the lox! Strangely enough, one of the biggest problems revolved around religion. A few of the black Christians were upset that some of their friends had converted to the Muslim faith. Now, don't get me wrong—none of us had anything against the Muslims. But these particular guys weren't interested in becoming "true" Muslims. They found out that the Muslims were allowed to leave work to attend prayer services. So they decided to convert. Hell, some of the guys couldn't even pronounce Mecca and Medina but if it meant getting off work detail—they were willing to pray in that direction several times a day. I'm not a particularly religious kind of guy, so I stayed out of that dispute. I wasn't about to get involved in a "holy war!"

But a few of the black guys sure raised a stink about me. They thought I was getting "special gym privileges" because I was white, which wasn't true. I might have been getting special gym privileges because I was Pete Rose but being white had nothing to do with it. So I went to Billy Guide and told him that I didn't want to cause any friction between the inmates. I remembered what it felt like to be discriminated against during my rookie year and I wanted no part of anything like that. Guide suggested that I referee the prison basketball games in order to smooth things out. It turned out to be a good suggestion because it gave me a chance to exercise and to show the other inmates that I was willing to make a contribution with my time. During the first few basketball games, I took a lot of crap for making what they thought were bad calls. But I never made any bad calls. I blew the whistle when I saw a violation. If a guy traveled—I called traveling. If a guy made a foul—I called a foul. I figured the guys would test me to see how much shit I was willing to take because that was the law of the jungle. The warden tested the captains. The captains tested the lieutenants. The lieutenants tested the guards. The guards tested the convicts and if there had been anybody lower on the totem pole, then that sumbitch would've been tested, too. But once they saw that I didn't back down, they left me alone.

By the time the second weekend rolled around, I was really starting to miss my family. Visiting hours were from 9 to 3 on Saturday and Sundays. Carol and the kids caught a plane from Plant City, Florida, to Atlanta, then took a puddle-jumper to Paducah, where they rented a car and drove to Carbondale. All totaled, they spent about 10 hours of traveling time. They wanted to arrive at 9 o'clock sharp, so we could spend the full 6 hours together. But since Count wasn't officially over until noon on weekends, I made damn sure they didn't arrive before then. Like I said, there was no way I'd let the guards humiliate me in front of my family. I watched as Carol's car drove through the entrance and along the winding road as they approached the parking area. I watched as the guards searched the car and then allowed them to approach the visitation area, where they were all searched individually. Cara was in diapers and Tyler was only 6 years old but they had to be searched as well. Upon entering the room, I was allowed to kiss my wife once but no touching was allowed after that.

"The whole process was sickening," said Carol. "They treated the guests like criminals as well. So, right away, I started to cry, which didn't go over too well with Pete. He doesn't like to see people cry, so I just gathered my emotions and tried to remain positive. But I felt so sorry for him because he was drawn and skinny. He'd lost about 10 pounds in just 2 weeks."

Hell, I was just happy to see my family. I played with Tyler for a while and then let him go outside with the other inmates' sons, who played tag on the prison grounds. Tyler was having a tough time. He didn't understand why his dad was not at home. He was taking a lot of teasing from the kids at his new school in Florida. They'd circle around him on the playground and call out, "Your daddy's a jailbird . . . your daddy's a jailbird." He'd come home after school and start to cry. My daughter Cara was just one year old, so she had no idea what was going on. Mostly, I just tried to reassure Carol that everything would be all right. I told her that things would change for the better after I got out of prison. But she just got more and more emotional until finally, I couldn't take it any more. I looked her in the eye and said, "Carol, I have a confession to make." Carol wiped her tears and tried her best to pay attention. "After 2 weeks in prison, I've come to the conclusion that . . . well . . . I'm gay." Hell, she busted a gut laughing so hard that I was worried the guards were going to terminate her visit for "inappropriate behavior."

I introduced Carol to Guide, Catfish, and Brady. She was happy to see that I had made some friends and had settled into a tolerable routine. Fred, my brother-in-law, was also a cop. So Carol took comfort knowing that I was in familiar company. Then, something happened that changed the way I looked at my incarceration. I smelled a powerful odor coming from Carol's diaper bag—but not what you think. This was a pleasant odor . . . the odor of food . . . not prison chow but real food. I reckon the guards didn't check her diaper bag too closely because there was a Big Mac in there, which was left over from Tyler's lunch. I knew that we weren't allowed to receive anything from our visitors. Anything other than prison chow was considered "contraband" and would be taken away. I knew that if I got caught, Carol's visit would be terminated and I would get reprimanded and sent back to the barracks. But the powerful smell of that Big Mac was just too much to resist. It was the first time in my life where I can remember being really hungry. It reminded me of a time when I was managing the Reds in an extra inning game . . .

. . . A great umpire, John McSherry, was working the bases. I knew that John loved to eat stadium hot dogs. I also knew that if John got too hungry late in the game, he'd make some quick calls, so he could get his ass back into the clubhouse to eat. Sure enough, John made a horseshit call and the fans just started booing like crazy. Some fan threw a hot dog and hit John right in the back. John turned around but he wasn't looking at the fan—he was licking his chops and staring at that hot dog! Finally, while the fans kept booing, I walked over to John and said, "If you promise not to make any more horseshit calls, I'll ask all 30,000 of these fans to turn their heads so you can eat that goddamn hot dog." John stabbed me with a look and in a split second, I swear he actually considered it.

Anyway, a split second was all I needed because as soon as the guards turned their heads, I grabbed that Big Mac and swallowed it whole in world record time. I mean one bite and that sumbitch was gone! Carol started laughing because she had never seen anybody eat so fast. But it was my first satisfying meal in 2 weeks and I was not to be denied. Right away, Guide stood up and ran interference. He squinted, held his nose, and started acting like Cara needed a diaper change, knowing that the guards would keep their distance. He didn't want the guards to come close enough to smell that sandwich. The whole experience gave me a chance at having fun—a shot at some excitement. So I asked Carol to bring something extra on her next trip—Grecian formula. Carol got really nervous because she was afraid of getting caught. But Guide and Catfish assured her that they knew how to handle the situation. Now, before I go on—I know what you're thinking: "Why did you need hair color in prison, Pete?" Hell, I was feeling a little depressed and, having a certain vanity about my appearance, I wanted a psychological boost. Not that I wanted to look good for my fellow inmates because I was just joking about being gay. I was 49 years old, limping on bad knees, and I figured looking younger might make me feel younger. Sure enough, on her next visit, Carol smuggled the hair color in one of Cara's diapers. Guide showed me where to stash my contraband until I could get back over to the barracks to apply the color. "Either Pete got rushed with the process or he left the color on too long because when he walked out of the barracks the next time I saw him, his hair was jet black . . . just like Elvis," said Carol. "The whole thing was hilarious because . . . well, let's just say the difference wasn't subtle. Pete got called in and questioned about what he did to his hair. But he was defiant. 'What are you talking about?' he said. They kept asking questions but Pete just blamed the whole transformation on some mysterious chemicals in the prison water. Catfish destroyed the package and the plastic bottles, so there was no evidence to prove anything. Pete was not going to admit to that hair color no matter what, which tells you something about how stubborn he can be. Pete hates to admit it but he is just like his mother. They had identical personalities. Rosie was cocky . . . aggressive . . . and if she had a thought, she'd speak her mind. She wasn't really affectionate but neither is Pete. But both of them have a great sense of humor. Years later, when Rosie came to visit, she and Pete would just butt heads. They'd tease and cuss at each other for hours at a time. They were just a riot to watch. Tyler, Cara, and I would just sit back and laugh so hard that we'd get tears in our eyes. Neither of them could ever back down from a challenge."

The hardest time of my entire prison stay came when the visits were over. Carol and Tyler started crying, which only made matters worse for me. Finally, the guards escorted my family from the visitor's room back to their car. Then, I realized why the entrance road was so full of curves. At first, I thought it was a chance for extra surveillance. But as I watched my son hanging out the car window, waving and crying along that winding road, I realized they just wanted to prolong the misery of saying good-bye. Watching my son leave the compound was the hardest thing I ever had to do. The whole drive probably only took 3 minutes. But those were the longest 3 minutes of my life. Then I started crying myself. It was the only time in my life that I ever felt helpless.

But like I said, I've never been one to dwell on the past. I just got back into my daily routine of sweeping floors in the welding department and tried to focus on the things that I had control over—which was nothing. I mean there is only so much sweeping a man can do until the goddamn floor is clean. Once I got it clean, I had to keep on sweeping until I got it cleaner. Once I got it cleaner, I had to keep on sweeping until I got it cleanest. Once I got it cleanest, I took a break and made coffee or hot chocolate for the welders in my department. The guys enjoyed drinking coffee and bullshitting about the past. Just about everybody had a question they wanted to ask . . . about this game or that game . . . or about a certain play in the World Series or All-Star game. So I'd tell a few stories to keep them entertained. One of the welders was really superstitious, so we used to tease him pretty good. Since ballplayers are the most superstitious guys on the planet, I only had about a dozen stories on that subject—like the time we were playing in Wrigley Field in Chicago . . .

. . . Wrigley must have been built back in the 18th century because nothing ever worked in that stadium. There was never any hot water for the showers unless you flushed the toilet, which caused the water temperature to get so hot we'd all get scalded. I think the Cubs kept it that way on purpose just to keep the visiting players in a bad mood. Anyway, Davey Concepcion was going through a terrible slump at that time. I think he was 0-for-30, or something like that. We were in the locker room before the game and Davey was just desperate to break out of his slump. He looked across the locker and saw a big industrial-type dryer, which they used for drying the towels and uniforms. Being superstitious, Davey got a great idea. He figured the best way to get "hot" again was to crawl inside the dryer and allow the heat to penetrate into his body, thus ending his "cold" streak. Hell, the idea made perfect sense to me! Either way, I'd come out a winner. If it worked—Davey would help the team. If it didn't work—I'd tease his ass for years to come. Sure enough, Concepcion crawled into that dryer and just sat there all crunched up. Just at that time, Tony Perez comes stomping into the room, pissed off about something and slams his fist against the wall. Like I said, nothing ever worked in Wrigley. So the force from Tony's fist triggered a short in the electrical wiring, which caused the dryer to turn on—full speed. Hell, Johnny Bench and I pulled on the dryer door but the damn thing was stuck. I looked inside and saw Davey just tumbling around like a pile of laundry. His eyes were as big as the Roadrunner from the cartoons. So, I ran outside to get some help. Finally, I found a janitor, who was able to shut off the circuit breaker. By the time we got Davey out of that dryer, every single hair on his body had been scorched off. He'd lost his sense of balance and was wobbling around the locker room like a hairless dog on a trampoline. If it hadn't been so scary, it would've been funny. The whole process must have been successful, though, because Davey went 4-for-4 that afternoon. But to this day, he can't even drive past a laundromat without going into seizures. I don't reckon my stories changed any ideas about each inmate's particular superstition. But my stories kept us entertained and for a few minutes a day kept our minds off of where we were—federal prison.

About once a week, Pete Hall would get a series of phone calls, telling him that the "old man" was on his way up to the welding department for inspection. Pete Hall, like the foremen in each department, wanted to impress the warden with the way he ran his department. So, between the times Mr. Hall got his advance warning calls until the time the warden arrived, we'd all bust our ass to make sure our unit was spic-and-span. If the warden gave Pete Hall a solid commendation, then Mr. Hall would pass along the favor and gives us all a break. If the warden didn't like what he saw, life was miserable for everybody. In fact, every time the warden got to the welding department, Pete Hall would look over at me and say, "You must be working your ass off, Pete, because that's the cleanest goddamn floor I've ever seen." The warden would just look down at the floor, crack a little smile, and then walk away with his team of guards. We never once failed to pass inspection. And I made sure that all of my welders had a steady supply of fresh coffee and funny stories so they could concentrate on their work. Like I said, I was the best floor sweeper that prison had ever seen!

After standing for evening Count and ignoring my stale supper as usual, I found a new diversion that really kept me going—tennis. The prison had one concrete tennis court, which had stress cracks from the extreme hot and cold weather conditions. That concrete court was the worst thing for my knees but I enjoyed the competition so much that I played almost every night. Prison rules allowed for the winner to stay on court until he lost a set or until lights out at 9:15, whichever came first. Besides the "early bird" club in Cincinnati, the last time I had played tennis was during *The Superstars* competition, which was a popular television show back in the 1970s. Each celebrity athlete would compete in a series of sports other than his own. I beat Karl Schranz, the champion skier, in a set that became my trademark for the show. I talked so much trash that Schranz thought I was a maniac. Hell, I was a maniac. The set came down to the last shot, which I made by diving across the court. I really got scraped up by diving but there was money and fame on the line. So I had to go for it. I wasn't going to dive on the prison tennis court, that's for damn sure. But since the fundamentals of swinging a racket were about the same as swinging a bat, I became a really strong player. And since I was a switch-hitter, my backhand was just as strong as my forehand, which made me very tough to beat. Because of my bad knees, I was slower with my side-to-side motion. But I could really swat that fuzzy ball. I'd hit that sumbitch so hard they couldn't return the thing. I got to the point where I reinvented my aggressive trademark. I started to talk trash during the game. I tried to wilt their spirit by pure aggression—especially after a great shot. "You didn't even see that one coming did you, Guide?" I'd yell. "Hell, no, you can't hit what you can't see!" Eventually, the other inmates lined up for a shot at the title but I never lost a set. The loser had to give up the court and then sit and wait for another turn. As I mentioned, I hate to lose. I hated the idea of giving up the court, so I made damn sure that I didn't. In fact, I heard that a few of the inmates pooled a meager fund from their commissary account for the first guy to beat me in a set—a fund that was never in jeopardy. After each set, the guys would walk off the court defeated but thoroughly entertained. I gave them a show with each ass-whuppin' so as not to create any hard feelings. Now, before I go on—I know what you're thinking: No, I didn't gamble on the tennis matches. Hell, no—there was no money in prison, just the little amounts we were allowed to keep in our commissary account for incidentals. No cigarettes. No magazines. We weren't allowed to have anything. So, we just played for fun . . . recreation . . . escape from the drudgery. Although years later, I heard that another ex-athlete who went to prison was actually running a bookmaking operation from the prison pay phone. He had reportedly hocked his wife's wedding ring and sold his house to fund his gambling habits. But I wasn't that type of gambler. I never gambled on a sport that I was playing because of the competition—just the actual playing gave me all the rush I needed. But I learned real quickly how other people might confuse the difference.

You see this was October . . . and October meant just one thing to me—the World Series. The Oakland A's were playing in the Fall Classic against the Cincinnati Reds, the team that I had managed the year before. All of the inmates gathered in front of the TV each night to watch the games. I can't even begin to tell you how humbled I was by that experience. But like everything else, I kept those feelings to myself. I had brought all of those players along for 5 years and just when they hit their peak—I got kicked outta baseball! I had made a slew of bad choices that kept me from becoming a world champion manager—a crown I would like to have earned. I knew all of the Reds players and I understood their strengths and weaknesses. I knew how each player matched up against Oakland's pitchers. I knew how Oakland's hitters matched up against the Reds pitchers—which was heavy in our favor. Our three aces, Charlton, Meyers, and Dibble, weren't called the "Nasty Boys" for nothing. Rob Dibble was my right-handed reliever. I clocked Dibbs in the high 90s. Earlier in the year, Nolan Ryan had pitched his sixth no-hitter against the A's, so I knew they would have trouble against Dibble's heat as well. Lou Pinella took over for me as manager and made three roster changes. He acquired Billy Hatcher, Randy Meyers, and Glenn Bragg—three players who had career years. On top of that, Larkin, O'Neill, Sabo, Davis, and Duncan were all on one helluva hitting streak. The Reds swept Oakland in four straight games. Most folks said that Pete Rose's team won that World Series. But that isn't true. Hatcher, Meyers, and Bragg made a huge difference. As the games progressed, I began to predict the pitching changes, the hit-and-run strategies, and the pinch-hitter situations—all of which kept Guide, Catfish, and the other inmates entertained. "Watching the World Series with Pete Rose was an amazing experience," said Guide. "His enthusiasm was contagious. Pete predicted every move that Pinella made an inning before he made it. We had an older guy nick-named the 'Wizard of Odds,' who got busted for running a gambling syndicate. The wizard was harmless but he kept asking Pete what he thought about this game or that game. Then all of a sudden, Pete just clammed up. I think the wizard reminded Pete of some of the mistakes he had made in the past."

I was just having fun with the strategy of the World Series game. I honestly never gave it a second thought until the wizard started asking the personal questions. That's when I realized someone else might have motives that could get me into trouble. Hell, I was already in trouble. I was in jail, for chrissakes. But that was one of the first times that I even became "aware" of the potential for trouble. In years past, I had been oblivious to it. You see, I've always been pretty impulsive—no, very im-pulsive. If I have a thought—it'll damn sure roll off my lips. I knew that certain folks might take advantage. But that's the way I've always been. Maybe it's due to the ADHD because I don't always pay attention when people are talking to me. Maybe I'm just too trusting with other people. Either way, that aspect of my life has created more than a few problems. But while my impulsiveness led me to a gambling problem and eventu-ally to betting on baseball, it never led me to fixing a game. It might seem easy to do. A manager might pull a pitcher an inning too soon or leave him in the game an inning too long. He might take the bat out of a hitter's hands by calling for a bunt or a take. He might call for a hit and run at a risky time or pinch-hit against the wrong pitching matchup. He might even try to steal against a catcher who has a rocket arm. Hell, I reckon there's a bunch of ways for a player or manager to try and tank a ball game—all of which would be obvious to the rest of his team. You see, people aren't stupid and neither am I. Management, players, and fans would see right through that kind of thing in a heartbeat. It would destroy any credibility the player or manager might have—which reminds me of a story that has never quite been told.

Ray Schalk played catcher for the Chicago White Sox from 1912 to 1928. He caught four no-hitters and one perfect game. Ray finished with a lifetime average of only .253 but held some pretty impressive statistics as a defensive specialist. Ray Schalk was inducted into the Baseball Hall of Fame in 1955 despite the fact that he was a member of the 1919 "Black Sox"—the biggest scandal, next to mine, in baseball history. Now I'm a pretty good baseball historian. But since I wasn't even alive back then, I'll have to rely on some other first-hand accounts. Russell Schalk is a friend I met through the horse-breeding business. He runs a reputable little outfit up in Baltimore called Raintree Racing. Russell is also Ray Schalk's nephew. As a kid, Russell was pretty close to his Uncle Ray, who shared his recollections about the events that took place. Ray never discussed the scandal in public, but I reckon he wanted to make sure the truth got passed down through the family. Apparently, there were some gamblers who wanted to try and fix the 1919 World Series between the Chicago White Sox and the—talk about ironic—Cincinnati Reds. The gamblers were evaluating all of the players to try and determine which guys would be most willing to accept a payoff to blow the series. Catcher Ray Schalk was not on their list of candidates. So they passed him by. Instead, they got to most of the pitchers—guys most capable of controlling a game and less obvious to the public. Apparently, the owner of the White Sox—old man Comiskey—was a real prick. Most of the players hated him because he reportedly cheated them out of their bonuses and never paid market value for his players. So I guess, in part, the guys wanted to get back at an owner that they felt had it coming. Unlike today's players, who are all millionaires, the White Sox were living day to day. Most of them—especially

Shoeless Joe Jackson—really needed the money. Ray Schalk was behind the dish, calling the game, when he discovered that the pitcher was blowing off all of his signals. If Ray signaled for a fastball down and in— the pitcher threw a curve. If Ray called for a curveball—the pitcher threw a fastball. You can imagine how frustrating he must have felt knowing that he was being ignored on every call. It didn't take Ray too long to figure out what was going on. So after the first game, Ray took the pitcher under the stands and got into a shouting match, which eventually turned into a brawl. After that, Ray played it straight. He kept himself above the fray but with all the pitchers on the take, he had no options. He couldn't fight them all. So Ray Schalk dummied up. But he was also very impressed with Shoeless Joe Jackson because Joe decided to swing away throughout the series. I reckon Joe figured that a guy could only flub a fly ball or tank a grounder so often before the fans caught on. Joe must have figured that with the pitchers serving up gofer balls, his performance would have no effect on the outcome of the game. Joe hit .375 for the series, which tells you something about his hitting ability and his character. But the interesting thing about the fix was that the one other guy they never approached was the manager, Kid Gleason. I reckon the gamblers figured that the Kid had less ability to affect the game than his players, which goes to prove my point about managers and gambling.

It all boils down to good old-fashioned trust and credibility, which I seem to have lost in the hearts and minds of certain folks. But those same folks will put trust and credibility in other professionals without the same degree of scrutiny—something that has puzzled me during my 14 years in exile. For instance, what happened to the executives at Enron, who bilked millions from the company stockholders? Back in the days when I had a stock portfolio, I heard talk about "insider trading" on a regular basis. Hell, I didn't even know what it meant until I found out that it cost me money. What happened to Alex Karras and Paul Hornung after they made bets on football? Both guys paid a fine and got suspended for a year. The last I checked, the NFL survived the scandal. And it's a damn good thing because Karras and Hornung are both great guys—guys who made a mistake but were allowed to get on with their lives. Paul Hornung is now a broadcaster for Notre Dame football. Steve Howe and Darryl Strawberry violated baseball's drug policy—numerous times. Both men got suspended—numerous times. Baseball paid for their rehabilitation—numerous times. Yet I'm banned for life?

Truth is, some folks are held accountable and some aren't. Nobody said life is fair. I bet on baseball and I have to take responsibility for my actions. So let me start by saying this: I would rather die than lose a baseball game. I hate to lose. There is no temptation on the planet Earth that could ever get me to fix a game—none—end of story. Second, I never gambled for money. I gambled for the "action high," which I got from putting big bucks on the line in an effort to win. So, even if I was on a cold streak and down large to a bookie, I would never be tempted to tank a game because winning money was never my main objective. I was making almost two million dollars per year in those days. I didn't need money. I wagered the dollar amounts—large dollar amounts—that gave me the rush I needed. The money provided the "risk" not the "reason."

I read some bad publicity over Michael Jordan allegedly losing a half million dollars while playing blackjack in the Bahamas. But they failed to comment on the seven hundred thousand he reportedly won the following night. His net gain was two hundred grand. But even if he had lost, what difference is two hundred grand to a man who is earning over forty million dollars per year? I know guys who lost ten times that much in the stock market but had nowhere near the fun I had going to the racetrack . . . or the fun Jordan had on the blackjack tables. In fact, when Jordan's golf-course gambling came under scrutiny, Commissioner David Stern justified Jordan's gambling habits during an interview with Bob Costas.

In my experience, most athletes like to gamble. And just because an athlete gambles large amounts of money doesn't mean he's likely to fix a game. In fact the experts say there is no connection between the two. Professional athletes thrive on the day-to-day competition of their individual sport. We crave the action. We are driven to extremes. We thrive on winning. We play for world championship stakes. We play to win—not to throw games. But when the game is over, our competitive drive is still in full gear . . . just raring to go. Most of us will seek an outlet for all of that energy. Some guys play golf. Some drive race cars or fly jets. Some guys drink booze or chase women. Some guys go to church. Others drink booze, chase women, and go to church all at the same time! My outlet was gambling. It was my hobby and my passion. When I gambled, I always looked for an edge . . . a jockey who knew how to hug the rail . . . a trainer who had a great work ethic . . . a horse that could break fast and finish strong . . . a receiver who could cut across the middle without hearing footsteps . . . a boxer who could take a punch. Every bet I ever made, regardless of the sport, I made with the intention of winning the event, not the money. In fact, if I found out that a jockey was betting on himself to win, I'd bet that jockey every goddamn time. So, the idea of betting to "lose" is about as foreign to me as living on Mars. As out of control as I got with my gambling, I never bet against my own team—ever. I reckon if I could have been tempted to fix a game, I would've been tempted way back in 1987 when I was down six figures to the bookmakers. The idea never entered my mind. I'm just not wired that way. In fact, even the runners and bookmakers who testified against me swore that I never took any unusual advantage or used any inside information from injuries that affected my betting—the very thing that Rule #21 was designed to prevent.

Over the years, I've heard a lot of talk about the "integrity of the game" and how baseball could never let anyone break the gambling rules. Some folks have even implied that I am unworthy to set foot on a baseball field because of what I'd done. I've never really understood that way of thinking. But I understand now. I've had 14 years to think about the rules. Rule 21 is there to prevent even the appearance of corruption as well actual corruption. My actions, which I thought were benign, call the integrity of the game into question. And there's no excuse for that, but there's also no reason to punish me forever.

Danny Sheridan has been a friend for many years. I asked for his advice when I was offered a seven-figure salary to help promote legalized off-shore gambling. I turned down the offer even though I needed the money. I mean, who doesn't need a million dollars a year? But I knew that being associated with casino gambling would not help me to get back into the good graces of Major League Baseball. Danny is very knowledgeable in the world of sports and is currently the sports analyst for *USA Today*. "There was never any game that Pete Rose played in or managed that was ever taken off the board in Nevada," says Danny. "Although, I don't make any illegal bets, I know just about every legal and illegal bookmaker in the country. Believe me, if there had been even a hint of corruption, the big-time sports books would've heard about it within minutes. The American public wagers hundreds of millions of dollars every year on college and professional sports. In fact, wagers for college basketball has now exceeded wagers for the Super Bowl. With all the many sophisticated mechanisms in place, a person could not fix a regular season baseball game without being caught. The same goes triple for the LCS or World Series. The days of a Black Sox scandal are over. In fact, after knowing him for the last 14 years, I'd say the days of a Pete Rose scandal are over as well."

12

PUSHING THE ENVELOPE

"It's not that Pete refused to back down—he was incapable."
—BILLY GUIDE,
former police officer and fellow inmate

Most folks might look upon their incarceration as an opportunity for "emotional growth." But given my stubborn personality, I remained steadfastly resistant to any such growth. And I felt justified in my convictions because prison was not about rehabilitation. It was not about teaching or reform or anything that might actually help the inmates and that's why I felt obliged to bend a few rules. It was midwinter, and I had reached the point where I was getting sick and tired of standing naked in the snow one day each week at 6 o'clock in the morning waiting for the prison guard to stick his finger up my ass! I mean, what the hell was he looking for, a hacksaw? Hell, there weren't any bars on the barracks windows, so if someone really wanted to escape, he wouldn't need to stash a lethal weapon where the sun don't shine. The only pleasure I got from standing out there in the morning was watching the geese fly south for the winter.

I reckon I'd seen geese in the past. But I never really paid much attention until I lost my own freedom. Funny how you can take such simple pleasures for granted. But since I only had a short time left on my sentence, I was just trying to bide my time until I was done serving my time. Needless to say, I was getting a little antsy. And y'all know what happens when a feller gets antsy.

I reckon I had lost about 20 pounds by that time and my craving for good food was growing stronger by the day. So, just before Carol's last visit, I decided to splurge. Carol entered the visitor's area wearing a heavy winter coat. Maybe they thought she was pregnant because they let her pass without a body search. Ex-cop Larry Brady had been on the inside the longest. He knew all the guards and got tips on their comings and goings. As soon as Brady signaled the all-clear, Carol opened her coat—revealing 3 pounds of turkey, 2 pounds of roast beef, 2 pounds of cheese, and a loaf of fresh bread, which was all taped to her waist. Guide kept an eye out for the hacks while Brady distributed the food for my going-away feast. I don't know what I enjoyed more—eating the meal or watching the look on my friends' faces when Carol revealed all that grub. Their eyes lit up just like slot machines. In some ways, it was like going to the racetrack. I loved to take my friends to the track, especially if they'd never been before. I loved to bet the favorites for them—bets I knew they'd win just to see the look on their faces. You'd be surprised how excited a person could get from picking a winning horse—even when a $2 ticket paid just $3. In the same way, the excitement of getting the food in prison was greater than the food itself. We didn't eat as quickly as when I devoured that Big Mac but we came damn close. I'd say that within 2 minutes, every morsel was gone, which was a good thing because as soon as we finished, the guards came back for surveillance. This time, they smelled the food. The guards started sniffing around, looking for evidence but since Brady, Guide, and Catfish were all ex-cops, there was not one shred of evidence to be found. Lucky for us. You see the guards would rotate every 2 months from level six to level one, and there were different rules for security every time the new guards arrived. This particular batch had a hard-on for the campers. They liked to treat us the same way they treated the hardened criminals on level six. Brady had been in the joint for 20 years, so he explained why the new security was so tight. Back in the early 1980s, Marion had been an open penitentiary. Each prisoner was allowed to move around freely but had to sleep in his own cell, which was left unlocked during the night. But the inmates got rebellious, started a riot, and killed two prison guards. They stabbed one and decapitated another. After prisoners cut off the guard's head, they rolled it down the cellblock for everyone to see. The lieutenant on this particular watch was the son of that decapitated guard. You can just imagine how he felt about inmates. Brady told me to avoid him at all costs, which I honestly tried to do. But when it comes to the eye of a storm, I'm usually the first in line to drive right in it.

Catfish had scheduled a softball game with a team from the outside— the Salukis from Southern Illinois University, located right around the corner in Carbondale. After the game, he accepted a new windbreaker as a gift from the other coach and gave the windbreaker to me. Like I said, we weren't allowed to have any personal items in prison. So, when I got caught wearing the windbreaker, I was taken in for interrogation. The hacks wanted to know where I got my "contraband." I understood that the guards had a job to do. I understood that they had to keep some type of order. But can someone please tell me why in the hell wearing a windbreaker in 12° weather is considered a crime? I was just trying to keep from catching pneumonia. You'd thought I was trying to smuggle explosives into the main prison. They asked me the same goddamn questions over and over until I thought I was going to get accused of assassinating President Kennedy. Hell, at that point, I would have confessed just to be left alone. But I played dumb. I told the hacks that I found the windbreaker over at the softball field and offered to give it back. But they didn't believe me because they didn't *have* to believe me. I was a prisoner and they were the guards. The guards were always right and the inmates were always wrong—regardless of who was right or wrong.

"Pete really showed his true colors throughout that interrogation," said Guide. "He refused to give up Catfish, which tells you a lot about his loyalty. But I was worried about what might happen. Pete only had a short time left on his sentence. Catfish and I still had 5 years to serve. So Catfish went over to the lieutenant and confessed just to try and get Pete off the hook."

For our misdeeds, Catfish and I each got a "shot" against our records, which taught me a valuable lesson about just how selfish I had been. In fact, that whole "windbreaker scandal" was very instrumental toward helping me to turn my life around. It taught me to recognize those deep dark rebellious forces, which kept knocking my life off-track during pivotal times. I was so ashamed of my behavior that I was determined to correct the error of my ways and get back on the path of righteousness. Hallelujah, brothers and sisters, I had seen the light! I would not be tempted again to seek warmth and comfort from the freezing Illinois winter. I'd stand naked in the prison yard and catch my death of cold! "Amen, hallelujah," I said with tongue planted firmly in cheek. "Pete Rose would sin no more! Can I get an 'Amen' from all you fine folks out there in the book-reading public?"—Amen.

A few days later, I found myself in another tight spot. A fellow inmate, a friend of Guide's from Chicago, was going through a tough time. His son was dying of leukemia and the authorities wouldn't allow him to go home for a visit. So I tried to persuade the guards to do the right thing. "This is his son," I said. "Why don't you let the man out on a 2-day pass and then give him extra work detail when he comes back?" But they wouldn't listen. In fact, the guards got pissed off at me for standing up for the guy. They told me to mind my own business. So I did. Catfish brought me a softball, which I autographed. Catfish took the ball and hid it just outside the prison gates. The next day, his friend from the motor pool was supposed to pick up the ball and send it to the dying kid as a souvenir.

"I was proud of Pete for what he did," said Guide. "But it was another example of just how naïve he could be. The gesture was harmless but nothing went outside the prison gates without serious consequences. As an ex-cop, I had a lot of experience with informants. They were the worst kind of scum but a necessary evil to effective police work. The prison population was filled with squealers, who traded information for privilege. So, I knew someone was bound to rat him out."

Guide was right. Sure enough, later that day, the guards stormed into the barracks and rousted me out of my bunk. "Rose," one screamed. "Stand up and put your fuckin' hands behind your head." I think it was the lieutenant who slapped the handcuffs on me while another guard rifled through my footlocker. "What are you looking for?" I asked. "Contraband," he said. "You ain't gonna find no goddamn contraband in there," I replied. The guard started screaming and yelling . . . creating a big scene in front of everybody. Then he led me out, shoved me into the cop car and drove me over to the main prison. "I'd seen this kind of intimidation in the past but never quite so intense," said Guide. "That guard really had it in for Pete. He had just come down from level six, where the pressures of dealing with the hardcore prisoners had taken its toll. Maybe the guard was just blowing off steam. But Pete was a camper, for chrissakes. He shouldn't have signed the softball but he didn't deserve to be sent to the hole for it. I didn't see what happened after they took him away. But I knew Pete wouldn't back down. He was standing handcuffed, nose-to-nose with an irate guard, who was looking for any excuse to bust him. But Pete didn't even flinch. He was either oblivious to the whole thing or else he had ice in his veins. Either way, I was worried about his safety. When those hacks flew off the handle, there was no telling what they might do."

The yelling and screaming went on and on. The guard was trying to put the fear of God in me. But just before they dragged me over to the hole, the captain arrived on the scene and took control of the situation. "What the hell is going on here?" demanded the captain. The guard tried to explain that I was involved in a "conspiracy to smuggle contraband" off the prison grounds. But that excuse didn't fly. Hell, I had already told the captain what I did that afternoon. "Take those goddamn handcuffs off," screamed the captain. "Since when do you take it on yourself to run this prison?" The guard was busted. He thought he was going to take me out behind the woodshed and show me who's boss. But he couldn't buck the captain's orders. Hell, if he'd taken the handcuffs off me and called off his dogs, I would've been obliged to give him an ass-whuppin' myself. But the captain turned to me and said, "I'm sorry about this, Pete. This guy won't bother you any more." Then it was all over.

When I got back to the barracks, everyone was glad to see that I'd come back alive. "I thought I told you not to push the envelope with these guards," said Guide. "What, for signing a softball?" I replied. "Hell, the guard was more embarrassed than I was." When you think about it—you had to feel kind of sorry for the guards. I mean, what else were they going to do for excitement besides hassle the inmates . . . go to the Saluki basketball games? I love college basketball as much as anybody but when that's the biggest attraction in town, you're starved for excitement! Being a prison guard was a pretty dreary occupation. In fact, the only difference between them and us was that the guards got to go home at night!

"In all my years as a detective, I have never seen anyone like Pete Rose," said Guide. "Pete had to win at everything . . . softball . . . tennis . . . basketball—it didn't matter. Pete had to win. His showdown with that guard taught me a lot about his personality. Most people would have apologized, sucked up to the guards, or made some attempt to get off the hook. But not Pete Rose. In his own mind, he had done nothing wrong—just like wearing the windbreaker. It wasn't that Pete refused to back down—he was *incapable.*"

Hell, I never gave it a second thought at the time. If the guards couldn't see fit to help a man whose son was dying of leukemia, then they had a problem—not me! I damn sure wasn't going to apologize for doing the right thing. I never backed down from a fight in my life and I wasn't about to start with prison hacks.

But looking back on it now, I reckon I could see where Guide thought I was pushing the envelope. Maybe because he had already served 5 years . . . or maybe because I was a ballplayer and saw things from a different perspective—"Pete Rose logic." Either way, I wasn't about to change. Pushing the envelope came as natural to me as breathing. It had been my stock in trade for over 30 years . . .

. . . It was August of 1981 and the strike-shortened season was driving me crazy. I was 40 years old and every baseball game I missed was a game I'd never play! It was the year Laffit Pincay Jr. rode John Henry in the Santa Anita Handicap. I was playing for the Philadelphia Phillies and on the day after the strike ended, I got my 3,631st hit off Mark Littell of the St. Louis Cardinals. It took 19 years, but I had just broken Stan Musial's National League record for career hits. Stan "The Man" himself came out on the field and congratulated me along with my teammates Mike Schmidt, Lefty Carlton, and Larry Bowa. After the game, I held a press conference with a couple hundred reporters who had crowded into Veteran's Stadium. I was busy answering questions about what it felt like to be the new champ. Then, they handed me the telephone, which was hooked up to the stadium speakers. "Please hold for the president," said the voice from the White House. So, I held . . . and held . . . and held . . . until finally, the voice says, "I'm sorry Mr. Rose, he'll have to call you right back." So, I hung up the phone and went back to my press conference.

The phone rang three or four more times but each time we got disconnected or interrupted by some technical problem. Finally, on the last try, I heard this voice: "Pete Rose?" asked President Reagan. "Yeah, how ya doin?" I replied. "I'm glad a missile wasn't on the way!" All the reporters started laughing while I spoke with Mr. Reagan. But later, some guy made a stink, saying that I was disrespectful to the president of the United States. What the hell was I supposed to say? I waited my whole life to break that record and he kept interrupting my press conference. I mean . . . he interrupted *my* party. I appreciated the call and I understood his position of respect. But that doesn't mean I'm suppose to kneel in front of him. After that episode, writers from all over the country wrote negative things about me in the papers. They said I was arrogant . . . that I didn't appreciate being "upstaged" by the president. But I wasn't arrogant. Hell, I never called the White House to interrupt Ronald Reagan while he was having one of his meetings with Gorbachev.

"There is an obvious difference between being cordial and kneeling down," says teammate and Hall of Famer Mike Schmidt. "But Pete's perception of the two shows his true competitive nature. Pete has a hitter's mentality, which means he is notoriously selfish—but in a good way. Selfishness is an essential part of a great hitter's success. In most cases, it carries over into other aspects of life . . . especially with Pete."

Throughout my career, other players have often described my behavior as something out of the ordinary. But I never understood their point of view. I was just being true to myself. In an ESPN television broadcast, writer Frank Deford quoted Richie Ashburn as saying, "Whether it's baseball, gambling, or sex, I've never seen anyone more obsessed than Pete Rose." Ashburn was right in his observation. I had huge appetites and I was always hungry. Red Smith described me in this way: "He waited to hit that ball in his low crouch with an almost lascivious enthusiasm." I don't even know what "lascivious" means, but it sounds good!

I was at an autograph show recently, which was held for former World Series MVPs. I ran into my old friend Ron Cey. I can call Ron a friend now but he was no friend when he played for the Dodgers. Back in those days, I used to go to extremes to get an edge on the competition. Ron Cey, Bill Russell, Steve Garvey, and Davey Lopes were all young up-and-comers at that time. Eventually, they would set a major league record for playing together for over eight seasons. But at that time, I didn't want them to think they had a prayer against the Reds. I had forgotten exactly what happened but Ron reminded me of our first meeting at Dodger Stadium. "I was in the cage, taking batting practice before our game against the Reds," said Cey. "I had never even met Pete Rose but this was the heyday of the Big Red Machine, so his reputation preceded him. Pete struts right up to our cage and without even saying hello takes a look at two or three of my swings. Then he says: 'I've seen enough. The only way you guys are going to win the pennant is if our fuckin' plane goes down.' Then Pete walked away. I was a rookie at the time and I was just blown away. But that was Pete Rose—fiercely competitive." If the "Penguin" says that's how it happened then by God, that's how it happened. Truth is, I'm surprised I even took the time to watch him swing the bat. I knew Ron Cey could hit. But I wanted to plant the seed of defeat in his head before the game even got started.

. . . In 1973, I was voted the League MVP. I won my third batting title with a .338 average and led the league with 230 hits. The Reds won their division title and were heading into the playoffs against the Mets, who were coached by one of my favorite people—Yogi Berra. As y'all know, Yogi caught for the Yankees during some of their best dynasty years. But seeing Yogi in that Met's uniform was like putting earrings on a hog—completely unnatural! Yogi Berra was a Yankee—not a Met. They had another great player who was out of uniform, too—Willie Mays. So right away, I knew we had the advantage. I figured the Mets were having an "identity crisis" because several of their players were dressed in disguise. But I knew we were in for an exciting series because baseball in New York is always exciting. New York fans are second only to Cincinnati fans in their enthusiasm for the game. New Yorkers, though, are in sole possession of first place when it comes to being crazy. Bench and I both hit home runs in the last two innings to win the first game of the series. But the Mets shut us out to take the second game. Their bats stayed hot because they were smoking us 9-2 in the third game. I came to the plate in the top of the fifth. We had the meat of our batting order coming up, so I was looking to start a rally. Hell, I started more than a rally. I started a riot. Actually, I didn't start it—I finished it. I hit safely for a single. Then Joe Morgan hit a strong grounder to Milner, who threw to second to get the lead out. I slid hard into second base to break up the double play but when I came up off the bag, I accidentally hit Bud Harrelson in the face. He was wearing flip-up sunglasses, which must have cut his forehead. When he saw the blood, he looked over at me and said, "You cocksucker!" If he'd called me an asshole or a sonfabitch, I'd a just left him alone. But nobody calls me a cocksucker and gets away with it. So I grabbed him and took him to the ground. I was 35 pounds heavier than Bud, so I wasn't looking to kick his ass. It would not have been a fair fight. I just wanted to point out the error in Bud's choice of vocabulary. But before I could even do anything, Red Garrett comes running over from third base and tackles me from the blind side. Talk about dirty! That's what started the whole brawl. Before I knew it, both benches emptied onto the field and we had ourselves a humdinger of a fight. My buddy Pedro Borbon was the first guy out of the Reds bull pen. He slapped a knot on Buzz Capra's head that escalated the whole brawl. The two of them really went after each other. Pedro ripped a hunk of hair out of Capra's head and threw it on the ground. Jon Matlack threw a punch at me but I didn't get a chance to fight back because I was on the bottom of the pile. Finally, big Ted Kluszewski, one of the Reds coaches, pulled me off the fray. The whole scuffle lasted for over 20 minutes. Pedro Borbon backed off and put Capra's baseball cap on his own head by mistake. When Pedro realized he was wearing a Met's cap, he started growling like an animal and took little bites out of the bill and spit them on the ground. Capra followed him around and started picking up the pieces. I reckon the Met's budget must have been real tight because they wouldn't give Capra a new hat unless he turned in the old one—even in little pieces! Eventually, we got back to playing the baseball game . . . or so I thought. By the time I got out to left field for the next inning, the New York fans started showering me with their appreciation—beer cans, hot dogs, and everything but the kitchen sink. Hell, I did what any red-blooded American would do. I threw the stuff right back at them. Then, I got bombarded with just about everything you could imagine. There was so much shit flying in the air that Shea Stadium looked like Times Square on New Year's Eve. One guy threw a bottle of Jack Daniels that barely missed my head. Just like a New York fan— sumbitch was empty. Now, I'd been hit by stuff before so I wasn't too concerned. Once in Chicago, some guy threw a crutch at me from the upper deck. I wasn't worried for myself. But if that guy needed crutches to get to the stadium, how'd he get back home? Anyway, the confetti kept flying at Shea until finally, Sparky Andersen came onto the field and waved us all into the dugout. He wasn't going to take a chance on getting any of his players hurt. I heard that someone called in Chub Feeney, the N.L. president, to try and stop the game from going to forfeit due to a lack of crowd control. But the fans didn't back down. Eventually, Tom Seaver and Willie Mays had to go out into left field along with a dozen of New York's finest to stop the ruckus. By the time I came to bat in the ninth inning, I could still hear the fans booing their asses off. But that didn't stop me. It made me stronger. The fans didn't know it but they were actually helping me. Unlike most folks, I thrive on conflict. Conflict inspires me. So I hit a single, which infuriated the fans even more. Once I got on base, Ed Sudol, the first-base umpire, looked at me and said, "Be careful when this is all over, Pete." Hell, I didn't want it to be over. We were down 9-2 but I thought we still had time to rally and win the game. I mean, wouldn't a come-from-behind victory be the perfect way to shut up the fans? Then, I looked over and saw my teammates, who were holding their bats in the dugout. I guaran-damn-tee they weren't getting ready for batting practice. They were preparing for a potential post-game riot. But our rally fizzled out and the Mets won that game 9-2. I ran off the field as quickly as I could. That night, I was told by management not to go out to dinner. They were hanging up Pete Rose "Wanted—Dead or Alive" posters in Queens. So I stayed in the hotel and ordered a steak from room service. The steak was an hour late and burnt to a crisp—compliments of the cook, who happened to be a Mets fan. The next day, Reds GM, Bob Howsam, came to me and asked if I would meet at home plate and shake hands with Bud Harrelson before the start of the next game as a gesture of good sportsmanship. Bob said the act would help settle down the angry New York fans and make me look good at the same time. Bob was right about one thing. It would have been an "act." "Hell no," I said. "I ain't shaking hands in the middle of a playoff series. I don't care how it makes me look. I came here to win a series—not a popularity contest." I never shook hands with Bud Harrelson. Truth is, it wasn't the right thing to do. It would have been phony. And the one thing New York people hate is phony. As it turned out, I made the right choice. The next game wasn't played against the Mets—it was played against the entire city of New York. The fans were jeering me throughout the whole ballgame. But I got my reckoning. In the bottom of the 12th, I broke a 1-1 tie with a game-winning home run. I ran the bases like I owned them and then stomped on home plate with both feet just to defy the bastards. Then the damnedest thing happened. Over half of the people in Shea Stadium started cheering. The same fans that were ready to kill me the night before were now paying their respects. It didn't make any sense. But then it made perfect sense. The fans hated to see their team lose but they loved to watch good baseball, which is what I'd given them. It confirmed what I already knew about the people of New York and about life—you couldn't be phony. You gotta do what comes natural. Years later, a young pitcher named John Rocker came to New York with a great fastball and a wild attitude. But Rocker made a mistake that I never made. He criticized the *people* of New York.

New York was a good distance from Marion federal prison and those play-off days were long past. But since the joint was in Carbondale, Illinois—the home of former Cleveland Indians' catcher, Ray Fosse—I hope you'll indulge me with the last, and most famous, example of pushing the envelope.

The year was 1970—the year of the grand opening of Riverfront Stadium and the year the Cincinnati Reds hosted the All-Star game. After 7 years in the big leagues, I had earned some pretty good statistics—Rookie of the Year in 1963, closing in on 1,500 hits, my fifth All-Star game, won the batting crown in 1968 and 1969, hitting .335 and .348 respectively. I was also the league's *first* $100,000 singles hitter. My reputation for hard work and determination made me a favorite with the Cincinnati fans, which convinced the Reds I was worth the money. I was a blue-collar kid who played all-out and balls-to-the-wall—which is what the fans paid to see. The night before the All-Star game, I invited Sam McDowell and his wife out to dinner at the Sycamore Shores restaurant. Sam asked if he could bring along a young catcher by the name of Ray Fosse. I said, "Sure, bring the kid along." Kid—hell, I was only 29 years old myself. After dinner, we all went back to my house where we talked baseball until about 3:30 in the morning. Fosse idolized Johnny Bench. What young catcher didn't? Bench was on track to hit over 40 home runs that year—a feat unheard of until Mike Piazza and Pudge Rodriguez came along. Fosse kept asking me questions about how Bench did this . . . or how Bench did that, until finally, I just fell asleep on the couch. Apparently, I had a little trouble waking up the next day because we were losing the All-Star game 3-1 going into the ninth inning. Then, Catfish Hunter served up a gofer ball to Dick Dietz and Roberto Clemente capped off our rally with a single that tied the score at four apiece. I reckon if we had been playing in Milwaukee in 2002, we would have called it quits, got on our private jets, and flown to New York for the ESPY Awards! But this was 1970, when players came to the All-Star game to win—not tie.

In the bottom of the 12th inning, Joe Torre and Roberto Clemente grounded out, which was not unusual with American League infielders like Brooks Robinson, Carl Yastrzemski, and Sandy Alomar. Then I came up to bat against Clyde Wright of the Angels, who had pitched two goose-egg innings. Clyde was a big farm boy from Tennessee, who had a curve-ball that matched his nasty temper. Clyde tried to fool me with a breaking ball, but I waited on it and drove a shot to centerfield. Then, Billy Grabarkewitz hit a single, which moved me over to second base. The first thing that came to mind was that my dad was in the stands, watching to see if I learned what he taught me about base running. With two outs, I wanted to score the winning run in front of my hometown fans. I'm thinking, "anything hit on the ground ends the inning. But anything hit to the outfield gives me a chance to score." A chance is all I wanted. So I took a big lead. On the next pitch, Jim Hickman hit a rope to centerfield that Amos Otis must have played on a one-hop. But I was already on a tear. Third-base coach Leo Durocher waved me on, but even if he hadn't, I was heading toward home. Ray Fosse moved up the baseline and blocked the plate, which is exactly what a catcher is supposed to do—exactly what his idol Johnny Bench would've done. As the throw came in from Otis, I had no choice but to lower my shoulder and barrel into Fosse—a crash that sent us both ass-over-elbows. I didn't know it at the time but the ball never touched Fosse's glove. I slapped home plate, which gave the National League a 5-4 victory. Needless to say, the crowd went wild. I reckon most of the 65 million television viewers felt the same way because at that time, ours was the highest rated All-Star game ever.

After the collision, I asked Ray if he was okay. He nodded but I could tell that he was hurt. Hell, I was hurt. I only missed 10 games during that entire decade and 3 of them came from that one play! Ray didn't miss any games. He probably should have. He suffered a separated shoulder that plagued him throughout the rest of his career, which didn't last too long after that. In those days, guys had to play through their injuries. We didn't have guaranteed contracts. So being a young star, whose career was on the rise, Fosse sucked it up and played with the pain. Today, Ray would've had an MRI and been put on the disabled list for 6 weeks, which probably would have saved his career. Hell, can you imagine what would have happened if Ray had caught the ball and tagged me out? He would've been the All-Star game hero and I would've been the goat. But I was 195 pounds, the son of a football player, charging toward the end zone with a full head of steam. Ray was standing still. Do the math. Like every catcher, Ray knew the risk involved in blocking the plate. He never blamed me for getting hurt. But I caught a ton of flack from the American League fans who thought I was too aggressive. Too aggressive? Hell, we weren't playing girls' volleyball. My dad taught me to play aggressive and that's the only way I knew how to play. I told the fans what I told the press: "I play to win—period." Who would've thought that 20 years later, I'd be sitting in prison in Ray Fosse's hometown?

Looking back on the highlights of my baseball career, I've come to the conclusion that I was very competitive. Competitive—hell, I was obsessed. You have to be obsessed to accomplish what I did. Frank Sinatra was obsessed. So was Elvis . . . Belushi . . . Ruth . . . Michael Jordan . . .

Cobb . . . and a bunch of other athletes, entertainers, and businessmen who would not—or could not—accept losing. The Wright Brothers were obsessed with flying. Henry Ford was obsessed with cars. I was obsessed with winning. The "never back down from a fight" attitude, which I got from my mom . . . and the perfectionist work ethic, which I got from my dad, served me pretty damn well on the baseball field. But that attitude has also wreaked havoc in my personal life—havoc that I've been trying to come to grips with.

According to Arnold Wexler, from the Council on Compulsive Gambling of New Jersey, "The typical compulsive gambler is someone with *unreasonable optimism*. They believe that they can accomplish anything. At times, during the peak of their sensation, they are oblivious to the circumstances surrounding them. They believe that they can't lose . . . that they are invincible."

I reckon "unreasonable optimism" accurately describe parts of my sports gambling and most of my baseball showdowns, including some I had with them prison guards. But during all that time, I never considered my attitude as anything but positive. "Unreasonable optimism" accounted for 4,256 hits—the most in baseball history. "Unreasonable optimism" accounted for 3,215 singles—the most in baseball history. "Unreasonable optimism" accounted for 14,053 at-bats and 7 other major league records—none of which are likely to be broken in my lifetime. Hell, can you imagine what I could have accomplished had I just been "reasonable?"

13

THE LONG ROAD BACK

*"It wasn't until I got to the halfway house
that I realized how well the prison was run."*
—PETE ROSE

They say that all good things must come to an end. And so it was with my
stay in the prison camp at the federal penitentiary in Marion. As it turned
out, I never got to meet Colonel Klink. But I met some good friends—
friends who weren't interested in my athletic accomplishments, my
celebrity status, or the way I threw my money around. Guide, Catfish, and
Brady were all stand-up guys, who had nothing to gain from being my
friend. I couldn't get them free tickets to the ballgames, take them out to
dinner at expensive restaurants, or introduce them to sexy women. Still,
they offered their friendship and support without asking or expecting anything in return. They helped me get through one of the toughest times of
my life. And for that, I was much obliged. But I had served my time and I
was ready to get back on with my life. I said goodbye to all the guys and
wished them well. I gave them my phone number and promised to stay in

touch. I told them to call if they ever needed any help on the outside. Just before I left, I pulled my last piece of "contraband" out of my pocket and gave it to Guide for good luck—a "Get out of jail free" card from my son's Monopoly game, which Carol brought during her last visit. Guide laughed . . . thanked me for doing him a "solid."

On January 7, 1991, I was given a heavy winter coat by the prison authorities. I thought: "How in the hell could they *give* me a heavy coat to wear home yet bust my ass for wearing a flimsy windbreaker while I was on the inside?" I reckon it was okay to catch pneumonia as a prisoner but not as a civilian! Grinning at the absurdity, I walked out of the federal penitentiary in Marion a free man. Two dozen reporters were camped outside but prison security kept them at a distance of 50 yards. The media was looking for a hot story. But I didn't give them one. In fact, for the first time in my life, I said nothing at all. I just walked across the street and got into my wife's car. I was tired of being the lead story. For the first time since 1960, I was just a "regular guy." Reuven Katz had arranged for a private plane to fly us back to Cincinnati. The drive to the Paducah airport was nothing like the drive going into prison 5 months earlier. I wasn't dreading this trip—I was looking forward to it. I never even closed my eyes. I looked—no, stared at everything—trees, buildings, horses, even the geese. I remembered the geese. But this time, I was able to watch for more than just a few seconds before they flew over the prison walls.

Upon arriving back in Cincinnati, Carol and I drove over to the Precinct restaurant, where my friend Jeff Ruby arranged for a private lunch. The "welcome home" signs were a reminder of happier times. I ate my first decent meal in 5 months, shared a few laughs, and got caught up on some local news. Then I went to the corner of the bar to read the sports page, a daily ritual that I missed during my stay in prison. I was anxious to get caught up on all the teams, so I grabbed a *Cincinnati Enquirer*, turned to the sports page, and saw something that caught my attention—

an ad from Premier Sports, Janszen's company, hawking "Pete Rose autographed baseballs." These were the ones he said were meant to be Christmas presents for all the employees at his friend's company. The ad reminded me of a bad joke. But I wasn't angry anymore. I was amused. Earlier in the day, Carol reminded me that my sportswriter friend never returned her calls while I was in prison. I reckon that since I was kicked out of baseball, he didn't feel the need to repay his $20,000 debt. But he had to live with his choices just as I had to live with mine. Either way, I had no time to dwell on the past. I had to get on with the future.

I felt relieved to be out of prison but I was not out of the woods. In addition to my 5 months at Marion, I was sentenced to 3 months in a halfway house, 1,000 hours of community service, and 1 year of probation with continued treatment for my gambling disorder. I had to report to the Talbert House in Mount Auburn, the ghetto section of Cincinnati, by 5 o'clock that afternoon. By the time I arrived, dozens of reporters and hundreds of fans were standing behind the police barricades, waiting to get the scoop on my release from prison. I pushed past the crowd and entered the halfway house—one of the biggest shocks of my life. I wasn't expecting to stay at the Hilton but I sure wasn't expecting to be stuck in a hellhole either. The whole environment just upset me. The lady who ran the place thought she was a prison warden. She brought me into her office on the first day and said, "I don't care who you are—you're going to do as you're told!" Hell, I hadn't even said a word and I was already being treated like a troublemaker. I was taken upstairs and given an army cot in the corner of a dingy old room. Like prison, I didn't sleep much during the first night. I was a little distracted by the constant sound of police sirens, gunshots, and the scampering noise from the rats in the attic. When I woke up the next morning—all of my clothes had been stolen. The halfway house was filled with robbers, rapists, and killers—guys who committed state, not federal, crimes. Every other word out of their mouths was "fuck this" and "fuck that." The inmates were all big-mouthed, hardened criminals, who had no regard for anyone. They were the worst people I had ever been around in my life. I thought about teaching them some respect but if I got caught in a fight—I'd get sent right back to prison. So I decided to bide my time and make the best of a bad situation. Carol wanted to bring Tyler and Cara for a visit but I refused to let my family come anywhere near that environment. It was no place for adults, let alone women and children. I didn't realize how well the prison was run until I lived in the halfway house. At times, I was ordered to provide a random urine sample for drug and alcohol tests. I had to urinate into a bottle in front of a counselor, who watched to make sure the sample wasn't tampered with. I explained that I never used drugs or alcohol. But the counselor didn't care. "Rules are rules," he said.

I left the Talbert House at 6:30 every morning, Monday through Friday, to report to my weekday job as an assistant gym teacher. I was assigned to rotate between five of the inner city's low-achieving elementary schools—all part of the 1984 Bronson desegregation agreement. I was actually looking forward to working with the kids. Obviously, teaching gym was going to be a whole lot better than sweeping floors in the prison. But I was shocked by the condition of the school system. There wasn't a day that went by where I didn't see a teacher get assaulted by a student—white or black. All the teachers through the sixth grade were female. So the kids walked all over them . . . disrespected everything that was taught. Some kids were nice but a lot of them acted like real animals—had big chips on their shoulders. They wanted to show the world how tough they were. I didn't want to mislead anyone or pretend that I was on a mission to rescue those kids from a bad environment. But after 5 months in federal prison and three World Championships, I felt like I had something to offer in the way of advice. But how was I supposed to get the message across to a bunch of first and second graders who were too young to understand anything about life. None of them were even old enough to have seen me play baseball.

My wife, Carol, was furious with the situation. She was under the impression that the halfway house was supposed to provide the opportunity for a man to reunite with his family and his community. I wasn't reunited with either. I was put into a position where I could do the least possible good. So Carol paid a surprise visit to Judge Arthur Spiegel and asked him to grant permission for me to perform my community service in Florida, where I could be near my family. But Judge Spiegel told Carol that "Pete Rose owed a debt to Cincinnati." Finally, Carol asked why I wasn't placed in the local high schools, where I could have an impact on the older kids. But Judge Spiegel had no answer. As it turned out, Judge Spiegel's wife, Louise, was a member of the Bronson Community Task Force, which is why I was placed in her coalition of schools. But when Carol accused the judge of "playing politics" with my community service, the judge felt insulted and threatened to place her in contempt of court. I told Carol to drop the whole matter because arguing with a judge was like arguing with a prison guard. "You can't win," I said. "Like prison, the halfway house is not about rehabilitation or reform. It's about humiliation and control."

While living in the ghetto, I got hit with another devastating blow. Baseball commissioner Fay Vincent went to the board of directors of the Hall of Fame and persuaded them to pass a new rule. On February 4, 1991, the board unanimously agreed that any player on the suspended list was no longer eligible for consideration into the Hall of Fame. Under the previous rule, I would have been in my first year of eligibility because I retired from the active roster in 1986. But with the rule change, I would no longer be eligible until the commissioner lifted my suspension. The press called it "The Pete Rose Rule"—another example that baseball felt no obligation to live up to the agreement signed by Mr. Giamatti. I entered into my contract in good faith with the understanding that I would be considered for reinstatement after one year. But baseball had absolute authority to change the rules—God-like power. It was just another reminder that "permanently" is a long, long time.

During evenings and weekends, I was allowed out of the halfway house for specific visits but had to be back before 9 o'clock curfew. I was also allowed "medical leave" in order to perform rehabilitation exercises on my knees. During that time, I would visit with my wife and kids or spend time with some longtime friends like Arnie Metz. Arnie brought my lunch from Montgomery Inn almost everyday. I told him not to go out of his way but Arnie was determined to do me a solid. He said he wanted to pay me back for everything I'd done for him.

"Nobody knows about this," said Metz, "but Pete always went out of his way to help the little people. He just never allowed any of us to talk about it. On the night he broke Ty Cobb's record, he was scheduled to attend a big celebration at the Waterfront restaurant. At the time, my wife was still in the hospital with our son, Matthew, who was born three weeks premature. Pete knew that things were touch-and-go with our baby, so after he finished his press conference at the stadium, Pete drove over to Good Samaritan Hospital and visited with us for about a half an hour. Everyone in the hospital was shocked to see him. I'm thinking: 'Pete just broke one of the biggest records in the history of baseball, and instead of going out on the town, he's visiting with me and my family!' Geesus, I couldn't ask for a better friend than Pete Rose. Of course, I brought his lunch over to the halfway house. Hell, I would've brought him breakfast and dinner too if he'd asked."

My son Pete Jr. was not playing baseball during the winter, so I got an opportunity to visit with him. On the way back from the gym, we stopped off at the Ball Game batting cage, where Pete Jr. and I had spent a lot of time practicing over the years. Pete took me over to the center cage and challenged me to face the 90 mph pitching machine. I hadn't picked up a bat in over 18 months. But I always felt comfortable with a baseball bat in my hands. I took a few practice swings, started to draw a crowd, then settled in for the pitch. On the first cut—I drove the ball right into the middle of the ball machine and knocked it off the ground, disabling the motor. I put down my bat and received a round of applause from the crowd, who had gathered to watch. I decided my first swing would also be my last. Pete Jr. just grinned and said, "Some things never change!" Petey was right about my swing—it hadn't changed. It was the most rock-solid, dependable talent I had. But in all honesty, other things had changed. The overall reception to my return to Cincinnati was mixed. The Queen City had been my oyster for 26 years but many of the local folks needed time to heal from the wounds that were created from my scandal. My roots ran too deep in the city to allow for a return to life as I once knew it. But that didn't stop me from trying. In many ways, I wanted to give something back to the community.

I continued with my weekly job 5 days a week for 3 months. I was never late, and I never called in sick. I was told to teach gym, and that's exactly what I did. In fact, I got along well with most of the kids.

In April of 1991, I completed my 3 month stint at the halfway house and began serving the remainder of my community service at the LeBlond Boys and Girls Club in Over-the-Rhine, Cincinnati. Within a few short days, I realized that the Boys and Girls Club had something that the school system was missing—discipline. During that time, I gave several fundraising speeches and suggested the school system find a way to get the inner city kids to react with the same enthusiasm for life as the kids from the Boys and Girls Club. This was my first experience with any organization outside of baseball. So I was at a loss for coming up with a solution to the problem. But at least I was willing to help. Truth is—most of the kids just needed some direction. But there just weren't enough qualified teachers to provide what was needed. I urged everybody in the community to pitch in because the city really needed help in that area. The kids at the club had more privileges and opportunities, which created a better atmosphere for success. If enough people got involved and offered their support, I knew progress could be made with the inner-city school system.

During the remainder of my community service, I was allowed to attend weekend card and memorabilia shows, which provided a means of earning a living. I was also given a local talk show with WCKY radio—"On the Ball with Pete Rose." The Reds were coming off their World Series championship, so expectations and enthusiasm were running high on Opening Day. Even though I was not allowed direct contact with the Reds, I was able to keep in contact with the fans, who called in to ask questions and voice their opinions. The entire experience was very positive—the first real steps toward reuniting with my community. I answered questions about my playing career, the Reds pitching rotation, and even the unlikely potential of a player's salary cap. Throughout the show, I tried my best to answer honestly and give the fans their money's worth. I got the strong impression that most of them were supportive and willing to forgive and forget. But others wanted to pry into the past and dig up old evidence. While on the air, I apologized for my mistakes and accepted responsibility. "It was my fault," I said. "And I'm very sorry that I disappointed my fans. But I'm doing the right thing now and I'm optimistic about my business opportunities outside of baseball. I just want to go on and live a normal life." I also made a point of thanking my wife and family for their support during my 16-month ordeal. But after everything I'd been through with the investigation and going to prison, I had no interest in re-hashing the past.

Within a few weeks, I was invited to appear on NBC's *Real Life with Jane Pauley*. It would be my first television appearance since getting out of prison and I was a little anxious. I wasn't sure if the national audience would be as forgiving as the local folks. Jane Pauley asked some pretty tough questions. She tried to spin the discussion toward betting on baseball. But I closed the door on that issue when I signed my agreement, which stated that the "Commissioner will not make any formal findings or determinations on any matter including without limitation the allegation that Peter Edward Rose bet on any Major League Baseball game." I spent over a million dollars to get that finding and I damn sure wasn't going to throw it all away and open a whole new can of worms. Still, I kept my sense of humor and talked honestly about prison and the halfway house—aspects of my future, not my past. I also took the blame and admitted to learning from my mistakes.

After I completed my community service, I decided that I would be better off moving to Florida. My family needed to escape the constant harassment they were getting around town. So we put some distance between my past and me. I wasn't running away from anything but living in exile from baseball would be easier if I was away from the great memories that surrounded me in Cincinnati. I had to sell my interest in the Precinct and Waterfront restaurants because as an ex-con, I could not hold a liquor license. I moved to Boca Raton and joined my family in our two-bedroom crackerbox apartment. I told Carol, "It won't always be like this." But she didn't seem too concerned. The thrills of being a mother kept her content. She didn't miss the big house, the fancy cars, or the money. She was completely happy with raising our young kids Tyler and Cara. Unlike me, Carol didn't crave life in the fast lane. She was a down-home girl with simple tastes. I didn't realize it at the time but she would provide the basic foundation for keeping my life grounded. How many women would stick with their man after he'd lost his fortune and went to prison? Damn few—that's for sure.

I was an ex-con with no formal education and no job prospects. I had no idea how I would earn a living. But I knew two things—I wasn't going to be in baseball and I wasn't going to make any illegal bets. Based on the type of person I am, I believed that someone would take a chance on me. During that time, my son Pete Jr. was playing for the White Sox organization in Sarasota. So I got a chance to watch him play baseball on a regular basis—something I missed during his childhood years. He was just 22 years old and loaded with potential. He was hitting .300 and seemed to be more relaxed after all the publicity from my scandal had settled down. I was optimistic that he would soon be in the majors, where I could watch him play the same way my dad watched me.

I tried my luck at playing golf but that particular sport is too slow for my taste. I spent a lot of free time with Carol and the kids—went to the zoo and to the beach. But I'm not a typical stay-at-home dad. I'm too hyperactive to stay in one place for very long. I need challenges to stay motivated. I need "action." Within a few days, I was invited to appear on the Johnny Carson show in Burbank, California. As I was announced, Doc Severinsen, the band leader, played "Take Me Out to the Ballgame." After I took my seat next to Johnny, I looked over at Doc and said, "Thanks for not playing 'Jail House Rock'!" Johnny broke into a big laugh, which made me feel like a king. Hell, I was the king—The Hit King! But in that split second, I learned that by laughing at my own mistakes, the crowd would laugh with, not *at*, me. I got the same response that George Brett of the Royals received when he said, "My hemorrhoid problems are all behind me now," during the 1980 World Series . . . which was won by my Phillies teammates and me. After I finished my interview on the *Tonight Show*, I felt confident that somehow I would land on my feet and survive my future outside of baseball.

When I returned to Florida, I remembered what my dad said when he knocked his son-in-law out on the front lawn: "A man who doesn't take care of his own family ain't a real man." I also remembered my love for horses. With that in mind I decided to take a stab at one of my lifelong dreams—horse breeding. I made a call to my good friend Wayne

Lyster. Outside of my family, Wayne was the only friend that I allowed to visit while I was in prison. I first met Wayne toward the end of my playing career. He was a big baseball fan but we became friends based on our mutual love for horses. Wayne grew up in the horse breeding business and owned Ashview Farms in Versailles, just outside of Lexington, Kentucky. Together, Wayne and I owned two race horses and shared a great deal of fun by trying to reach the winner's circle. Our colt actually won a race at Turfway Park, which turned out to be the highlight of our racing career. But Wayne and I were ready to move on to bigger and better opportunities.

We decided to pool our meager resources and try our luck in the breeding business. But we needed a game plan. As chairman of the Kentucky Racing Commission, Wayne had access to lots of great people—and lots of great advice. Wayne invited me for the annual train ride to the Derby. Shortly there after, we went to Keeneland for the yearling sale and began our efforts to put together a first-class breeding and racing program.

Every year, there are hundreds of good horses out there. But only a handful ever make it to the top. Most folks get into racing for the sport of it. But people who go into the racing business have to accept the fact that they are going to lose money—unless they get lucky enough to find some really good horses their first time out. There are some success stories out there—like Funny Cide, who was bought for peanuts by a group of high school buddies. But those stories are few and far between. First you have to buy a good broodmare. After you breed the mare to a stallion, you wait 11 months before the colt arrives. After the colt comes, you still have to wait because he can't run until he's 2 years old. So if you're breeding to race, you have to wait a total of 3 years. During that time, you're spending a lot of money with nothing coming back into the coffers. To stay in business, you need enough broodmares and colts to pick a few of the choice ones to keep, and then sell the rest. It takes a huge amount of time, experience, and money. At 50 years of age, I was beyond the stage of spending years in the "minor leagues," while waiting for a break. I was ready to shoot for the moon. To start a successful breeding business, you need between $5 and $10 million per year for 3 years. In order to get that kind of money, you need credibility.

To get "credibility," we took a page out of the playbook of the most successful trainer in horseracing history—D. Wayne Lukas, who also had a great passion for horses. He began training quarterhorses in the southwest and after achieving a certain amount of success, moved on to thoroughbreds. One of D. Wayne's first customers was Gene Klein, who owned the San Diego Chargers. Gene took an immediate liking to D. Wayne Lukas and funded his first efforts into the racing business. Together, they went to Keeneland and bought some really good young horses, which was D. Wayne's specialty. He was always successful at picking the best young horses and getting them ready to race. As a result, he always attracted the same kind of investors—the kind who were willing to pay for the top 2-year-olds. In a very short period of time, D. Wayne Lukas rose to the top of the thoroughbred business. Today, he holds a lot of very impressive records in the racing world. He has won the Derby, the Breeders' Cup, and the Preakness. The only race he hasn't won is the Belmont but eventually, he'll win that one as well.

But since D. Wayne Lukas had a history of working with celebrity clients, I decided to add my name to his list. After just one phone call, D. Wayne Lukas agreed to partner with Wayne Lyster and me—instant "credibility." Our game plan was developing.

I wanted to accomplish the same goals in breeding that I accomplished as a hitter. Each year, I set my goals for 200 hits and 100 runs scored. I knew that I had to get 650 at-bats to accomplish that goal, so I always conditioned myself to stay healthy. I had a precise game plan for the entire season, which began before I left for spring training. Trying to make it to the Derby or the Preakness or the Breeder's Cup is like trying to catch lightning in a bottle. But since I had caught "lightning in a bottle" throughout my playing career, I believed that I could do it again— "unreasonable optimism." As is the case with any top breeder, D. Wayne has won his share of races. But he has also had horses that break down. So I looked at the breeding business as like trying to hit .300. Baseball is the only sport where a player can fail 7 outta 10 times and still make it to the Hall of Fame—well okay, *some* players. If you're a doctor and you fail 7 outta 10 times—you're a horseshit doctor! If you're a lawyer who loses 7 outta 10 cases—you're a horseshit lawyer! But a baseball player only has to be successful 3 outta 10 times to become a star. I figured if I could reach the same batting average in horse breeding as I did as a hitter—I'd be rich and successful. But in breeding, you have to allow for the fact that 9 outta 10 horses won't pan out or earn money. But that one horse that pans out will more than make up for the rest that go bust. One great racehorse is like a Nolan Ryan, Sandy Koufax, or Hank Aaron. They pay dividends that last for years and years.

During the 1930s, a horse of Seabiscuit's caliber ran 3 times in 2 weeks—unheard of today. Today, a horse of Seabiscuit's caliber is lucky to run 12 times per year! That's because the stud fees have become so outrageous. Most colts that get put out to stud will have raced only 9 or 10 times in their career, but they will have won $2 or $3 million in purses. Once a pony gets to the million-dollar mark and has won a grade I, grade II, or grade III race, he's ready for the real exciting end of racing. Most investors want to cash out early on their investment, and stud fees is where that cash is. War Emblem, who won the Derby and the Preakness, just missed the Triple Crown. He was put out to stud at $35,000 per fee at 100 mares per year—$3.5 million. Thunder Gulch, another one of D. Wayne's horses, won the Derby and the Preakness. He came back at $65,000 per fee at 100 mares per year—$6.5 million. But the record goes to Aladar. He came back at $200,000 per fee at 90 mares per year—$18 million! That's why when I die, I'd like to come back as a racehorse. You get to fuck all day and get paid big bucks for doing it!

With D. Wayne Lukas and "credibility" on board, our next step was to acquire a major investor. At that time, Donald Trump was on top of the financial world. He was the largest real estate developer in Manhattan, with investments in land, airlines, hotels, office buildings, and casinos. I first met Donald at his Trump Plaza Hotel and Casino in Atlantic City, New Jersey, where I appeared at several autograph shows. He and I hit it off right away because we both went after what we wanted in life and refused to let anyone stand in our way. So I called Mr. Trump and asked for a meeting in New York.

Wayne and I arrived in Manhattan and checked into The Waldorf Towers, one of my favorite hotels—a place that brought back memories of my playing days against the Mets. We asked for a modest room but when the manager heard that I was there, he bumped us up to the Douglas MacArthur Suite, free of charge. Since Sparky Anderson always compared me to the General, I looked at that gesture as a good omen. That night, Wayne and I went over our business plan and began to prepare ourselves for our meeting with Mr. Trump and D. Wayne Lukas. It was the most nervous I had ever been. I played in 17 All-Star games and won three World Championships, yet I was nervous as hell. This was my first stab at making a living outside of baseball and I didn't want to screw it up. Deep down, in a place where I didn't want to go, I was concerned that Mr. Trump might not want to invest with an ex-con who had been kicked out of baseball. But Wayne reassured me that everything would be fine. He was the technical expert who could answer all of Mr. Trump's questions, D. Wayne Lukas was the world-class trainer, and I was . . . well, I was Pete Rose. Hell, no wonder I was nervous! I was going into a meeting with the

richest man in the world, asking him for $30 million with no other qual-
ifications than having played baseball for 24 years. Off that stark realiza-
tion, Wayne and I decided to take a break and have dinner in the hotel
restaurant. We laughed and talked about baseball and horses, which took
our minds off the business at hand. About halfway through dinner, I received an invitation, which reminded me of another part of my past. The
concierge came over to our table and mentioned that he received several
"discreet" calls from local women who were interested in coming up to
my room for a "party." Most folks know about my reputation with the
ladies—temptations that were just too plentiful and too hard to resist. But
I was in town for business—not pleasure. And believe it or not, I was actually trying to turn my life around. So I declined all offers from the local
female population and returned to our suite, where Wayne and I continued to pore over our business plan. Just imagine—Pete Rose, celibacy,
and an evening in New York—nobody would ever believe it!

We left the hotel early the next morning and went straight to Fifth
Avenue where we entered Trump Towers. Although I never cared for
pink, I was immediately impressed with all the marble and the 80-foot wa-
terfall that filled the lobby. I knew that I was in the right place. Mr. Trump
was very gracious and well-prepared. He asked all the right questions and
even complimented us on what he thought was a first-class proposal.
Wayne and D. Wayne were right on top of things, which put Mr. Trump
at ease. Of course, I cracked a few jokes and acted like "Pete Rose," which
turned out to be exactly what I was supposed to do. Mr. Trump was a big
baseball fan and well aware of my hitting records. I didn't need to try and
impress him. The meeting went far better than expected. Mr. Trump
seemed very interested in our proposal but wanted to confer with his close
friend Allen Paulson before making a commitment. Mr. Paulson sold his
stock in Gulfstream Aerospace for hundreds of millions and settled into
Lexington as one of the biggest "Gentleman Farmers" in the state. Mr.

Paulson also kept a home in Bel Air and Del Mar, where he could watch his California horses race during the winter. Since Wayne and D. Wayne were both familiar with Mr. Paulson, we looked at the prospect of an outside advisor as being a positive influence. It proved that Mr. Trump was serious. Within two weeks, Mr. Trump invited us back to New York for a second meeting. We met with his advisors and discussed the particulars of our business proposal. Afterward, Mr. Trump gave me a big hug and expressed a genuine interest in standing in the winner's circle of the Kentucky Derby. We left the second meeting with a very positive feeling. But within days after returning to Cincinnati, we read in the newspaper that Ivana Trump had just caught The Donald in the company of a young beauty named Marla Maples. The scandal got front-page coverage and also cost us a chance at completing our deal. Later, a spokesman told us that Mr. Trump would not be getting involved with any new business ventures until after his pending divorce was final. Needless to say, Wayne and I were very disappointed. We gave it our best shot but came away with nothing but goodwill. At the time, the decline in real estate values had reduced Mr. Trump's net worth to one-third of what it had previously been. So it wasn't a good time for him to be looking for risky investments. Within weeks, the rest of the economy went into a serious recession and the opportunity for investment dollars went dry as a bone. But my biggest disappointment came in how my endeavor was portrayed in the press. Folks in the Cincinnati media suggested that my involvement was somehow related to gambling rather than profit. They took a legitimate venture with well-respected businessmen and twisted it around to manipulate the public into thinking that I was some kind of inveterate horse player looking to make a score. Hell, I made my share of mistakes but trying to hook up with Donald Trump and D. Wayne Lukas was not one of them. After the backlash from my gambling investigation, the press was still treating me like "the boy who cried wolf"—they didn't believe a word

I said. Afterward, I sold my interest in the two remaining racehorses and returned to Florida.

After arriving in Florida, I was back to square one. I was disappointed but not disheartened. Within days, I was introduced to Tom Walsh, the owner of Ocean Properties. Tom had an idea for a restaurant and wanted to discuss the possibilities of a partnership. I met with Tom and described the success I had with both the Precinct and Waterfront restaurants in Cincinnati. Both places had performed great based in part on the popularity of my co-owners, Boomer Esiason, Cris Collinsworth, Jeff Ruby, and me. We held special events like "Celebrity Bartender Night" to attract customers on a weekly basis. Boca Raton is especially busy during spring training and I believed that I could bring in baseball players, owners, and managers, which in turn, would draw a lot of other loyal customers. I explained to Tom that whether it was the World Series or spring training, I always gave the fans their money's worth. I never got involved in any business proposition where I didn't commit to its success. Tom Walsh liked what I had to say and decided to take a chance with me. Tom put up the money and offered me a base salary and performance bonuses in a restaurant called the Pete Rose Ballpark Café. It would take 6 months to remodel the property but I stayed involved with the entire building process.

During that time, my building contractor, Larry Shawe, introduced me to another feller who had a few good ideas about my future—Warren Greene. Warren owned a company that specialized in sports marketing and represented some top clients. As I gave Warren a tour of my restaurant, we talked about the possibilities of working together. "Unlike most athletes, Pete didn't try to impress me with how important he was," said Warren. "I asked Pete what he wanted to achieve with his future and he was very honest. Pete said, 'I'm not a businessman or a business operator. I'm a people person. I'm Pete Rose. That's all I know how to do.'" At first,

Warren and I decided to take it slow because I was still trying to cut some contractual ties with other people from my past. But within a few months, Warren got me my first gig at a sports memorabilia show in Detroit. I flew in for the weekend, met with all the sponsors, and cooperated in every way. By the end of the show, the promoter stopped by and gave me a bonus check for surpassing my signing guarantee. It was the first bonus money I had ever received in the memorabilia business. Warren told me to keep the entire check as a gesture of good faith.

Within months, we opened the Pete Rose Ballpark Café and Tom's investment started to pay dividends. I greeted the customers every night and signed autographs. We also opened a souvenir gift shop, which sold a great deal of sports memorabilia. I told the staff that I expected consistency in the front and back of the restaurant. "People will come back if they like the food and the service," I said. At the end of their meal, I asked the customers if they were satisfied with their experience. If they had a complaint, I wrote it down and made changes the very next day. If they were pleased with everything, I passed along the praise to the rest of the staff so they could feel appreciated for a job well done. I invited other baseball players, who brought in their family and friends as well. But the ballplayers always ate for free—a gesture of thanks for their patronage. We were a success from the first day.

Shortly after we opened the restaurant, Rollie Fingers and Tom Seaver were announced as the newest inductees into the Baseball Hall of Fame. Seaver received 98.8 percent of the total votes—surpassing a record held by Ty Cobb. I received 41 write-in votes even though I wasn't eligible due to the "Pete Rose Rule." The TV announcement drew a round of applause from the restaurant patrons. It was also the first indication that "time heals all wounds." A few years later, we opened another Ballpark Café in Boynton, a few miles down the street. We did one helluva public relations job with both of those restaurants. I didn't earn huge money but it was enough to support my family and move us into a new condo-minium. I was earning a good living outside of baseball and proved that I could land on my feet.

Once the restaurant got going and we built our reputation, I became more and more involved in other business opportunities. A gentleman from Sports Fan National Radio Network came into the restaurant one night and asked if I would be interested in hosting a syndicated sports talk show, where I would field questions from callers and interview various sports stars all broadcast live from the Pete Rose Ballpark Café. My 2-hour show, "Talk Sports with Pete Rose," went on the air five nights a week from 6 to 8 P.M. on WJNO-AM. We started out with only 21 sta-tions but added new stations and grew in the ratings every week. My first guest was Indiana University basketball coach and longtime friend Bobby Knight. Bobby was the perfect first guest because he loved to talk and didn't need much prompting. I just sat back, grinned, and listened to Bobby talk about basketball, fishing, and war—subjects he understood thoroughly.

After my first show, I thought, "Damn, this radio stuff is a piece of cake." But not every guest was as talkative or as cooperative as Coach Knight. Some guests were nervous or failed to call in on time, which meant that I had to pick up the slack. But within a few days, I got better and better with cracking jokes and telling some pretty crazy stories on the spur of the moment.

Eventually, my show became a big ratings success and was picked up by WSAI-AM in Cincinnati and pitted against Cris Collinsworth and Andy Furman, a pair of old friends who hosted their own radio talk show on WLW. My show had no way of competing with a major station like WLW but that didn't stop me from trying. I started calling on friends to make sure I got the top guests to appear on my show. If Cris and Andy got Bob Huggins—I got John Wooden. If they got Johnny Bench—I got Ted

Williams. If they got Jack Twyman—I got Oscar Robertson. If they got Sam Wyche—I got Mike Ditka. We created some pretty healthy competition but it was all in the name of good fun and strong ratings. I wasn't living in Cincinnati but I damn sure wanted to compete for the city's attention.

After experiencing some success in the restaurant and radio business, I started looking to expand my business opportunities. But I had one strict rule: no associations with shady characters. At one point, a gentleman from Virginia came into the restaurant and captured my imagination—R. Alan Fuentes, a self-made millionaire. Like me, Alan earned bad grades as a kid but didn't let "school" interfere with his "education." Alan joined the Army, fought in Vietnam, and returned to start a company called Computer Dynamics Inc., which by 1987 became the tenth largest minority-owned contracting business in the country. In his spare time, Alan traveled the world and fulfilled his craving for adventure by climbing Machu Picchu in Peru and Kilimanjaro in Africa. I liked Alan even though he hated baseball. He was into sports that involved "speed"—powerboat racing. Alan liked to drive his speedboat along the bridges of the inland waterways and rev his engines until a passing sports car took part in an "unofficial" drag race.

Alan had a boat called "The Executioner," a 40-foot Vee-hull powerboat, which went undefeated during the previous racing season. But Alan didn't compete in enough races to actually win the national championship. Alan thought I might be the missing ingredient to help him win the title. He described the thrill and excitement of trying to out-maneuver an opponent, who was only inches away at 90 mph. Alan mentioned that many athletes and entertainers, like Chuck Norris, Joe Theismann, and Don Johnson had been successful in powerboat racing and asked if I wanted to give it a try. Growing up 50 yards from the Ohio River, I was exposed to boat racing at an early age. My dad always took me to the boat regattas during the summer, so I accepted Alan's invitation for a trial run. As soon as we got out on the ocean, he cut right into the crest of a strong wave, which caused us to jump 30 feet out of the water. When we landed back down, I thought we were going to break in half. Within minutes, I was hooked. Powerboat racing, which had been in existence for over 60 years, became my new drug of choice. I agreed to join the racing team but I had one stipulation—I had to drive the boat! Alan agreed to be the throttle man and kept his other navigator to fill our three-man crew. I wore a vest, which was rigged with kill switches, so that if I ever got thrown from the boat, the engines would shut down automatically for safety purposes. But I never got thrown. My hand-eye coordination served me well in racing just as it had in baseball. In many ways, driving a boat at high speeds was like staring down a 95 mph fastball. It also reminded me of the first time I got laid—pure excitement in a short period of time!

Alan renamed his boat the "Hit King" and painted **14** on the bow. We had two 1250 Mercury Cruisers with 2,000 horsepower and topped out at 120 mph, which qualified us for the Super V, the fastest of three different speed classifications. A typical race covered 10 laps over a 12-mile course so there was little room for error. As the driver, it was my job to steer the boat, maintain proper fuel levels, and keep the crew aware of the condition of the engines, which proved to be the most important aspect of racing.

My first race was the $100,000 Virginia Beach Offshore Grand Prix III in Alan's hometown of Virginia Beach. I arrived early to take my physical and earn my competition card by taking instructions in boat safety and first aid. I assured Craig Andrews, a board member of the American Offshore Power Boat Association, that I was taking the sport seriously and would cooperate with all the rules and regulations. I wasn't there to get publicity—I was there to compete! We won the preliminary race on Saturday, which meant that we became the parade leader for the big race on Sunday. But during the prelim, I had a little fun with former football star

Joe Theismann, who drove the Zuba boat. Joe was not in direct competition with me because he was in a lower speed classification. But I lapped him once just to let him know how much power I had under the hull. Then, Joe showed me why he was a quarterback. He didn't appreciate being shown up, so he went out and set a new record for his speed classification. After the race, Joe said, "Thanks for getting me motivated, Pete!"

We jumped out to a big lead on Sunday and averaged 85 mph on our first few laps. But after 10 laps, we ruptured a hose, which filters sea water needed to keep the engines cool. After we discovered the problem, we turned off a valve, which stopped the leak. But it was too late to finish the race because the boat had already taken in too much water. Since we finished with the fastest time, we were declared the winner over Steve Ballard's "Success Express," which only completed eight laps due to engine failure. I felt good that we won the race but a part of me was pissed off that we didn't finish those final two laps. I complained about not taking better precautions with our engines. But Alan explained that such accidents are unavoidable with powerful engines at high speeds. "Even the most experienced racers will often break down . . . even get killed due to accidents that involve engine failure," said Alan. "It's part of the thrill of racing." Still, I couldn't help but look at the mishap the same way I looked at making an error—avoidable!

After returning to Boca Raton, I parked the boat in the parking lot of the Pete Rose Ballpark Café. The showcase provided great advertising for the racing team as well as our restaurant. Fans who followed the racing circuit came from all over the state to celebrate our success. The whole scene reminded me of the atmosphere we created in Cincinnati with the loyal Reds fans. During the season, we raced in Sarasota, Miami, Fort Myers, and even on the lake outside of Chicago. Within a short period of time, we climbed to #1 nationwide. But our biggest problem was money—or the lack of it. At one time, Alan had over 500 employees in his company but cutbacks with his government contracts caused problems with his cashflow. We were racing against the likes of Reggie Fountain, owner of Fountain Powerboats, who had huge sponsorship money. Reggie could afford to race a new boat every week, whereas we had to rebuild our engines before each race. And even then there was no guarantee that we wouldn't break down during the race. Eventually, the proposition became too expensive. There were no available TV contracts and I couldn't afford to sponsor the team with my own money.

Still, I hung on for as long as possible. Finally, I read the handwriting on the wall. We were in Sarasota for another big race. But after we put out to sea, I noticed there was no oil pressure coming from our gauges. So I tapped on the dash to see if there was a short in the wiring. At the same time, I looked back and noticed a 4-foot flame shooting out of one of our engines. We were just heading out to race, so all three of our gas tanks were full. If one of the tanks caught fire—KABOOM! We were goners. So Alan called to abandon ship. Just before we bailed, the Coast Guard came to our aid and gave us an extra extinguisher to help put out the fire. But afterward, we waited for over an hour before the tow-boat arrived to take us back to shore. We were tossing and weaving in the high seas to the point where I got so sick, I wanted to die. My face turned green and I vomited about a dozen times. I have no tolerance, patience, or under-standing whatsoever when it comes to being sick to my stomach. The whole boat racing experience taught me a very valuable lesson—the high seas were no place for a baseball player!

14

MY PRISON WITHOUT BARS

"I was suspended from baseball—not the city of Cooperstown."
—PETE ROSE

In 1993, I received a phone call from Tommy Catal, who operated a little business called "Mickey's Place" in Cooperstown, New York—right down the street from the Baseball Hall of Fame. The store featured a Mickey Mantle museum on the second floor and drew a large crowd of visitors throughout the summer. Tommy and his manager, Andrew Vilacky, invited me to make a public appearance during the 4-day weekend of the Hall of Fame Induction Ceremony. I called my agent to get his opinion on the proposition. Warren was immediately in favor of me doing an appearance in Cooperstown—just not during Hall of Fame Week! He thought my presence would be misconstrued by Major League Baseball. So I accepted the invitation immediately—"Pete Rose logic." If someone tells me that I can't, I'll damn sure prove that I can. It turned out to be a great idea. We set up a signing table and attracted more than 1,000 customers during the first day. I earned over $40,000 for the 4-day event. The attraction became so popular that I was invited back for an annual event. The fans would attend the formal ceremonies and then slip across the street to visit with me. I shook hands with grown-ups and kids alike. I talked with the fans, kissed babies, and took photos like a politician running for office. At the end of the day, one fan came back for a second autograph. He was disappointed with the treatment he received from the Hall of Fame players across the street. He said, "Pete, you're the only player out here who looks up from signing and talks with us. Some of the other players are downright rude." I said, "Sir, the only connection I have left with baseball is with the fans. I'm not going to take that opportunity for granted!"

During the second day, many of the 50 Hall of Fame players who attended the formal ceremony slipped by and asked if they could sign autographs next to me. They said, "Pete, you're drawing the biggest share of the audience." Reggie Jackson, Harmon Killebrew, and Ted Williams were among the players who came by to visit. But they weren't just there for autographs. They stopped by to pay their respects and to say hello. The players always remained friendly with me. They never held a grudge over my past mistakes. But the press had a field day. They made it appear like I was the only player signing autographs outside of the induction ceremony. As Warren predicted, they accused me of "prostituting myself." Apparently, my appearance didn't set too well with members of the Hall of Fame's board of directors either. But since I was already banned for life, what more could they do to me . . . ban me again? The event became so successful that Andrew Vilacky bought the entire building and opened a Pete Rose collectibles museum, which has grown in business every year. During those years, fans from around the National League have stopped by to share the highlights of certain games and individual plays that had an impact on their lives. Those memories have helped me to cope with living in exile. But the biggest highlight came from a surprise visit from a

76-year-old lady, who was in town for a book signing. I was sitting at my booth, when I saw her approaching from across the street. As soon as she spoke, I knew exactly who she was. My knees started knocking. I've met Presidents Nixon, Ford, Carter, Reagan, and Bush. I've stood before federal judges who held my life in their hands, but nothing made me more nervous than standing before her. She said, "Pete, I've walked three blocks just to say hello to you. My father died of throat cancer in 1939. But if he were alive, I think he would have enjoyed watching you play baseball. He liked men who played hard and lived hard." I wanted to speak but I got a sudden case of cotton mouth. Finally, I said, "Ma'am, your dad was the greatest player who ever walked the planet. I would have flown to Mars just to meet him." After paying me the best compliment of my life, that lady smiled and gave me a kiss. She was Julia Ruth Stevens—the daughter of George Herman Ruth—The Babe!

Over the years, Cooperstown provided me with several great experiences, including a surprise from Mike Schmidt. Mike took the first steps toward my reinstatement in 1995, when he, Nolan Ryan, and George Brett were inducted into the Hall of Fame. Mike scheduled a meeting with Reggie Jackson and Joe Morgan to discuss some ideas that he wanted to take to the commissioner to try and get the process started. During the previous year, Leo Durocher was voted into the Hall of Fame by the Committee on Baseball Veterans after having been suspended in 1947 for "associating with known gamblers." There was just one problem—Leo died the year before! So he never even got to enjoy the honor of being inducted. That made no sense to me. I wanted to enjoy my Hall of Fame induction ceremony while I was still alive! Mike Schmidt felt that since public attitudes toward gambling were changing, the timing might be right for me as well. He scheduled a meeting but I called at the last minute and backed out. I spoke with Mike about an hour before the dinner and told him that something else had come up. At that time, Mr. Selig still held "interim" status as Baseball Commissioner. My attorney Roger Makley and I didn't believe an interim commissioner would be willing to tackle such a controversial issue as "reinstating Pete Rose." Really, though, my heart just wasn't in it at the time. I wasn't ready to face the possibility of being rejected again. But despite my reluctance, Mike continued his efforts and shocked everyone during his own induction speech. He said, " . . . I stand before you as a man totally humbled by the magnitude of this entire experience. And I join millions of baseball fans around the world in hoping that some day very soon, Pete Rose will be standing right here." The crowd gave Mike a big round of applause. Afterward, he took a lot of heat from baseball for mentioning my name. But Mike stood his ground, which explains a lot about Mike Schmidt's character. After all, how many folks would initiate a meeting for someone else to get into the Hall during the same week he was getting inducted himself?

Three months later, President Jimmy Carter wrote a beautiful letter in *USA Today*, urging the commissioner to consider my reinstatement: ". . . There was a vast abyss last fall with no World Series and still a diminished luster on the game as players and owners prepare to resume their endless contract disputes," wrote the President. "But there was something else amiss, underscored by the heroic achievements of Cal Ripken Jr. and Greg Maddox. An equally remarkable player—Pete Rose— is barred from recognition in the Baseball Hall of Fame. Election to the Hall of Fame has never been an affirmation of impeccable character, but rather a recognition of extraordinary achievements on the diamond. This is what makes the case of Pete Rose, one of the greatest players of all time, so agonizing. . . . For at least five generations, our family members have been avid baseball fans. We were particularly proud of Ty Cobb, a fellow Georgian, and simply let the negative aspects of his character fade into relative unimportance when compared to his achievements on the diamond. It was with mixed emotions that we observed Pete Rose getting his

4,192nd hit on September 11, 1985, breaking one of Cobb's seemingly in-
vulnerable records. But we recognized Rose's extraordinary spirit and determination. Few players ever made greater use of their natural talents or
brought more enthusiasm to the game. . . . Pete Rose served his prison
time as required and has subsequently led the life of a proper and law-
abiding citizen. He is gainfully employed and has complied with the special restraints placed on him by Commissioner Giamatti. In painful
dignity, he has suffered many other actual and indirect punishments. . . .
A 1994 article in *Sports Illustrated* reported a telephone poll of Americans
in which 97 percent of respondents said that Pete Rose should be in the
Hall of Fame. I have found no fans who disagree. I have never met or
communicated with Pete Rose but would like to join with other Americans to help give him—and the game of baseball—this opportunity for re-
demption."

◆ ◆ ◆

As my radio show became more popular, I flew to Las Vegas once a
month, where I would broadcast live from the MGM Grand Casino. I
would usually take my wife and family, which gave them an opportunity
to enjoy the perks and live entertainment. As a result, my daughter Cara
became smitten with the entertainment industry. She began taking
singing, dancing, and acting lessons and showed a real commitment and
work ethic that reminded me of my own. By 1994, she was ready to try
her luck at the big time. We decided to move to Los Angeles to help Cara
get started with her career. With the help of some good friends, we found
a home close to the best schools in Sherman Oaks. Within a year, Cara
found a good agent and landed her first role on *The Ellen Show*, followed
by guest-starring roles on *Touched by an Angel*, *Pretender*, and *Melrose Place*.
After 4 years of steady work, she became a regular on the daytime soap

opera *Passions* and, much to my surprise, began earning more money than me! Gradually, Los Angeles became our primary home. But I kept my condo in Florida, where I could maintain my commitment to the Ballpark Café. But since both restaurants were operating at full capacity, I didn't need to be available as much as I did in the beginning stages. The monthly trip to Las Vegas for my radio show was a quick flight from Los Angeles, so it became convenient to be "bicoastal." The West Coast home was also more convenient for traveling to the corporate functions, where I became more and more popular as a "hospitality guest"—a celebrity who would meet and entertain corporate clients during business conventions. My knees had been getting worse and worse. All those years of playing hard had taken their toll. Most kinds of physical activity became uncomfortable, and you can imagine how frustrating that is for me! I was often a corporate "golf guest," but I rarely played. I'd ride along on the cart with various CEOs, tell stories, and keep their clients' big egos in check. I had several sarcastic one-liners for anyone who took golf too seriously or made the mistake of duffing a shot while I was watching. "For chrissakes," I'd scream! "With a swing like that, you should play from the ladies' tees!" I'd continue to cuss and tease until finally some frustrated executive would get pissed off, hand me his golf club, and say: "Here, Pete, if you're so damn great, let's see you try it!" I'd usually act nervous just to put the foursome in a good mood. Then I'd take a few goofy warm-up strokes, as if I'd never played golf before. Then I'd wait until they started to make wagers on the outcome of my shot. But since swinging a golf club is the same mechanics as swinging a bat, I was pretty damn good. After driving a shot 260 yards straight down the middle of the fairway, I'd get a bunch of slack-jawed expressions from the foursome. "How in the hell did you do that, Pete?" they'd ask. After collecting my winnings, I'd grin and say, "Boys, I got 4,256 hits swinging at a ball that traveled at 95 mph. The goddamn golf ball was standing still! How hard can it be?" Throughout the day, I'd make plenty of jokes and meaningless wagers, and by the end of the round, everyone walked off the course thoroughly entertained, regardless of how well they scored.

Pretty soon my corporate entertaining business had gone onto the big time. I was being invited back year after year to the same events, and, before long, I was getting invitations to be a keynote speaker at major functions.

"Pete Rose, Keynote Speaker" sure had a nice ring to it. I discovered that, although I'm not a polished public speaker, I could entertain folks with my outrageous stories. Whether it was the Men's Club in Detroit or the Greater Cincinnati Chapter of the Cystic Fibrosis Foundation, I tried to be the best speaker they ever had. I had to rely on my instincts and react on the spur of the moment. But I always gave the public their money's worth and I always told the truth. My favorite story, one that I told often, involves an investor who came to visit me after the show. While I was broadcasting the show from the MGM Grand, I was introduced to a businessman from Sacramento . . . who will remain nameless for obvious reasons. My friend Doug Drabin arranged the meeting after the gentleman approached him with an idea for investing in a series of "Pete Rose Batting Cages," which he wanted to build throughout California. Doug mentioned that the gentleman, whom I'll call "Mr. X," was well financed and respected in his community. After the radio show, I returned to my room at the MGM Grand, where Doug was watching a "Show-Girl" awards banquet on television. When Mr. X arrived, Doug turned the television to "mute." But that didn't stop me from watching out of the corner of my eye because the ladies were all dressed in skimpy little outfits. Mr. X entered wearing a brand new suit and started talking about baseball and how much he enjoyed watching me play . . . typical "get to know each other" talk. Then all of a sudden, Mr. X broke down and started crying. I looked over at Doug to see if he had any clue about what might be wrong. But

Doug was just as shocked as I was. Mr. X was sobbing uncontrollably! Then Mr. X explained that 13 years earlier, someone had left a little baby on his doorstep. Not knowing what to do, he kept the little boy and raised him as his own son. Now that the kid was turning 13 years old, Mr. X was afraid that someone might come along to claim him, which might cause the boy to hate him for not revealing that he was adopted in the first place. Most folks know that I'm not a warm-and-fuzzy type guy. But I'll be damned if I didn't start to cry myself! But I wasn't crying over the impact of the story. I was crying to keep from laughing over what Doug and I were looking at. The new suit Mr. X had bought from the hotel men's shop had not been fully stitched. The inner lining to the pant leg was open all the way up to his crotch. And because of his emotional dilemma, Mr. X forgot to wear his jockey shorts. So as he sat there spilling his guts, his balls were spilling out of his pants! Between watching the bizarre awards show on TV, listening to Mr. X's heartfelt confession, and watching his balls dangle in the air—I was crying just to keep from laughing! Finally, Mr. X stopped crying and apologized for breaking down. Then, he said that he was amazed by my sensitivity. "I've always heard that Pete Rose was a real tough bastard," he said. "But anyone who would cry over hearing a sob story from a total stranger is one helluva caring man!" Then I confessed that I wasn't crying over the nature of his dilemma. After I made a gesture toward his crotch, Mr. X turned got so embarrassed that he wanted to run and hide. But I told him not to worry. "Any father who feels that strongly about his son has no reason to feel ashamed," I said. "If that young kid ever discovers that he was left on the doorstep, I hope he also discovers that he got a great Dad out of the deal." Mr. X never followed through with his investment proposal. But a few years later, I returned to Las Vegas for an autograph show and was approached by Mr. X once again. He mentioned that everything was still fine with his son. Then he opened a bag, gave me the original suit pants that he wore during our first meeting and asked me to autograph them. I grinned and signed, "You're Nuts! Pete Rose."

I continued to perform my radio show from Las Vegas . . . and continued to take heat for being in "casinos" even though I rarely gambled in them. All totaled, I performed on the radio for 7 years and eventually became the highest-paid sports-talk-show host in the country. We were picked up by over 250 stations. But I priced myself right out of the market. When my salary reached 350,000 per year, the network decided they could get other sports personalities for a fraction of the cost. But I was proud of the work I did in the radio business. My guests always knew what to expect and trusted me to treat them fairly. I never took cheap shots on the air.

Even though I had success in all my business ventures, I was still a fish out of water. I had success in radio but I was not a true radio personality . . . or boat racer . . . or restaurant entrepreneur. In my heart, I was still a baseball man . . . and I was feeling the need to get back to my roots.

On Labor Day of 1997, I flew from Miami to Cincinnati to watch my son Pete Rose Jr. make his playing debut with the Reds. Pete Jr. had been playing well in the minors and was the only player to be brought up from Triple A. He hit .300 practically every year and was finally getting his chance to show his stuff. It was my first visit to a baseball stadium since my lifetime ban. I bought four tickets and sat next to the owner, Marge Schott, a longtime friend. As soon as I walked into the stadium and my picture was shown on the big stadium screen, I received a standing ovation from the crowd. After the game, Pete Jr. told me that he heard the ovation from within the locker room. "When I heard that roar, I knew you had arrived," said Petey. The Reds had only been drawing about 18,000 fans per game but this game had 34,000 in attendance. Pete went 1-for-3 and made two good plays in the field at third base. He got his only hit off of Kevin Appier. Manager Jack McKeon sat

Pete Jr. on the bench the next day because the Reds were facing a left-hander. But late in the game, he brought Petey in to pinch-hit with no warning or warm-up. After Petey struck out, McKeon said, "I guess I've seen all I need to see of that Rose kid." Afterward, Petey was sent back down to Triple A and then released the following year. It was not my place to get involved and question Jack McKeon or General Manager Jim Bowden. But I believed they were unfair in their treatment of my son. Petey was six feet three and 225 pounds with some of the best statistics in Triple A. He should have been given a fair chance. I can't prove that he's been discriminated against because of what happened to me. But he's had trouble sticking with a team over the years and it hasn't been because of a lack of talent. It's true that he hasn't had a breakthrough year when he needed it . . . and he has had some untimely injuries. But he has hit consistently in the .300s and is well liked by his teammates. Years later, he was invited to spring training, where he hit .500 with the Phillies. But as soon as the regular season started, Petey was given his release. He was disappointed but like me, Petey thrives on challenge. He never lets adversity affect him the wrong way. I've had talks with him about maintaining his confidence and he has handled his setbacks like a man. "I keep putting up the numbers, Dad" said Pete Jr. "But I just can't catch a break." At one point, he even changed his roster name to P. J. Rose, which helped to relieve the pressure of playing in my shadow. But Petey wasn't comfortable with hiding his identity and changed it back. Some coaches have used his "age" as an excuse but the big league rosters are filled with 32-year-old players—some with less talent than Petey.

Recently, I received a call from Larry Bowa, who wanted to sign Jim Thome to the Phillies roster. Thome was a free agent who said publicly that I was one of his favorite players. Bowa asked me to place a call and talk about the advantages of playing with the Phillies, which I agreed to do. I have always considered myself the best ambassador that baseball has.

And I have nothing but great memories from playing in Philadelphia. Shortly after I spoke with Jim Thome, he signed with the Phillies. I asked Thome if he could put in a word and ask the Phillies to invite Pete Jr. to spring training for another tryout. But I never heard back from anyone in the Philadelphia organization. I was disappointed but not surprised. Over the years, friends have consistently called and asked for favors. Throughout those years, I've never turned down a friend. Yet when it comes time for me to ask, I'm suddenly the guy who was banished from baseball, unworthy of consideration. To this day, my sportswriter friend has refused to honor his $20,000 debt, even though my loan kept him out of jail. Go figure!

Being back at Riverfront Stadium in Cincinnati and watching Pete Jr. play baseball brought back great memories. So I decided to make a stab at getting my life back. Since Commissioner Selig's "interim" status had finally been removed, I asked my attorney to draw up a formal letter requesting reinstatement. After 8 years, the impact from my scandal seemed to have softened with the acceptance of gambling as a part of our everyday culture. Wagers on college sports alone topped billions in annual revenue. Off-shore casinos, Indian casinos, state-run lotteries, office betting pools, and church bingo were more popular than ever before. Major League Baseball even allowed the casinos to advertise inside their stadiums. Mr. Ilitch, who owns the Detroit Tigers, also owned an interest in a gambling casino. Mr. Galbreath, who owned the Pittsburgh Pirates, also owned Darby Dan Farm, which was one of the most successful breeding stables in Ohio. I knew firsthand because Mr. Galbreath offered me two of his top brood mares during our contract negotiations in 1978. Mr. Steinbrenner, who owned the Yankees, also owned a racetrack. All in all, it seemed hypocritical of baseball to allow certain privileges to the owners and to permit the casinos to advertise but to condemn me for taking part in the services they provide! But Mr. Selig never "officially" responded to my letter. He acknowledged receiving my application and then made a very harsh public statement: "I see no reason to change baseball's position on the ban of Pete Rose."

◆ ◆ ◆

On July 13, 1999, I traveled back to Boston to make a corporate appearance for one of the largest pharmaceutical companies in the world. While eating dinner in the hotel, I ran into many of the 100 living players who had been nominated for the Mastercard MLB All-Century Team. They were in town for the All-Star game and to choose the members of the All-Century Team. I was on the ballot, in the program, and on the advertising banner. But I was not allowed to be a part of the All-Star celebration, which was being held at Fenway Park. At that time, Mr. Selig made another harsh public announcement: "I don't think there is anything new that would cause me to change what Bart Giamatti did by kicking Pete Rose out of baseball." But since Mastercard was paying huge endorsement dollars for their campaign, they insisted that I be placed on the voting ballot. Mr. Selig graciously agreed to their request.

After being voted onto the Mastercard MLB All-Century Team, I received a letter from Mr. Selig congratulating me on the honor and inviting me to share in the ceremony, which was being held in Atlanta during the 1999 World Series between the Yankees and the Braves. It would be my first official contact with baseball in over 10 years. Needless to say, I was excited. Hell, I was ecstatic. Of course, John Dowd went public with his objections to my being allowed to participate. After 10 years, Dowd was still trying to make a name for himself. But baseball told him to stay out of matters that were none of his business.

Several months earlier, I committed to participating in a ceremony honoring the living members of the 3,000 Hit Club, which was being held on the same weekend in Atlantic City. I joined Stan Musial, Willie Mays, Hank Aaron, Lou Brock, and Carl Yastrzemski for the 2-day event. Although all the other ballplayers spent their free time in the casino, I was the only one who was singled out in the press for playing blackjack. Due to my signing commitment, I was unable to leave for Atlanta until Sunday, which caused me to miss the main press conference for the All-Century Team. Of course, the press made it sound like I was deliberately snubbing the ceremony for a gambling spree in Atlantic City. Nothing could have been further from the truth. Like Musial, Mays, and the others, I was fulfilling a contract that had been negotiated months in advance. Afterward, I flew directly to Atlanta with my agent and my son Tyler, who was 14 at the time. We went straight to the hotel to check in and get dressed for the occasion. As soon as we pulled into the stadium, I was greeted by the head of baseball security, Kevin Hallinan, who could not have been more cordial. But right next to Kevin was Jim Gray. I barely got out of the limo before Jim Gray pulled Warren aside and said, "I already spoke with Mike Schmidt and told him that I want to interview Pete as soon as he gets off the stage from the ceremony," said Gray. "I have inside information that this interview could be the best thing Pete ever does." I looked over at Warren and nodded in agreement. I was still in shock over being at the stadium and didn't give the idea much thought. Then I was escorted inside the stadium for a press conference, where I fielded some pretty tough questions. Many reporters asked if I thought it was "fair" for me to be included in the ceremony. I believed that since the fans voted me in and Mr. Selig had invited me, I had every right to be there. "Why would I snub such an outstanding gesture?" I asked. After the press conference, Mike Schmidt approached and told me that Jim Gray had been pestering him about an exclusive interview . . . saying he had "inside information." At that point, I got a little nervous and asked Warren to talk to Jim Gray and to set the ground rules. I was there to take part in the ceremony—not talk about gambling. Warren spoke with Gray and asked if his interview would include gambling. Jim Gray said, "No, don't worry. I mean, I'm one of Pete's guys. Pete's my man. I would never do that to Pete!"

Just before the ceremony, I met up with Mark McGwire and Hank Aaron and started laughing and joking about hitting the long ball. The two Homerun Champs couldn't have been more different in size and style. But they sure had some interesting stories—1,338 home runs between them! Then President Jimmy Carter arrived with Ted Turner and asked for a group photo. But before settling in for the pose, I made a point of thanking Mr. Carter for his beautiful letter back in 1995. Then, Mr. Carter stood right next to me and Hank Aaron in the middle of a large group that included Willie Mays, Ted Williams, and Stan Musial. Mr. Carter insisted on standing in the middle of the photo. Afterward, Stan laughed when he caught onto Mr. Carter's logic. "Ain't that just like a politician," said Musial. "He stands right in the middle so they can't crop him out of the goddamn picture!" Everybody laughed, and then Mr. Carter replied, "Mr. Musial, that's the difference between a baseball player and a president!"

Afterward, I talked with Bobby Cox, Ryan Klesko, and several of the Braves players. It was just like the good old days. I was having the time of my life. Then my son Tyler nudged me and pointed toward the commissioner. I had never met Mr. Selig but I went right up to him and thanked him for giving me the opportunity to be a part of the ceremony. "You're welcome, Pete," said Bud. "The fans voted you onto the team and you deserve to be here." Then I introduced Mr. Selig to my son Tyler. They shook hands and talked a little baseball. It was a very proud moment. Throughout most of his life, my son heard all about what a louse I was. But finally he was getting the chance to see his dad for what he really was—a great baseball player, respected by his peers and the fans.

The ceremony itself was too impressive for words. Just before I went on stage, they gave me a Cincinnati Reds baseball cap, something I hadn't been able to wear in 10 years. Then, as they announced my name, I just went numb. The crowd stood and applauded for over 3 minutes—the longest ovation of any player. I was overwhelmed by the show of support. I had to clench my jaw to hold back the emotion. Later, Hank Aaron joked that he couldn't believe that I got a bigger ovation than him in his home-town of Atlanta. I said, "Damn, Hank, they see you in the ballpark every week. They haven't seen me in 10 years!" It was one of the greatest mo-ments of my life.

Then, as I walked off stage, Jim Gray ambushed me on live television. He asked that since the fans were very forgiving, would I show some con-trition and "apologize to the fans for betting on baseball" I was shocked by his contentious attitude. I just stared at him and said, "No, not at all, Jim . . . can't you just let a man enjoy his evening?" Then, I walked away and threw my hands in the air. I looked over at my agent and said, "That little bastard double-crossed us. He talked about nothing but gambling!" As I approached the Yankees locker room, I was greeted by Derek Jeter and the Reverend Jesse Jackson. Both spoke words of encouragement but the crowd noise was too loud for me to hear what they said. Besides, I was still too shocked to speak. Once I got inside the clubhouse, all the umpires congratulated me. They had been watching the ceremony on live televi-sion and couldn't believe what they saw. They called Jim Gray every dirty name in the book. Then Craig Sager approached me and apologized. Craig said that Jim Gray's behavior was the worst thing he'd ever seen in broadcasting. Then I did a very positive interview with Charlie Steiner from ESPN Radio, which gave me some time to settle down and reflect on the honor of being named to the All-Century Team. Afterward, I spoke with Mike Schmidt and explained that I wasn't angry with the gambling question itself. I had been asked about gambling for years. I knew how to respond. But I was pissed off by the way Jim Gray lied to get the interview. I could have talked with a dozen different reporters but I gave the exclusive to Gray because he said he had "inside information." I told Mike, "What the hell was Jim Gray thinking? Did he actually believe that after 26 years in the majors, 17 major league records, 5 months in federal prison, and 10 years in exile, that suddenly I had gone soft . . . that I was going to break down and confess to a TV reporter?" *Even in the Catholic Church*, the sinner is supposed to confess to the priest—not the whole congregation! My "priest" was Commissioner Selig—not Jim Gray! Afterward, I only stayed to watch two innings of the World Series game. I was too upset to enjoy the evening. I went back to the hotel, packed my things, and left for the airport. The next day, my agent received calls from officials from Mastercard and Joe Morgan of NBC, saying they had no idea Jim Gray was going to pull such a stunt. But as it turned out, Jim Gray got his comeuppance. During the next game, he apologized to the fans for his behavior but not to me. At the end of the game, Gray approached Shane Spencer of the Yankees after he hit his game-winning home run. Spencer said, "After talking with all the guys on the team, we decided not to talk with you after what you did to Pete." Then Shane Spencer walked away, leaving Jim Gray standing alone with egg on his face on national television.

After receiving the warm reception from the fans in Atlanta, we asked for a meeting with Mr. Selig to discuss the possibility of my reinstatement. He sent his top executive, Bob Dupuy, to meet with my attorney Roger Makley. Bob flew into Dayton and discussed the evidence that Roger had gathered from his many investigations. Roger and Bob spoke for several hours. But Mr. Dupuy did not want to hear anything about evidence. He wanted to see signs of a "reconfigured life." Mr. Makley discussed the changes in my gambling habits and my legitimate business interests. But Mr. Dupuy was not receptive. Rumors about my racetrack gambling and public appearances at casinos must have raised some red flags. After the meeting, we called Mr. Dupuy to ask permission to attend the 1975 World Series reunion ceremony with the Cincinnati Reds and the 1980 World Series reunion ceremony with the Philadelphia Phillies. But Mr. Dupuy did not return our phone calls. Once again, I felt like I'd been slapped in the face. But this time, I wasn't alone. Players from both teams complained publicly over the way I was treated. I was allowed to participate in a major ceremony where baseball earned millions in endorsements but was denied the chance to participate in two small ceremonies where baseball didn't benefit financially from my presence. Within weeks, we held a press conference in New York and launched a new Web site— Sportcut.com, which allowed fans to add their names to a petition for my reinstatement. We set an Internet record of 1.2 million hits in one day. President Clinton even added his name for support. "Pete Rose has definitely paid the price," he said. "He deserves to be in the Hall. I'd like to see it worked out." The message from the public was just as clear: "Enough is enough. Give the man his due. In an era when top performers are jacked up on performance-enhancing drugs, indicted for murder, or in and out of drug rehab, how does the commissioner justify a lifetime ban for Pete Rose?"

From that point forward, I enjoyed an enormous amount of public support. I even made the jump from "Hospitality Guest" to "Spokesman" in the world of corporate America. Maaco signed me to be their pitchman—my first national television commercial in over 12 years. I also signed a major deal with PONY Baseball, who launched a nationwide campaign to push for my consideration in the Hall of Fame. But baseball would not budge from its position. It was like I was dead. Another reminder that "permanently" is a long, long time.

"That was the beginning of our most difficult times," says Carol Rose. "It was like baseball opened the door and then slammed it in our face. The whole experience really affected Pete in a negative way. It was like they ripped the soul right out of him. During the investigation, Pete's first wife, Karolyn, said, 'It would kill Pete if they took baseball away from him.' At that point, I was beginning to think it might. But there was nothing I could do or say to make him feel better. I wanted him to be more at peace . . . and relaxed like he was in the past. I wanted him to enjoy life . . . see his outrageous sense of humor come back. But he missed baseball terribly and he didn't know what to do with himself. Pete was bored . . . and he's not the typical family man who can just stay at home. Pete's just never content unless he's involved in a challenge. He has an obsessive personality but he's not cruel. He doesn't mean to hurt anyone. He just has to compete at full throttle in everything he does in order to feel satisfied, which is not really his fault. It's just the way he is. That's why it's so hard to say anything about the racetrack . . . because there isn't anything else for him to do. That's what he enjoys . . . that's his pleasure."

When asked what it would take for me to get back into baseball, Mr. Giamatti said that I needed to show a "redirected, reconfigured, or re-habilitated life." Obviously, there was a big discrepancy between base-ball's interpretation and mine. I stopped making illegal bets and hanging around with undesirables, which is what I was told to do. Hell, nobody said I had to become a monk! And yes, I continued to visit the racetrack but I only went three or four times a month—not everyday like I used to do. And I always stayed within my means. If I lost what I took to the track, I went home. When the opportunity presented itself, I tried my luck at a Pick-Six. The California tracks are usually alive with a Pick-Six jackpot that will grow as high as $500,000 after a carryover. I find it ex-citing to match my wits against the track with those kinds of stakes. But I wasn't betting with the money I used to pay my mortgage or my monthly expenses. And I never stayed all day to bet every race in the program. I was just going to the track and betting legally like millions of other Americans. During that same time, I was offered a 2-year contract at $1 million a year to promote an Internet gambling Web site. Although I needed the money, I turned down the offer because I didn't want to promote gambling for a profession. I wouldn't let my son visit those Web sites, so I wasn't going to lend my name to their cause. Besides, I knew the deal would put a nail in the coffin for my chances of reinstatement. If turning down $2 million isn't proof that I was "redirected" then what more did I need to prove?

Recently, I read where two college basketball players were caught shaving points to earn money to pay for their cocaine habit. Throughout the scandal, no one talked about the "integrity of the game"—only the nature of their "medical problem." I bet on my team to win—never shaved points or fixed a game. But my mistake was considered worse than fixing a game to buy cocaine. Come on! I hadn't made a bet on baseball since before I got busted. I felt no temptation whatsoever to try it again! I just reached the point where I was sick and tired of the double standard. I was tired of defending my lifestyle as if I was the only gambler on the planet. I never raised a hand to either of my wives or any of my children. Yet there are wife beaters in the Hall of Fame. I never drank, smoked, or used drugs. Yet there are addicts in the Hall of Fame.

Throughout that time, I was approached by a number of high-profile attorneys who wanted to handle my case on a contingent basis. They believed that even though baseball operated by a set of rules, those rules did not allow them to break the law. The attorneys wanted to fight my lifetime ban based on a number of legal issues, including "restraint of trade," and "being deprived of my livelihood without due process." I'm no lawyer but the arguments made good sense. They advised me that Mr. Giamatti broke our contract within hours after signing, which made the agreement "voidable under the law." Furthermore, if a company wanted to hire the members of the Big Red Machine for a commercial endorsement, they would need permission from Major League Baseball to use team logos. Without Pete Rose, the whole deal might fall through. As a result, Joe Morgan, Johnny Bench, Tony Perez, and I could each sue for damages from lost income. But the idea of a lawsuit also opened up a big can of worms. I had already been through a series of bitter court battles with baseball and wasn't anxious to do it again. I wanted to settle my dispute without going to court and without public embarrassment. I wanted to take the high road. Suing baseball would have only hurt me and the game, no matter how many dream teams of attorneys approached me. Either way, I was still living in a prison without bars.

15

TURNING POINT

"No matter how hard I tried, I couldn't control it."
—*JIM EISENREICH,*
World Series champion

I've been fortunate to have achieved a lot of firsts in my life. On July 1, 1970, I hit the first triple in Riverfront Stadium, just after hitting the last triple in the history of Crosley Field. During the exhibition season of 1982, I became the first player to get a hit inside the Metrodome in Minneapolis. The Phillies were playing the Twins and as the leadoff hitter, I drove a frozen rope into centerfield, which was fielded on the one-hop by a young rookie named Jim Eisenreich. During the bottom half of the inning, Eisenreich became the first Twins player to get a hit inside the dome. He pulled an inside pitch that sailed over my head and into right field. Twenty years later, I discovered that I had more in common with Eisenreich than just base hits.

Eisenreich continued to hit well throughout the exhibition season of 1982. In fact, he was on track to win Rookie of the Year. But every time he took the field, his body went into such weird contortions that he could barely play his position. Finally, after running off the field during the middle of the inning in Fenway Park, Jim's career hit the skids. Like me, Jimmy was brought up to the big leagues early—straight from class-A ball. Jim was a talented hitter with a magical bat. But he had a strange problem. Ever since he was 6 years old, Jim made "involuntary jerking movements and guttural snorting sounds." "No matter how hard I tried," said Jim, "I couldn't control it."

Like me, Jim had a great dad who tried to get some help for his son. But all the doctors said the same thing: "Don't worry," they said. "He's just a little hyperactive. He'll grow out of it." But Jim didn't grow out of it. His condition got worse. Throughout his life, Jim was teased for being "different" from all the other kids. The nuns at his Catholic grade school even brought in doctors from the state mental hospital, who timed his twitches with a stopwatch in front of the whole class. Fortunately, Jimmy had a gift. He could hit a baseball. And playing baseball became Jim's way of coping with the pain of being "different." But while playing the outfield in Fenway Park, the pain got too much for him to handle. An irate fan threw a beer bottle that almost hit Jim in the head—kinda like my experience with the Mets fans in Shea Stadium. But instead of fielding the line drive, Jimmy ran off the field in the middle of the inning. Afterward, the Twins checked him into a psychiatric ward for observation. Everyone thought Jim was crazy. But the doctors couldn't treat or diagnose his strange condition. For the next 3 years, they put Jimmy through a living hell. They shot him up with tranquilizers, gave him biofeedback, hypnotherapy, and even brought in an evangelist to "cast out the demons"! Hell, if it had been me, I'd have told the doctors to go fuck themselves! But Jimmy was the real quiet type—he never said anything to offend anybody. Finally, Jim retired from baseball and took up residence in the basement of his dad's house. He was so embarrassed, he could barely function. But his dad,

"Eike," never gave up hope. He kept right on hunting until he found a doctor who could help his son. Eventually, Eike took Jimmy to a specialist, who diagnosed him with Tourette's syndrome—"a neurological condition caused by the inability to properly metabolize the brain chemical dopamine." Sound familiar? After another 2 years of experimenting with medication to treat his condition, Jimmy returned to baseball, where he hit home runs in two different World Series. In 1996, Eisenreich led the league with a .361 batting average but was six at-bats shy of qualifying for the title, which was won by Tony Gwynn, who hit .353.

I heard another inspirational story from my writer, who spent a great deal of his spare time coaching young athletes in his community. Rick coached a young kid who averaged over 45 points per game in his basketball league. The kid was so gifted that he could score at will—unstoppable. During one game, he scored 50 points in his team's 58–8 victory! The boy had a gift. But he also had a problem. "Sometimes, when the pace didn't suit his needs," said Rick, "the kid would steal the ball from his own teammates, drive to the hoop, and score." He had boundless energy, which drove him to take control of every aspect of the game, regardless of the rules. The young boy was diagnosed with an obsessive-compulsive personality due to a deficiency in the brain chemical dopamine. But when asked how to deal with the condition, the doctors told his parents, "Just give him all your love and support and try to teach him some acceptable boundaries. He's liable to be the next Michael Jordan."

An expert by the name of Oliver Sacks wrote a book called *Awakenings*, which explains "the relationship between dopamine and human behavior." They even made a movie based on the book, which starred two of my favorite actors, Robin Williams and Robert DeNiro. In the movie, the character played by DeNiro suffered from something called "sleeping sickness." But when Dr. Sayer (played by Robin Williams) gave him massive doses of dopamine, he came out of his coma and lived as a normal human being—until the medicine started to wear off. Then he began to twitch and jerk uncontrollably, much like Jim Eisenreich. No matter how hard he tried, he couldn't control it.

Recently, Oliver Sacks gave a speech in Pasadena, California, where he talked about "the uncanny dysfunctions of the brain caused by the chemical dopamine." I was out of town during his lecture but I sure as hell took an interest in the subject matter. It seemed like every talk show, magazine cover, and newspaper article I saw talked about the subject of "brain chemistry"—why we do the things we do.

According to the experts, "dopamine is the brain chemical most responsible for the control of our emotions and behavior. When levels of dopamine are deficient, a person will have problems ranging anywhere from dyslexia, ADHD, Tourette's syndrome, oppositional-defiant, risk-craving, to obsessive-compulsive behavior. But people with this particular brain chemistry are also blessed with a gift. They have an extraordinary ability to focus on a given task. And when they find something they love, they will excel far, far above normal expectations."

I watched an interesting TV program recently, where celebrities talked about beating addictions. Ann Richards, the former governor of Texas, talked about her problems with alcohol. Actress Jamie Lee Curtis had a battle with the painkiller Vicodin. Actor Tom Arnold talked about his battle with alcohol and cocaine. Each one of them described being in "bondage to a craving that was nearly impossible to resist." Robert Downey Jr. expressed similar feelings after he was arrested for possession of cocaine. As I watched and listened, I was amazed by how willing those celebrities were to talk about their problems and reveal their vulnerabilities to the whole world. Then, it all made perfect sense. They worked in professions where it was okay, even necessary, to show their emotions. Vulnerability is the main tool in an actor's craft. Emotion is a powerful force in political appeal. But I was neither an actor nor a politician. I came from a world where vulnerability was a worthless human emotion. My dad raised me to be strong—and somewhat merciless. Even though I was impressed by the celebrities' willingness to discuss their problems, a part of me still looked at confession as an act of weakness, as backing down from a challenge—something I refused to do.

But as I listened to these stories about athletes and entertainers, I began to see similarities in my own life. The same dopamine that caused Jim Eisenreich to twitch caused my "risk-craving behavior." The same dopamine that caused the young basketball player to ignore the rules caused me to do the same. But just because the doctors had a fancy name for it didn't mean I could change it! I realized that those folks were all gifted in a certain area—just like me. They were all at the top of their profession—just like me. They all had obsessive habits that caused setbacks in their lives—just like me. But they all had something I didn't have. During the course of their TV interviews, Jamie Lee Curtis, Tom Arnold, and Ann Richards each talked about the importance of "hope"—something I was deprived of by Baseball's lifetime ban. They all said hope gave them the strength to carry on. Despite their problems or mistakes, Tom Arnold, Jamie Lee Curtis, Robert Downey Jr., and Winona Ryder were still allowed to make movies. Ann Richards was still involved in politics. Pat Summerall returned to television after recovering from alcoholism. Even Marv Albert returned to the broadcast booth with NBC after his brush with the law. They were all allowed to resume work in their individual professions. But I was not allowed to step foot on a baseball field. Banned for life without the possibility of parole. I had no hope. What was it Ray Schalk said about Shoeless Joe Jackson? Oh yeah, "The Hester Prynne of baseball forced to wear the 'scarlet letter' of scorn and rejection."

Regardless of the similarities in our conditions, I was faced with completely different circumstances. Admitting my guilt to anyone outside of baseball served no practical purpose. I wasn't going to confess to Jim Gray or on *Larry King Live!* I wasn't going to get down on my knees and beg forgiveness like a TV preacher. It wouldn't do any good! The commissioner of Baseball was the only person who could reinstate me. And he didn't answer my letters or my phone calls. Based on Baseball's long-standing position on Rule #21, I had no reason to believe that admitting my guilt to the public would change my lifetime ban. After all, I was accepted back into the world of corporate America, earning six figures a year from speaking engagements and enjoying the benefit of overwhelming public support. Hell, I was more popular by *not* being in the Hall of Fame!

"Pete has never been the kind of guy to talk man-to-man about anything of a personal nature," said friend and Hall of Fame player Mike Schmidt. "I was as close to Pete as any teammate and we never had any one-on-one conversations. Pete is simply a product of the generation in which he played. He saw himself as a larger-than-life hero and he believed in that image. His ego and his impression of himself were very strong. Pete was told by so many people that he was larger than life and in some ways, he was. Part of that behavior is not completely his fault. From high school on, athletes are coddled, pampered, and given special treatment. We get privilege and access to things and places that most folks can only dream of. Politicians and celebrities want to be our friends and nobody ever says no to us. We are led to believe that we can do no wrong. Then, the public wants to know why we make errors in judgment when our entire life has been shielded from the outside world, where the basis of good judgment is formed. As a Hall of Fame ballplayer, I understood the perks and privileges of being a celebrity. I knew that I could get out of a speeding ticket or not be held accountable for certain things. In fact, all of us have made bad choices and maybe never got caught—or had them jump up and bite us in the ass the way that gambling bit Pete. Pete just pushed the limit a little too far. On the other hand, Pete had made a good living from his reputation as the bad guy. He was aware that a great deal of the public liked that image. But the 'image' itself was part of the problem. I knew that Pete wasn't a religious guy. So his show of remorse or change in attitude was going to have to come from someplace else."

Mike Schmidt was right. I am a product of my generation, where men took stock in discipline and hard work—not wearing their hearts on their sleeves. I never talked one-on-one with any of my friends because I never felt the need. It's not that I didn't feel the emotions—I just never learned how to express them. I'm just not built that way. Sure, there's probably some real emotion buried somewhere deep inside. And I'd probably be a better person if I learned to express the emotions. But you're not reading this book to be my therapist, and frankly, there are places in all of us we just don't want to go. That's one for me. Let's move on.

◆ ◆ ◆

On April 1, 2000, I received a phone call from my sister Jackie in Cincinnati. "Mom died," said Jackie. "Her heart just finally gave out." Mom was 84 years old, so I can't honestly say that I wasn't expecting the call, but it still came as a shock. A death in the family is always a shock—especially when it's your mother. After my dad passed away, Mom married her childhood friend, Bob Noeth, who lost his wife at about the same time. Rosie spent Christmas, Thanksgiving, and most summers with Bob's family. So we just kinda grew apart after a while. Then, in 1973, Rosie and Bob moved to Thonotassa, Florida, which was about 25 miles east of Tampa, where the Reds had spring training. I always left six tickets for Rosie and her friends from the trailer park where she lived. She came to most of our games at Al Lopez Field and always cheered for me and the other players. Rosie was a big baseball fan and she was very proud of my accomplishments. But she was proud of all her kids. She always made a point to talk about Dave, Jackie, and Caryl, so that nobody felt less important due to my success. Rosie liked the fact that I never turned down an autograph to the fans and that I played with the same dedication as my dad. Still, I never got to see Mom very much during spring training because I was always on the field with the team. I invited her to my house in Florida, but Rosie always had an excuse not to come. "I'll get lost, Pete," she said. "I don't know how to get over to your house." Finally, I just drove over to her house one day and had dinner with her and Bob. Mom only had one piece of sports memorabilia hanging on her wall—a poster of me from Fan Appreciation Day, which was signed "To Mom, a great fan, I love you very much, Pete Rose." Rosie used to laugh when she showed the poster to her friends. "Isn't that a riot?" she said. "He signed it 'Pete Rose'—as if I didn't know his last name! But that's okay. I know he loves me."

That I did, but it didn't stop me from forgetting her birthday! I didn't do it on purpose—that's just how I am. I just can't seem to concentrate on things I'm not interested in. Usually I'd just give Mom a grand or two for Christmas. I'd say, "Here, Mom, take this and get something for yourself. I forgot to go shopping." Rosie never felt embarrassed about taking money instead of gifts because she knew I had money and that made her proud in itself. Hell, it made us both proud.

After Bob Noeth died in 1984, Rosie stayed in Florida for a while to be around her friends. She kept busy with arts and crafts and rode her bicycle 5 miles a day. She built a small table lamp and made miniature figurines, which she kept on her living room table. Rosie hated to sew or read or write letters. She was still pretty active—still outspoken and opinionated right up to the end. Finally, Rosie moved back to Cincinnati and lived with my sister Jackie Schwier and her husband, Al. She came down to Florida for Christmas one year but she really didn't like to travel. "I can't climb those stairs, Pete," she said. We used to tease and cuss at each other for hours at a time, but that was the nature of our relationship. We both had fun with it. Rosie lived 30 years after my dad passed away, which was a miracle, given her medical history. As Rosie got older, she lost her kidney, appendix, bladder, female organs, tonsils, and just about everything else the doctors could take out. She had more operations than anybody. She looked like a zipper, God rest her soul. In her last years, Rosie was always on the verge of dying from some mysterious ailment. But miraculously, she always pulled through. "By God, I'll outlive all you kids!" said Rosie. She almost did.

I flew back to Cincinnati and joined my brother Dave and my sisters Jackie and Caryl and their families. We all sat around the funeral parlor and talked about the good old days back in Anderson's Ferry. It wasn't a warm and fuzzy reunion. Nobody in the Rose family wants to put their burdens onto anybody else. But still, it was good to see the whole family together. All of my mom's friends were there to pay their respects, people she'd known all her life. Jackie showed everyone the photo of Rosie fishing off the front porch during the great flood of 1937. She reminded everyone that Rosie always wore a hairnet and loved to snack on Pringles potato chips before she went to bed. So just before the service, Jackie placed Rosie's hairnet and a can of Pringles in her casket. Then, she grinned and looked over at me. "See, Pete, she's not dead," said Jackie. "She's just getting ready for bed."

When I finally sat down for Rosie's funeral, I started to think about all the folks who weren't there. My mom's brothers, Al, George, and Buddy, had all passed away. Each one of them had been a big influence on my life. All three were mentors—guys who taught me the finer points of hitting and fielding. I especially missed flamboyant Buddy—the "Masked Marvel." I often wondered what he could have accomplished had he been able to stick with baseball. He might've been another Stan Musial because he certainly had the talent. But instead, he channeled his talent into me, and I was much obliged for his efforts.

As I sat there thinking, something else hit me pretty strong. I always pictured my mom sitting in the audience in Cooperstown when I finally got inducted into the Hall of Fame. But now she wouldn't have the chance. Then I felt someone take my hand—Marge Schott, former owner of the Cincinnati Reds. Marge drove all the way across town in the pouring rain, walked right over, and sat down next to me. She didn't say a word. But she held my hand throughout the entire service—one of the nicest things anyone has ever done for me. Afterward, we talked about the good old days. Marge had to be hospitalized twice in 1989 for stress-related ailments. But she never let anything keep her down for long. Throughout the investigation, she never once turned her back on me, which is not to say that I didn't give her fits. Marge and I had similar personalities, so we'd butt heads from time to time. When she first bought the team in '84, she hired me as the manager but made no bones about her concerns. "With Pete's mouth and my mouth, I don't know how we're going to handle all this." Marge had a St. Bernard named Schottzie, who became the team mascot—dog went everywhere Marge went. And every time I went over to Marge's house, Schottzie would plop his big ol' head on my lap and drool all over my pants. Finally I got fed up. "Hey Marge," I said. "Can you do something about your dog?" Marge just stabbed me with a look. "The dog lives here, Pete. You're just visiting." As the conversation continued, the subject of one of my pets came up. At that time, I had a pet lion, which I brought back from Japan during one of our barnstorming tours. When Marge asked me what the hell I wanted with a pet lion, I just grinned. "So it can eat your dog!" I couldn't help but think that Marge got a raw deal with the way she was forced to sell the Cincinnati Reds baseball team. Like me, Marge was a blue-collar person. Sophisticated folks didn't care much for Marge because she wasn't polished or educated. But Marge Schott was real. She was honest. And she was decent. And I know for a fact that she wasn't a racist. She was just a tough lady trying to compete in a man's world. The other owners never welcomed her into the fold, so she had to fend for herself. And she did a damn good job of it, too. Marge would try to answer questions from the media honestly, but many reporters would goad her into areas where they could take advantage. Some writers even waited until late at night to call her because they knew that Marge liked to sip a little vodka before she went to bed. Marge wasn't a heavy drinker—that's just how she liked to unwind from the pressures of the day. But the reporters figured that they could take advantage if Marge was tired or a little tipsy. But how many other owners would even take the time to field phone calls from reporters late at night? Very few, that's for damn sure. Marge was a great owner and a great person. She only came into my office one time in 5 years and that was just to wish me a happy birthday. She never complained and she never interfered with the way I ran the team. I only went to her office twice in 5 years—once to ask for more money to keep Dave Parker and again to ask for money to get Buddy Bell and Bill Gullickson. Marge okayed both requests. Like Rosie, Marge was a tough lady who ruffled feathers with "polite society." But neither of them ever backed down from a fight.

◆ ◆ ◆

"When Pete came back from his mother's funeral," said Pete's wife, Carol, "I could see some subtle changes. After 23 years, I've come to accept that Pete never talks about personal issues. But he started doing little things, like opening a car door for me, or calling ahead to make dinner reservations. It may not sound like much, but for Pete Rose, it's a major breakthrough!"

I'll admit that I was dealing with a few personal issues. I've never been the type to dwell on the past, but being back in Cincinnati and laying my mother to rest brought back some memories. Mostly, I was thinking about my kids. I was not a hug-and-kiss dad with Fawn and Pete Jr. I was too macho to say "I love you" back in those days, just like my dad. So I raised my kids the same way my dad raised me—tough. But that doesn't mean I was a bad father. I just wasn't around much. I was a professional ballplayer, who lived in a tough and aggressive world. I was always on the road or at the ballpark, so my kids missed out on certain things. Like the families of other athletes, entertainers, and politicians, my family took a backseat to my pursuit of greatness. But they also enjoyed many benefits that other families didn't have—like going to the ballpark every day, spring training trips to Florida, living with all the comforts that money could buy. Looking back, I don't know if it was a fair deal.

Because I was always playing baseball during the summer, I never saw Pete Jr. play any of his Little League games. But I took him to the ballpark every chance I got. I probably cheated my daughter Fawn more than anyone because she was a girl. I couldn't take her to the ballpark because there was no place to leave her. The stadiums didn't have "hospitality suites" for the players' families like they do today. But now with my second family, I wasn't playing baseball anymore. I had more free time to be at home, and I was learning to be more affectionate with my younger kids. I wasn't the same man at 60 that I was at 40—hell, nobody is! In some ways, I was learning how to be a parent for the first time. At the same time, I was learning about what makes me tick.

I helped coach Tyler's Little League teams and drove Cara to her acting and singing auditions. I even started taking my wife and daughter to the track—but not just for the races. We went to the stable area to visit with the trainers and watch the horses work out. At that time, Will Farish, from Lane's End Farms, ran into a little bad luck with a 4-year-old gelding by the name of Fort Point. The horse was purchased for $975,000 but after just a few races, developed breathing problems. They took the horse to John Kimmel, one of the top vets in the business, but Fort Point had a bad flapper, which couldn't be repaired with surgery. In time, Fort Point would heal and return to racing. But Lane's End was not interested in a $50,000 claimer—they wanted to win the Derby. So, rather than put the horse down, Will and his co-owners offered him to me. I boarded Fort Point at Del Mar, with my friend Bob Hess. Carol and Cara started visiting the horse on a regular basis and just fell in love with him. They fed him carrots and even gave him a nickname—Charlie Horsel. Then Bob let the exercise riders take him out for a few short runs. Before I knew it, Fort Point was running pretty strong. Afterward, Bob sent the horse to the vet, who put him on the treadmill and ran some tests. But he couldn't find anything wrong with the horse's breathing. So Bob and I brought him back to Del Mar and put him into training. I doubt if Fort Point will make it to any of the classic races, but if he runs well enough to make even a small comeback, it'll be a great success story. One I shared with my family.

My son Tyler had no interest in horses, but by the time he became a sophomore in high school, he grew to be six feet two and developed into a fine basketball player. He had a smooth jump shot and could dunk two-handed from the standstill position. I made a point of attending all of his games and practices. I got along great with his coach and all of his teammates, but I was shocked to see how the attitudes had changed since I was a kid. In my day, you never opened your mouth unless you could back it up. Several of the kids from the area spent as much time trash-talking as they did playing the game. Attitudes had changed with today's kids, and I tried to keep an open mind. Whenever I was in town, I went to every practice and every game. I watched as Tyler made great progress in basketball and loved every minute. Tyler doesn't cuss or fight—although sometimes I wish he did. During one particular game, he stole the ball for a breakaway layup and I screamed, "Dunk the sonafabitch!" I don't know if Tyler heard me, but everyone else in the gym sure did. Since he was playing for a private Catholic school, the folks were a bit surprised by my outburst. But I couldn't help myself. I get excited when it comes to watching sports—especially when my son does something great.

Tyler's coaches believed he had the potential to play on the college level. But like his dad, Tyler didn't like to study. He was the leading scorer on his team but was on the verge of becoming ineligible due to bad grades. Talk about déjà vu all over again! My folks didn't pressure me into hitting the books because they knew it wouldn't do any good. I was too headstrong to pay attention. Besides, I played baseball with such desire that even though I flunked out, I didn't drop out. My dad saw what I could accomplish when I set my mind to it, so he decided to keep me focused on sports. I understood how Tyler felt; I hated school, too. But if I had everything to do over again, I'd further my education. If I had gone to college, I don't think everything would've turned out the way it did, with gambling and such. I'm one of those guys who had success without an education because I had street smarts. I'm not sure my son does. I told my son that not getting an education was my mistake—a mistake he doesn't have to repeat. So with Tyler, I decided to get a little more involved than my parents did. No matter how hard I tried to impress upon him the need to study, Tyler didn't listen.

So in order to get Tyler back on the right track, I decided to take extreme measures, to bring in my "closer." My daughter Fawn is the first college graduate in my entire family. She got her degree in psychology and I asked her to put her education to good use. At the time, she was living in Cincinnati and waiting to start a new job. So I offered Fawn the job of tutoring my son Tyler. She accepted and agreed to live with us until she had to report for her new job in Seattle.

"I didn't realize it at the time, but it was one of the best decisions I ever made," says Fawn. "At first, I was surprised by Dad's request. In the past, he avoided certain issues that needed to be discussed. By addressing Tyler's schoolwork, I felt like Dad was making progress."

"When it comes to discipline for the kids," says Carol, "Pete is very lackadaisical, which is surprising given his strong personality. He usually delegates that task to me, especially with Tyler. I guess because it's a guy thing. I'm a little stricter, but Pete lets the leash out with him. I think it's because he feels guilty that he travels most of the time. He doesn't want to come off as the heavy and then leave home for 2 weeks, where he can't be around to enforce the rules."

Fawn surprised me. "I began teaching many of the things I learned from my dad," she says. "Dad was never late and he never missed a day of practice in his entire life. So Tyler had to complete all his work and be on time or face the consequences. At first, Tyler fought me to see what he could get away with. But after he saw that I didn't back down, he came around to my way of thinking. Dad and Carol were surprised by the way Tyler responded. By being a stepsister instead of a parent, I could accomplish some things they couldn't."

Fawn was a good influence on Tyler. Eventually, the tutoring sessions became an entire family experience. They even tried to drag me into the act. My daughter Cara was also being tutored because her acting and singing career kept her away from the classroom. While working on a term paper, she came to me with an interesting question. "Why do they make cars that go 140 mph but have speed limits of 65?" she asked. "Hell, darlin', I don't know," I said. "Why do they sing 'Take Me Out to the Ball Game' when you're already there? Why does a pizza arrive faster than an ambulance?" Some questions just weren't meant to be answered! But Cara was not to be denied. She kept pushing and prodding me for an answer until I got provoked, which most folks tend to avoid because nobody loves a good argument more than me. But kids have a way of pushing their parents' buttons. Finally, I thought back to the early days when I was a kid and came up with a sound explanation. "In the beginning," I replied, "the car manufacturers were just interested in building bigger and better engines. Then, after folks started getting into accidents, the insurance companies began to deal with the safety issues. In fact, they even put a 'governor' on the mascot tractor we used for the Big Red Machine to keep it from going too fast." I could tell by the surprised look on Cara's face that she was impressed with my answer. Hell, I was kinda proud of myself, too. But then, Cara started giggling. "They should make 'governors' for people," she said with a big grin. Well, right away, I could see what she was referring to. But everybody has their limits. And I wasn't about to let my daughter get in the last word. Cara and the other kids just kept giggling until I had no choice but to come up with a solution. I started a pillow fight until everyone forgot all about the subject. And by God, that was the last time they asked me for help with their homework! Still, it's funny the way your kids can make you think.

Each morning, before Fawn started her tutoring session, I'd meet her in the kitchen for coffee. We'd laugh and tell jokes. In fact, we laughed at just about everything. Fawn has many of the same personality traits as me but she is more expressive with her feelings. Hell, we even had a few wrestling matches on the floor like we did when she was a kid. "During that time," said Fawn, "I remembered the things I admired most about my dad: his dedication and work ethic—his ability to dream. He always taught me to strive for excellence in pursuing my dream. As a kid, I watched Dad sacrifice everything in his life for his dream. I learned from that experience and believed that I could find a balance of wanting to be successful and not forgetting my family and home. And after spending more time around him at this stage of his life, I saw a caring side that I never really saw before."

◆ ◆ ◆

As much as we tried, Tyler's grades didn't improve. He remained eligible for the basketball team, but barely. By his senior year, Tyler grew to be six feet four and was really making progress with his skills. But at the end of the season, he got himself into trouble. Besides being a good basketball player, Tyler has a talent for art. He likes to draw designs and paint pictures. He's no savant, but Tyler has talent. He drew a real nice design for the cover of a friend's notebook, which would have earned him an A had it been turned in for art class. But Tyler didn't turn in his work. Instead, he painted the design on the side of a vacant school locker. Why? I reckon he just wanted to show off. But somebody must have ratted him out because Tyler got suspended from school, pending a hearing before the dean. We received a formal letter from the school, which criticized his act of "vandalism" in such a way that made Tyler feel like he had committed a major crime. Hell, it was just a 6-inch art design, which easily could have been washed off. It wasn't like he destroyed the locker. Still, I was pissed off when I found out what Tyler did. Of course, I yelled at him, but after Tyler apologized, I forgave him. When he asked me how I wanted to handle the situation, I didn't have to think twice. "Go before the dean and admit your mistake," I replied. "Apologize and ask for a stiff punishment, like serving detention or yard cleanup." Ironic, huh?

I was out of town at the time, but Carol attended the meeting to hear the charges against him. The dean was not receptive to Tyler's apology. The dean explained that recent acts of graffiti on a nearby bridge had caused problems for the school. She suspected that Tyler was involved in the graffiti and wanted him to "name names." But Tyler was not involved with the graffiti on the bridge. He had no idea who was responsible. Even if he had known, I would not have allowed him to rat out his friends. Tyler was there to confess and apologize for painting on the locker—not to get turned into an informant. The dean suggested that graffiti could lead to more severe acts of "vandalism," which could also lead to a life of crime and even to potential suicide! Tyler and Carol were both shocked to hear the dean's reaction. How could an experienced school educator suggest that one act of bad judgment could turn my son into the next John Gotti?

Afterward, the dean scheduled a formal hearing before the principal and the eight-member committee of the disciplinary board. Tyler told me that another kid was recently caught smoking marijuana and was let off with a warning. Painting a small design on a locker was not as serious as smoking weed. So Tyler believed that by confessing the truth and apologizing before the board, he would be reinstated after serving his punishment. Carol and I were asked to attend the meeting but we were not allowed to speak. Tyler stood up, answered all their questions, and confessed to painting the design on the locker. He apologized for his mistake and asked for their forgiveness. But the members of the Board were all control freaks. They suggested that certain words that were found in Tyler's artwork had implications of being "gang-related." Eventually, Tyler got so upset that he started to cry. Then he asked for a second chance. At that point, I felt like they were trying to break my son's spirit, which really pissed me off. Tyler is a Rose—ain't nobody gonna break a Rose's spirit! The whole process reminded me of prison.

The board members spoke to Tyler like he was doomed to a life of crime. Tyler had never been in trouble during his 4 years in high school. Other than having bad grades and too many tardy slips, he had no misconduct records of any kind. He didn't drink, smoke, cuss, or use drugs. He was about as close to "gang-related" as I was to Mister Rogers! Still, they suspended Tyler from school without the possibility of an appeal. I wanted to stand up and give the bastards a piece of my mind. Tyler was a star basketball player with college potential—not a "gang member"! But I held my peace. Carol was not as patient. "How can a Christian school, which is supposed to teach forgiveness and understanding, be devoid of the very ethics they are supposed to teach?"

But the board members would not budge. They implied that they were doing Tyler a "favor" by kicking him out of school! Just 37 days before graduation, Tyler had to transfer to a public school to earn his high school diploma. It was one of the worst experiences of his life. He felt devastated and betrayed. Not one of the board members, who Tyler thought were his friends, stood up on his behalf. He just couldn't understand why "telling the truth" could be so demoralizing. Since there were no witnesses, the school couldn't prove that Tyler painted the design on the locker. But he did the ethical thing and told the truth. But as a parent, how could I explain the value in "telling the truth" when Tyler got a worse punishment than if he had lied? I had no logical answer. I had plenty of my own experiences to rely on, but nothing in the way of encouragement. As a sophomore in high school, I felt betrayed when the varsity coach denied me an opportunity to play football. Afterward, I rebelled and dropped out—not what I wanted for Tyler. Years later, I hid my involvement during Baseball's investigation and got permanently suspended. Tyler admitted his involvement and still got permanently suspended. Through my own actions, I showed Tyler the trouble that comes from not owning up to your mistakes. But now the world had just shown him that admitting them doesn't make things any better! Where in the hell was the justice? I felt like I made a turning point in my life, but what about my son? What was I supposed to tell him about ethics?

<u>16</u>

THE MEETING

"We all build our lives on the choices we make. And we all have to live with the consequences of those choices—good or bad. None of us make all the right choices. But we have to own up to them."
—BUD SELIG,
Commissioner of Baseball

Early in 2002, Joe Morgan, Mike Schmidt, and Reggie Jackson met again with Mr. Selig to discuss the possibility of a "Pete Rose reinstatement." But Mr. Selig was not interested in hearing any evidence that might rebut the Dowd Report. He had no interest in participating in a debate. Mr. Selig wanted to move forward—a major sign of encouragement. But shortly after that meeting, *Vanity Fair* magazine came out with a sleazy article, based on information provided by Tommy Gioiosa. I had not spoken with Gio since he got out of jail, so I had no idea what was going on in his life. Apparently, he was still trying to cash in on my fame. Gio was reportedly paid $50,000 for the article, which was filled with lies about corked bats and drug use— a bunch of bull. But the lies and garbage created a public relations disaster, which drove another wedge between me and the reinstatement process. Afterward, Baseball refused to answer my phone calls. It was like they wanted no dialogue or paper trail with me. I was very frustrated because I was hoping to move forward with some type of meeting. My lawyers believed that Baseball should at least be required to answer my calls. They suggested that we make a formal complaint to the commissioner's office based on legal ethics. But I decided not to rock the boat. I just couldn't accept that Baseball wouldn't give me a second chance.

On Labor Day of 2002, I ran into Joe Morgan, who coincidentally was booked into the same memorabilia show as me. As a Hall of Famer and one of the top broadcasters in the game, Joe had the commissioner's ear. He engaged the commissioner in several conversations over the years and was spearheading another attempt to get me before the commission. "I can't take a position one way or the other," said Joe. "But I spoke with the commissioner, and he's willing to meet, but he wants to hear a full confession. Are you ready to admit your involvement?" I got into a heated discussion with Joe for taking the liberty of speaking on my behalf. I wanted to meet with the commissioner personally—not through go-betweens. But Joe Morgan was right. I'd just thrived on conflict for so long that I didn't know any other way to respond. After years of waiting for the opportunity to confess, all of a sudden the idea of admitting my guilt didn't sit too well. Deep down, in a place where I didn't want to go, I was covering up my real fear. How would the public respond if they found out that I bet on baseball? Would they turn against me or would they understand that I just couldn't help myself? The very thought that I might lose public support was scary. Hell, it was downright intimidating. But I was running out of options. The only contact I had with baseball was through the fans. And how many more "All-Century" teams could there be? None in my lifetime! While in prison, I joked about the "deep dark rebellious forces that kept knocking my life off-track during pivotal times." But the time for joking was over. I had come to a crossroads in my life, and it was time to make a life-changing decision.

I spoke with my wife and kids and called my agent and lawyer. They offered their support, but in the end, neither my family nor my advisors could make the decision. I had to make it myself. I thought back to my days as a young River Rat, who loved playing baseball every day of his life. I thought about the thrill of going to the racetrack and breaking into the big leagues. I thought about batting titles, All-Star Games, and World Series Championships. Then I thought about my dad, and how all the folks from Anderson's Ferry gave me a daily reminder of my goal in life—a goal more important than 4,256 hits. "If you grow up to be half the man your father is," they said, "You'll be one helluva man." From that simple goal, I realized that confessing the truth was not an act of weakness, but an act of strength.

◆ ◆ ◆

After coming to my decision, I called Bob Dupuy and apologized for letting him down. I understood that Mike Schmidt, Joe Morgan, and many others had worked very hard on my behalf. Mr. Dupuy was very understanding. Afterward, Mr. Selig called Mike Schmidt and asked if he would act as a liaison between the two parties. Within a few weeks, Bob Dupuy flew to Florida, where he met with me, Mike Schmidt, and my agent, Warren Greene. I insisted that no lawyers be present. I didn't want the meeting to get bogged down in legalese. We met at a local hotel and discussed some parameters for my reinstatement. Mr. Dupuy made it very clear that he was not there to talk about the Dowd Report or the Makley Report. He wanted to know if I was prepared to move forward. I agreed to do whatever Mr. Selig felt was necessary. Mike Schmidt cooperated with every step of the process. He voiced only one objection to the issue of a 1-year "probation" period. He thought probation was unfair because I had already been on probation for 13 years. Then, Mr. Dupuy asked a few relevant questions that were prepared by Mr. Selig. "Do you owe any large sums of money, Pete?" he asked. "Do you mean undesirables?" I replied. "Yes, undesirables," he said. I knew that I had some real estate debt and a tax lien against my house, but I didn't consider the IRS an "undesirable." So I answered "No." I also remembered that I could have avoided the whole tax problem by keeping better records of my charitable speaking engagements, which could have been used as tax write-offs. But like I said, I'm better at breaking records than I am with keeping them. My agent had been in the process of working out a payment plan to lift the lien, so I knew the problem was on the verge of being solved. Mr. Dupuy continued to ask about my gambling habits, and I informed him of the events that I've described in my book. I told him that I was no longer making illegal bets or hanging out with undesirables. I hadn't made a bet on baseball since before I got busted. I assured him that I would not be tempted to try it again. I explained my lifelong love for the racetrack, where gambling is perfectly legal. And I explained that I often traveled to Las Vegas or Atlantic City, which host many of my speaking engagements and memorabilia shows. I confessed truthfully that I rarely gamble in casinos despite the many rumors to the contrary. "Just 2 weeks earlier," I said, "I flew to Las Vegas for an autograph show, got off the plane, and went straight to the convention center, where I signed autographs for 3 hours. Afterward, I got back on the plane and flew home. The next day, it was reported in the Cincinnati newspaper that I was in the casino playing blackjack. Truth is, I never set foot in the casino. I was there for a business opportunity, which is the only means I have to support my family. The pit boss even e-mailed the newspaper to verify that I was in the convention center, not the casino. But the paper refused to print a retraction." Mr.

Dupuy was aware of such bullshit and did not seem concerned. He implied that Mr. Selig had plenty of experience with the media regarding "misrepresentations." After our meeting, Mr. Dupuy flew back to Milwaukee and met with Bud Selig to discuss their options.

◆　◆　◆

On September 20, 2002, the Cincinnati Reds held their closing ceremony to say good-bye to Cinergy Field. The Reds played at Crosley Field for 58 years and then 32 more at Cinergy Field, the former Riverfront Stadium— 90 years of baseball history, and it all flashed before me in a blink of an eye. Since I was still on baseball's suspended list, I was not allowed to participate in the ceremony, which included all the former Reds players and managers. But I was in Cincinnati at the time and watched on television. At the end of the ceremony, someone placed a rose on third base in my honor. Then Tom Browning, who pitched throughout my 5-year career as the Reds manager, stepped up and did me a solid. Tom was my ace in 1985—a 20-game winner. He also won Game Three of the Reds four-game sweep of the Oakland A's in the 1990 World Series. Tommy was a scrapper just like me. He took out a can of red spray paint and painted #14 on the pitcher's mound. The packed crowd erupted into a chant of "Pete . . . Pete . . . Pete!" I wasn't there in person but it was nice to know that I was remembered.

Three days later, I hosted a celebrity softball game as the last official event in Riverfront Stadium. My team included all the members of the Big Red Machine—Bench, Morgan, Perez, Concepcion, Foster, Griffey, Tolan, Geronimo, and Helms. We played against an All-Star team, which included Mike Schmidt, Steve Garvey, Ryne Sandberg, Vince Coleman, Gary Carter, Andre Dawson, Dale Murphy, Dave Parker, Doc Gooden, and John Tudor. We played before a capacity crowd of 42,000, which sold out in just 2 hours and 20 minutes after we announced the game. We gave away 40,000 bobblehead dolls, paid $5,000 to each player, donated money to various charities, and still came away with a nice profit. We also attracted a larger crowd than any Major League game during that week. Early in the day, Mike Schmidt reminded me of what the fans wanted to see. I understood what he meant but I wasn't sure I'd be up for the task. Then, late in the game, I got a base hit and then advanced to second on a Tony Perez single. Then, Joe Morgan hit a pop-up to Doc Gooden in centerfield. I tagged up but when I saw Doc make an underhanded toss to Vince Coleman, the shortstop, my instincts took over. I took off with a vengeance and dove headfirst safely into third! The crowd cheered and gave me a standing ovation. Although it was well worth the effort, the slide took its toll on my arthritic knees and 61-year-old body. But it was my last game at Riverfront and I was determined to give the fans their money's worth. By the end of the game, we came up on the losing end of the scoreboard, 19–7. But what else could you expect? Among the 10 members of the Big Red Machine, we had over 600 years of baseball experience. Most of us were lucky to be breathing, let alone playing softball! Instead of running out for a beer after the game, we reached for the Ben-Gay and took a nap! Still, everyone had a great time. After the game, all the players thanked me for organizing the game. They played in many games at Riverfront Stadium throughout their careers and felt honored to be a part of the last "official" ceremony. They all had the time of their lives.

Bench, Morgan, Perez, and I took turns at the microphone and said our good-byes to the fans. We thanked them for all the great memories and soaked in some last-minute glory. The last thing I saw as I left the stadium was a sign in centerfield, which read: "Rose in the Hall—Bet on It!"

Months later, I watched on television as the dynamite explosions crumbled Riverfront Stadium to the ground. It was like watching a death in the family. But like I said: Change is inevitable. Sometimes, change is better.

Within a few weeks, MasterCard announced the second of its major advertising campaigns—"*MasterCard's Most Memorable Moments in Baseball History.*" Once again, since I was on the suspended list, I was allowed on the ballot but not in the campaign. During the following weeks, I watched as my fellow honorees were given the benefit of a very expensive advertising campaign. Hank Aaron, Babe Ruth, Lou Gehrig, Kirk Gibson, Jackie Robinson, and Cal Ripken Jr. appeared regularly on inspirational television commercials that featured their individual accomplishments. But there was no Pete Rose commercial, no magazine or radio ads to commemorate my 4,256 hits. I believed that I deserved to be included in the top 10, but without the benefit of the big advertising campaign given to the other players, I figured I had no chance. I figured Hank Aaron was the shoo-in for breaking Babe Ruth's record of 714 career home runs. But Ty Cobb's 4,191 hits was considered just as "unbreakable" as Ruth's record. So then I figured maybe I had a chance after all. Lou Gehrig had a good chance at winning because of his "Iron Horse" statistics, terrible disease, great speech at Yankee Stadium. Mark McGwire's 70 single-season home runs were also pretty impressive. But when the final tally was in, Cal Ripken Jr. won for breaking Lou Gehrig's record for consecutive games played. For my career record 4,256 hits, I was voted MasterCard's 6th Most Memorable Moment in Baseball History.

I received a nice letter from the commissioner, congratulating me on the honor. He invited me to participate in the ceremony, which was being held in San Francisco during the 2002 World Series between the Angels and the Giants. It had been 3 years since the All-Century celebration, and I was looking forward to another reunion. I arrived in San Francisco and ironically, checked in to the same hotel where I stayed the night I first met Joe DiMaggio.

When I arrived at the stadium on the night of the ceremony, I met with Hank Aaron and Kirk Gibson. We laughed and shared some stories about the good old days. I was having the time of my life. Then I was struck by a terrible thought: "What happens if Jim Gray comes lurking out of the shadows?"

When I stepped forward to accept my award, I felt a rush that I hadn't felt since breaking Cobb's record. The fans gave me a 3-minute standing ovation, which also caught the attention of Commissioner Bud Selig. I didn't realize it at the time, but Mr. Selig was in the process of making a major decision.

◆　◆　◆

I flew into Milwaukee on November 25, 2002. I was met by Baseball's security and local police, who escorted me from the plane and onto the tarmac, where I was taken by limo to a downtown Milwaukee hotel. Baseball had brought me in under a cloud of secrecy. But I'll be damned if after 13 years I was going to sit in my room and order room service just to avoid publicity. I met with Mike Schmidt and ate breakfast in a restaurant, which aroused suspicions with the local townfolk. Like I said, I'm not a nervous person, but I was a bit anxious. Mike and I talked about our 1980 World Series in Philadelphia and got caught up on the good old days. Then, just after breakfast, Mike gave me the reminder that I referred to in the beginning of this book—"Baseball needs Charlie Hustle."

Mike Schmidt, Bob Dupuy, my agent Warren Greene, and I entered Commissioner Selig's office. Once we got inside, Mr. Selig took charge and discussed some of his ideas. Right away, Bud Selig surprised me with his knowledge and love for the game. He talked about Cap Anson, Stan Musial, and how much he loved going to the ballpark as a kid. Then, we got on the subject of the 2002 All-Star Game and my sense of humor took over. I reminded Bud that he must have felt really bad when he got booed by his own fans in Milwaukee. Mr. Selig grinned and nodded his head. He knew that I meant no disrespect. He understood that I always say what's on my mind. With Pete Rose, "what you see is what you get." I just wanted to let him know that I understood how much it hurts to get booed when you're wearing the white jerseys. It was not the commissioner's fault that the managers of both teams ran out of pitchers. Mr. Selig understood what I meant and didn't take offense. Then, he discussed some ideas that might bring back the era of the "Ray Fosse–style" All-Star Games.

I played in 17 All-Star Games and won 16 of them. I considered the All-Star Game a privilege—an opportunity to give something back to the fans, to play for the love of the game. I remembered going to the All-Star Game in 1965 and playing behind Willie Mays, Roberto Clemente, and Frank Robinson. I never got in the game because I was the only guy on the team who could go behind the dish if the catcher got hurt. But I came up to bat in the 14th inning and got the game-winning hit. Over a decade later, I played in an All-Star Game where the starting outfield was me, Willie Davis, and Cesar Cedeno. The back-up players were Willie Mays, Hank Aaron, and Roberto Clemente! The fans were actually cheering for the manager to take the starters out of the game, so they could watch their heroes play! Hell, I was cheering, too. I wanted to watch them play! Neither age nor money had anything to do with how we approached the game in the 1960s and 1970s. Willie and Hank and Roberto hated sitting on the bench as much as I did. We all wanted to play in every inning of every game for the love of the sport. That's why I told Mr. Selig that I believed the change in attitude had to start with the players. Mr. Selig understood and appreciated my point of view. But he had already been working on a plan. Within days, he solved the problem by providing an incentive. He proposed home-field advantage in the World Series to the All-Star Game's winner—smart move!

◆ ◆ ◆

Finally, Mr. Selig changed gears and talked about how things might transpire. He spoke very eloquently about the fact that we all build our lives on the choices that we make. And that we all have to live with the consequences of those choices—good or bad. "None of us make all the right choices," said Bud. "But we all have to own up to them." Then Mr. Selig asked everyone to leave the room except me.

"As I stepped outside the commissioner's office," said Mike Schmidt, "I looked through the picture window and noticed the view of the surrounding lake. As beautiful as the lake was, my thoughts were not on the view. They were on the conversation inside Mr. Selig's office. All of the important details had been worked out in advance. But what it boiled down to was that the commissioner wanted to hear the truth from Pete's own mouth. Basically, Pete needed to get down from his high horse and show some humility. I never asked or expected to hear any details of Pete's gambling activity. So I wasn't there to counsel or criticize him. Whatever confession needed to be heard was going to be heard by Mr. Selig behind closed doors. I got involved in the process because I wanted to see Pete get reinstated to baseball. Pete was there to apologize for his choices with the hope that he would be forgiven. But the commissioner was definitely looking for a show of guilt or remorse. He wanted to know that Pete had cleaned up his life. The commissioner was willing to extend a new platform to Pete if he had the willingness to turn his life around."

Shortly after the others left Bud's office, I heard the telephone ring. I broke into a big grin because I thought it must be John Dowd on the other line, calling to complain about the meeting. But it was Mrs. Selig, calling to discuss dinner plans. When Bud hung up the phone, I responded with fake surprise. "I'm amazed to see that you actually have phones in Wisconsin," I said. "I knew the mailman didn't deliver!" Bud smiled and nodded. He appreciated my sarcastic reference to never having my phone calls returned or my mail answered over the previous 13 years.

But the time for humor was over. Mr. Selig looked at me and said, "I want to know one thing. Did you bet on baseball?" I looked him in the eye. "Sir, my daddy taught me two things in life—how to play baseball and how to take responsibility for my actions. I learned the first one pretty well. The other, I've had some trouble with. Yes, sir, I did bet on baseball." Mr. Selig nodded, understanding how difficult it was for me to speak those words. Then he took a deep breath. "How often?" He asked. "Four or five times a week," I replied. "But I never bet against my own team and I never made any bets from the clubhouse." Then, Mr. Selig took a moment to gather his thoughts. "Why?" he asked. I wanted to be as honest as possible, so I gave it to him straight: "I didn't think I'd get caught," I said. "I was always the type of gambler who believed in his team. I just thought that I would win every game that I managed. I was looking for an edge, some added excitement." Mr. Selig seemed satisfied with my answers. Then he recalled his conversations with his close friend Bart Giamatti during the investigation of 1989. He said that Bart was very troubled over the entire ordeal. "You could bring any other player in this office and tell me that he bet on baseball games and I would have understood," said Bart. "But not Pete Rose! Pete is synonymous with the game of baseball. How could he possibly commit such an act? Doesn't Pete understand that he's Pete Rose?" I didn't realize it at the time, but the answer to Mr. Giamatti's question was a big reason why I needed to write this book. I was aware of my records and my place in baseball history. But I was never aware of "boundaries" or able to control that part of my life. And admitting that I was out of control has been next to impossible for me. I was aware of my privileges, but not my responsibilities.

At that point, I expressed my regrets to Mr. Selig. But I couldn't change the past. "What's done is done," I said. "I paid an enormous price for my mistakes. They caused a great deal of misery in my life." Bud looked at me and said, "I appreciate you coming forward to tell the truth." I nodded and we shook hands. "I appreciate you taking the time to hear me out and to consider my reinstatement," I replied.

Mr. Selig likes to keep everyone in the loop. He wanted to consult with the baseball owners and members of the Hall of Fame before moving forward. He also wanted to speak with Bart Giamatti's family, to get their opinion on my reinstatement. I understood completely. But after the meeting, I had every reason to believe that I would be reinstated to baseball within a reasonable period of time. Mr. Selig said that it would take a "nuclear bomb" to make him change his mind.

Afterward, we stepped outside and joined the others for lunch. During that time, we sat around a big conference table, joked around, and talked baseball. It was one of the best days of my life. They say "confession is good for the soul." They were right. I felt like a load had been lifted from my shoulders.

During our lunch, Bud received a phone call warning him that there was a swarm of reporters waiting downstairs in the lobby. The "secret meeting" was no longer a secret. Word had apparently leaked out. If I had flown into Chicago for a meeting, no one would have noticed. But the sight of Pete Rose and Mike Schmidt having breakfast in a downtown Milwaukee restaurant started the rumor mill grinding. After lunch, baseball security escorted me and Mike Schmidt down the freight elevator and into the basement, where the limo drove us all the way to Chicago. Mr. Selig had our flights rerouted to avoid the swarm of reporters, who were waiting at the Milwaukee airport. As I drove off in the limo, I came away with a very clear understanding that Mr. Selig was a fair person and a good commissioner. He definitely loves baseball. He also gave me something I had been deprived of over the previous 13 years—hope!

Epilogue

MY DREAM

You know things have changed when the world's best rapper is white, the best golfer is black, the French call the Americans arrogant, and the Germans do *not* want to go to war! Some folks might add that things have changed when Pete Rose admits he bet on baseball. Truth is, I never thought those words would ever come out of my mouth. But like everything else in life, change is unavoidable. Sometimes, change is better, which is why I'm going to say something that I thought I'd never say: I'm glad I got caught. I'm glad Janszen squealed—not because there is any honor in squealing. I've never ratted out a friend in my life. But if Janszen hadn't squealed, someone else would have. Maybe not in 1989, but sooner or later, I would have kept pushing the limit until all hell broke loose. But as Mr. Giamatti said, "In the end, life is about rules." I broke them and I've decided to take responsibility. Although I have no practical use for John Dowd, I'd like to take just one page out of his playbook. In his report, he described the three convicted drug dealers who testified against me in this way: "Each has stood before the bar of justice and engaged in the most painful act of integrity—the admission of illegal acts." By God, Dowd got something right!

Unlike most folks in the literary world, I didn't set out to write a "self-help" book or go on a "journey of self-discovery." But as my life progressed, life itself jumped up and bit me in the ass. In the process, I learned a thing or two about a thing or two, which is why I needed to write this book. So I could make my peace with the game of baseball and all of its fans—especially the folks in Cincinnati and Philadelphia, who supported me throughout my career.

When asked what it would take for me to get back into baseball, Mr. Giamatti said that he expected me to show a "redirected, reconfigured, or rehabilitated life." I'm not going to lie to you folks and say that I have everything worked out, that I've solved all the problems in my life. It's a daily battle but I'm fighting every step of the way. I still enjoy gambling at the racetrack, which has always been my favorite pastime. But I've learned to distinguish between the legal and the illegal bets, which is what got me into trouble in the first place. There is a big difference between "getting" into trouble and "staying" in trouble. Elvis and John Belushi got themselves into trouble and they're both dead. I'm still alive and so are you. That alone is reason for hope. So, if there is anyone out there who might be having some problems in their life, maybe, just maybe, you folks can learn a valuable lesson from my mistakes. Whether you're struggling with the temptation of drugs, booze, gambling, or even an obsession with golf—call a friend. Talk about your problem and "listen" to good advice.

After a career record of 9,530 victories, Laffit Pincay Jr. recently retired from horse racing during a ceremony at Hollywood Park. At 56, Pincay wanted to race for another 2 years, but his doctors advised him against it because of injuries he got from a near-fatal spill. At his press conference, Pincay wiped away his tears and said: "I feel very sad because I'm leaving a sport I really love. I'll have a fire inside me that I cannot put out." I understood exactly what Pincay meant. I still feel the same fire inside me for baseball.

So before I continue, I know what you're thinking: "If we let you back into baseball, Pete, what's to stop you from gambling again?" Listen: There hasn't been a day in my life where I didn't regret making those bets. I wish I could take it all back. But I can't. What's done is done. In the past, I didn't distinguish between trusting my instincts to win a game or to win a bet—a talent that cut through my life like a "two-edged sword." That's right, I said it—a metaphor! It has taken me a lifetime to step out of the shadow of the "Masked Marvel," but now that I've done it, don't expect me to go on Oprah or Dr. Phil and spill my guts. Spilling them for this book has been hard enough!

I'm sure that I'm supposed to act all sorry or sad or guilty now that I've accepted that I've done something wrong. But you see, I'm just not built that way. Sure, there's probably some real emotion buried somewhere deep inside. And maybe I'd be a better person if I let that side of my personality come out. But it just doesn't surface too often. So let's leave it like this. I know I fucked up. All the shit that flowed from my bad decisions hurts and hurts big time. I'm sorry it happened and I'm sorry for all the people, fans, and family that it hurt. Let's move on.

For the last 14 years, I've consistently heard the statement, "If Pete Rose came clean, all would be forgiven." Well, I've done what you've asked. The rest is up to the commissioner and the big Umpire in the sky. So, to you folks who find it in your heart to forgive what I've done—I'll tip my hat and say, "Thank you kindly." To you folks who think that I've committed the "unpardonable sin"—I'll still tip my hat and just move on down the line. I reckon that'll put me right smack dab in the middle of Charles Barkley's 50-50 Rule. But according to a recent Internet poll, the fans have voted 80-20 in my favor, which is not bad for a scrappy little kid from the wrong side of the tracks.

At the time of this book, I'm 62 years young and looking forward to getting on with the next stage of my life. A stage that I hope will include baseball—if they'll have me. So, just in case a few of the "baseball purists" decide to protest: My reinstatement does not mean baseball condones gambling. It's not like the next player will come along and say, "Hey, they only gave 14 years to Pete Rose—I might as well bet on baseball, too!" The "deterrent factor" for future players is still firmly in place. And if there is any doubt, I'll be happy to discuss the matter and set the record straight. Nobody, I mean nobody, should ever experience what I've been through. Today, there are over 1,800 Web sites, that feature online gambling. Most of those sites are visited by teenagers, who are gambling with Daddy's credit card as well as their future. Maybe my story can have a strong impact on redirecting a few of their lives.

Rick Hill and I began writing this book on the afternoon of my 60th birthday. It was a good place to start and a good place to finish. I warned Rick that he had his work cut out for him because I would not be easy to work with. As a lifelong sufferer of ADHD, I get distracted easily and have trouble concentrating on nonbaseball subjects for more than a few minutes at a time. So, I want to thank Rick for staying the course and helping me find the words to express the feelings.

After talking about base hits, headfirst slides, and 90 degree vertical drops, Rick and I walked out to the backyard and joined the many guests who had come for the party. Rickelle Ruby and Charlotte Jacobs flew in from Cincinnati, along with my agent, Warren Greene, and a longtime friend, Fred Fenster. I was surprised by the size of the birthday cake that Carol ordered for the occasion. The cake featured an air-brushed baseball and bat, which read, "Hit King Hits 60." As you know, I'm not given to "matters of introspection," so I didn't dwell on the downside of turning 60 years old. I always said that you only live once, but if you do it right, once is enough! Throughout the day, Carol kept reminding me that my daughter Cara was planning to sing a special song in my honor. "What song?" I asked. "I don't know," said Carol. "It's a surprise." "I bet she'll sing 'My Way' by Frank Sinatra," I said. "No," said Carol. "She's a teenager . . . and a Rose. She'll try to steal the show. She'll sing something from Christina Aguilera or Beyoncé." After I cut the cake and joked with a few of the guests, I turned and listened as my daughter took the stage for her first public singing engagement. The song was of her own choosing:

> *"Amazing grace, how sweet the sound . . .*
> *that saved a wretch like me . . .*
> *I once was lost but now am found . . .*
> *was blind but now I see . . ."*